# Sanctification &
## Liberation

# Sanctification & Liberation

Liberation Theologies in Light of the
Wesleyan Tradition

### Edited by
### Theodore Runyon

Prepared under the Direction of the
World Methodist Council

Abingdon / Nashville

SANCTIFICATION AND LIBERATION

*Copyright © 1981 by Abingdon*

**Library of Congress Cataloging in Publication Data**

Oxford Institute on Methodist Theological Studies, 6th,
1977.
Sanctification and liberation.
Papers presented at the conference held under the
auspices of the World Methodist Council.
Bibliography: p.
1. Sanctification—History of doctrines—Congresses.
2. Liberation theology—Congresses. 3. Wesley, John,
1703–1791— Congresses. I. Runyon, Theodore. II.
World Methodist Council. III.    Title.
BT765.O93    1977        261.8        80-20287

**ISBN 0-687-36810-3**

MANUFACTURED BY THE PARTHENON PRESS AT
NASHVILLE, TENNESSEE, UNITED STATES OF AMERICA

# Contents

# CONTENTS

# Preface

Most of the chapters that follow were presented originally to the Sixth Oxford Institute on Methodist Theological Studies, held at Lincoln College, Oxford, in the summer of 1977. More than ninety theologians, historians, and others interested in theological education, from twenty-two nations of the first, second, and third worlds, assembled under the auspices of the World Methodist Council to reflect on the relationship of the Wesleyan heritage to the liberation theologies of today.

With its ivied walls, manicured lawns, and aura of tradition, Oxford University may have seemed an incongruous setting in which to deal with issues of liberation and revolution. Yet two-and-a-half centuries earlier, when John Wesley was a tutor at Lincoln College, the Holy Club provided the seedbed for another kind of revolution—one not unrelated historically to the yearnings and struggles of the oppressed, as these chapters will demonstrate.

The reader will find in these pages no uniform evaluation of Wesley, his doctrines, or his movement. The comparison with modern-day liberation theologies leads to very real differences of opinion—and these differences have not been papered over but left in their original lively and provocative form, in the hope of stimulating further reflection, research, and discussion.

*Sanctification and Liberation* joins those volumes that have emerged from previous sessions of the Institute under the able editorship of Dow Kirkpatrick: *The Doctrine of the Church* (1964), *The Finality of Christ* (1966), *The Living God* (1971), and *The Holy Spirit* (1974).

Special attention is called to the bibliography included in this volume, containing a comprehensive listing of secondary materials on Wesley's doctrine of sanctification and its social implications.

The warden for the Sixth Oxford Institute was Rena Karefa-Smart of Boston University; and Brian Beck of Wesley House, Cambridge University, and I served as co-chairpersons. Financial assistance was provided by the Overseas Division of British Methodism, the Board of Global Ministries, New York, and the World Methodist Council. Abingdon, publisher of most of the previous Oxford Institute volumes, cooperated to make publication possible. Special appreciation is due Phyllis Barker, Kathy Henderson, and Clarence Bence for their assistance in preparing the manuscript for publication.

Theodore Runyon
Emory University
Atlanta

# Introduction:
# Wesley and the Theologies
# of Liberation

*Theodore Runyon*

During the decade of the 1970s liberation theologies moved from the periphery of theological attention to its center. Their insistent questions have instigated a re-evaluation not only of traditional understandings of Christianity but of the function and methods of theology. Three types of liberation theology are represented in this volume: black theology, with its concern for the plight of those oppressed politically and economically because of racial barriers; feminist theology, with its sensitivity to male dominance and the shaping of culture to the detriment and disadvantage of half the human race; and Latin American theology, with its use of Marxist analysis to expose exploitation of third-world peoples by the privileged groups, classes, and systems that control economic power.

In spite of their obvious differences these theologies share a common *critical* approach. Their task, as they conceive it, is not to rationalize and justify doctrine and church practice but to ask, on the basis of the biblical vision of the kingdom of God and his righteousness, how Christian theology and practice have been consistent with that vision—or have thwarted it. Aware of the extent to which theology has served as an ideology to legitimize unjust social orders in the past, these theologians have a litmus test that they apply to any claim to theological truth: Does it advance the cause of human freedom? With Jürgen Moltmann, they find that "*the new criterion of theology and of faith is to be found in praxis.* . . . Truth must be practicable. Unless it contains initiative for the transformation of the world, it becomes a myth of the existing world."[1]

The thesis advanced by some of the writers of the following chapters is that there is a peculiar affinity between Wesleyan theology—especially Wesley's doctrine of sanctification—and movements for social change. When *Christian perfection* becomes the goal of the individual, a fundamental hope is engendered that the future can surpass the present. Concomitantly, a holy dissatisfaction is aroused with regard to any present state of affairs—a dissatisfaction that supplies the critical edge necessary to keep the process of individual transformation moving. Moreover, this holy dissatisfaction is readily transferable from the realm of the individual to that of society—as was evident in Wesley's own time—where it provides a persistent motivation for reform in the light of "a more perfect way" that transcends any status quo.

*Justification by faith,* the *leitmotiv* of the Reformation, remained for Wesley a fundamental component of salvation, as we shall see. But the role of justification is to provide the foundation in grace for the actual transformation of the person that is the divine intention. Justification restores us to God's favor; sanctification, to God's image.[2] Only with sanctification begins the renewal of creation that is explicit in the vision of the kingdom of God. A qualitative change in human existence is the divine objective in the process of reconciliation. From Wesley's standpoint, redemption, therefore, cannot be complete without it. *Entire* sanctification functions on the level of the individual as an eschatological goal, paralleling the kingdom on the social level. Though the realization of this goal is the gift of the Father's unfailing grace and not the product of human striving, entire sanctification is nevertheless a possibility within this world and this life.

It follows that Wesley, unlike most eighteenth-century

writers, does not view the kingdom of God as referring exclusively to heaven or to life after death. The first fruits of the Kingdom are available now. "A society [is] to be formed . . . to subsist first on earth, and afterwards with God in glory. In some places of Scriptures the phrase [kingdom of God] more particularly denotes the state of it on earth; in others, it signifies only the state of glory; but generally it includes both."[3] Therefore, when we pray "Thy kingdom come, thy will be done in earth as it is in heaven,"

> the meaning is, that all the inhabitants of the earth, even the whole race of mankind, may do the will of their Father which is in heaven, as *willingly* as the holy angels; that these may do it *continually,* . . . yes, and that they may do it *perfectly*—that "the God of peace through the blood of the everlasting covenant, may make them perfect in every good work to do his will, and work in them" all "which is well-pleasing in his sight." In other words, we pray that we and all mankind may do the whole will of God in all things.[4]

"Thy will be done in earth as it is in heaven" is *not* to be understood as it is "by the generality of men" as a phrase expressing only resignation, "a readiness to suffer the will of God, whatsoever it be, concerning us." On the contrary, we pray "not so much for a passive, as for an active, conformity to the will of God."

For Wesley this active conformity includes the responsibility to critique conditions in this world that are not in accord with the divine will. In the chapter "John Wesley on Economics," **Thomas Madron** details Wesley's attacks on the causes of poverty, such as the enclosure laws, which rationalized agriculture, denied the peasants access to common grazing lands, and drove them off the land and into the cities to become the great disenfranchised urban proletariat. Not content simply to *speak* against injustices, Wesley organized various self-help projects, cottage industries, literacy classes, credit unions, medical clinics, and other means of coping with the degrading and impoverishing impact of industrialization and early capitalism.

Wesley's sharpest attacks were directed against the slave trade, which he witnessed firsthand in Carolina (initially the Georgia colony prohibited slavery) and considered the worst abomination found in the Christian world. He cut through the pious rationalizations of the trade offered by his contemporaries—that it was, for instance, an economic necessity. "Better is honest poverty," he wrote, "than all the riches brought in by tears, sweat and blood of our fellow creatures." Or that it brought Africans the benefits of living in so-called civilized lands, to which Wesley retorted that no slave merchant actually operated with such motives. "To get money, not to save lives, is the whole spring of their motions."[5] The profit motive perpetuated the evil for all concerned. He was not impressed by the piety of some slaveholders.

> It is your money that pays the merchant, and through him the captain and the African butchers. You therefore are guilty, yea, principally guilty, of all these frauds, robberies and murders. You are the spring that puts all the rest in motion; they would not stir a step without you; therefore the blood of all these . . . lies upon your head.[6]

The last letter Wesley wrote was to William Wilberforce, who at the time was attempting to win passage of an antislavery bill in Parliament. Wesley did not hesitate to give Wilberforce's cause absolute status and transcendent sanction. "Unless God has raised you up for this very thing you will be worn out by the opposition of men and devils. But if God be for you, who can be against you? . . . Go on, in the name of God and in the power of his might, till even American slavery (the vilest that ever saw the sun) shall vanish away before it."[7]

Black liberation theology has found in Wesley a congenial figure, therefore, whose consistent championing of the rights of black people set an unambiguous standard for the movement he founded. Unfortunately, Wesley's example was not always followed by his sons and daughters, as **James Cone** and **Kwesi Dickson** show in their analyses of the development of Methodism in North America and in Africa. The Methodist witness often has been compromised by the socioeconomic structures of slavery and racism. Nevertheless, the abolitionist cause obtained much of its support in nineteenth-century America from the perfectionist orientation called into being by the Wesleyan revivals and frontier preaching, as **Timothy Smith** and **Donald Dayton** demonstrate. Moreover, the notions of sanctification and holiness proved more compatible with the style of worship and piety of black churches as they developed on American soil, than did Calvinism or Anglicanism.

Similarly, as **Nancy Hardesty** explains, feminist theology can point to the openness of both Wesley and the Wesleyans to the contributions of women and to the leadership roles women occupied in the movement, long before they won comparable recognition elsewhere in society. Though scarcely a champion of equal rights in the modern sense, Wesley was capable of passionate prose when arguing for the right of women to exercise ministries such as visitation of the sick.

> But may not *women* as well as men bear a part of this honorable service? Undoubtedly they may; nay, they ought—it is meet, right and their bounden duty. Herein there is no difference: "there is neither male nor female in Christ Jesus." Indeed it has long passed for a maxim with many that "women are only to be seen; not heard." Accordingly many of them are brought up in such a manner as if they were only designed for agreeable playthings! But is this doing honour to the sex? Or is it real kindness to them? No; it is the deepest unkindness; it is horrid cruelty; it is mere Turkish barbarity. And I know not how any women of sense and spirit can submit to it. Let all you that have it in your power assert the right which the God of nature has

given you. Yield not to that vile bondage any longer. You, as well as men, are rational creatures. You, like them, were made in the image of God: you are equally candidates for immortality.[8]

Thus with regard to the first two forms of liberation theology under discussion, the relation of Wesleyan doctrine to human liberation is fairly clear-cut; there is ample historical documentation to suggest a more than coincidental connection between sanctification and social reform. The case is not as clear when we turn to the third type; its criticism of the status quo is grounded not so much in traditional democratic egalitarianism as in Marxism.

## The Special Challenge of Latin American Theology

When we move from black and feminist theologies to Latin American liberationist thought, we move, as **Rupert Davies** observes, into a new arena. No straight line can be drawn from Wesley through nineteenth-century enlightened liberalism, or through evangelical perfectionism to the political liberation movements of today. The Wesley whose name lends legitimacy to movements for social reform cannot as readily be called upon to legitimize revolutions. The relationship necessarily becomes more complex and requires a more thorough introduction.

The crux of the problem from the Latin American standpoint is that Wesley was a reformer, but not a revolutionary. His witness may lend itself to increased justice *within* the politico-economic system, but can it endorse radical change? Is there not something in the very notion of sanctification that is meliorist and gradualist, and therefore not appropriate as a model in a situation that calls for more fundamental solutions? Wesley assumes that for the most part, in both church and state, the structures are already in place; that what is lacking is the power and the new content of righteousness. This assumption makes him attractive to the liberal reformer—but suspect to the Marxist, for whom liberal reforms may be worse than nothing since they relieve the pressures that otherwise would force the fundamental changes necessary for a new order.

Is it possible to read Wesley in a way that makes sense and that contributes to Christian understanding and action in those parts of the world influenced by the Marxist critique? To spell out the nature of the dilemma, we turn first to the so-called *Halévy thesis* to summarize the issues at stake.

Elie Halévy (1870–1937) was a French historian intrigued by the contrasting developments in England and France at the end of the eighteenth and the beginning of the nineteenth centuries. In the first volume of his monumental six-volume *History of the English People in the Nineteenth Century*, he sought to explain why, with similar conditions of impoverishment and unrest, France went through a bloody revolution, while England moved into the modern period without such violent upheaval.[9] In this and other writings, he concluded that

> England was spared the revolution toward which the contradictions in her polity and economy might otherwise have led her, through the stablilizing influence of evangelical religion, particularly Methodism. . . . The despair of the working class was the raw material to which Methodist doctrine and discipline gave a shape.[10]

The result was the rise of leaders within the proletariat and petty bourgeoisie who were committed to nonviolence and to the orderly achievement of social reforms in basic loyalty to the government. The influence of Methodism on the trade-union movement in Britain has often been remarked. Labor leaders received their training as class leaders and local preachers, and they adapted the methods of the class meeting and dues collection to the needs of the fledgling trade unions.[11] In his book *The Methodist Revolution,* Bernard Semmel has updated Halévy and argued, from the standpoint of a social historian, that sociologists should give Wesleyan theology the same careful attention accorded Calvinism by Tawney and Weber, because of Methodism's undeniable social impact.[12]

The Halévy thesis continues to exercise a fascination—not least of all because it is so ambiguous. Does it mean that Wesleyan doctrine and practice instigated profound socio-economic changes, which in other societies have been accomplished only by prolonged violence and bloody revolution? If so, Wesleyan doctrine conceivably could be touted as the answer to the third world's search for ideological alternatives to both capitalism and communism.[13] Or does it mean that Methodism's effect was to dampen the fires of revolution by redirecting discontent toward spiritual preoccupations, which would have left the external world unaffected, had it not been for other forces for change at work? Historians of a more critical and Marxist persuasion are inclined toward the latter theory. Their arguments run from the judgment that Methodism simply was not strong enough numerically (150,000 to 200,000 members) by the end of the eighteenth century to wield the kind of influence Halévy attributes to it and that by the time its numbers increased significantly, it had lost most of its identification with the working class and had become bourgeois (a view that **John Kent** [chapter 4] shares[14]), to the claim that Methodism was a retrogressive and reactionary force, preoccupied with individual morality and that it drove a wedge between converts and their fellow proletarians—between the chapel and the pub. "Energies and emotions which were dangerous to social order . . . were released in the harmless form of sporadic love-feasts, watch-nights, band-meetings or revivalist campaigns."[15] Hence it can be argued that, to the extent that Methodism did affect the working classes, it indoctrinated them in the conservative Toryism of its founder and prevented the kind of radical critique of economic and class structures that could have brought about a new and more just social order.

Wesley's political conservatism cannot be denied. He defended the monarchy, opposed the American colonists in their moves toward independence, and abhorred anarchy in any form. And with good reason. He had faced mobs and lawlessness, and he knew how to value the political structures that guaranteed order and relative freedom of speech. Moreover, he was convinced that under the monarchy and Parliament, in spite of corruptions, Britons enjoyed the greatest degree of freedom found anywhere. But this same conservatism caused him to oppose the new *laissez-faire* economic policies and to call upon the government to return to mercantilist practices, which would assure more just distribution (e.g., setting the price of bread at a level the poor could afford). Oppression lay not in the government as such, but in corruption where it existed—in the buying of votes, for instance, or in an economic policy that accepted unemployment as a matter of course. But the system was presumed to be reformable. True, Wesley's doctrine of universal depravity saw evidence of human folly everywhere, as his treatise "The Doctrine of Original Sin, According to Scripture, Reason and Experience" amply illustrates.[16] But sin can be rooted out; the sanctifying grace of God is given in order that the devil and all his works might be not only renounced but actively opposed and even destroyed.[17]

If we may press the theological analogy, Wesley assumed that the system was "justified"—in its basic lineaments capable of being conformed to the will and purpose of God. What remained was "sanctification," the practice of conformity to that will. Thus the appropriateness of the gradualist, meliorist approach. But what about lands where the regime is neither just nor subject to reform? Is sanctification then not an inappropriate category? Should not one demand instead a fundamental "conversion" before sanctification becomes a possibility? Meliorism does not commend itself to those who see radical change as the precondition of any genuine improvement in the lot of the masses. Gradualist reforms are, intentionally or unintentionally, always the ally of the present system. They relieve the worst inequalities and undercut pressure for revolution, thus insuring that exploitation will continue as before under those who control the wealth and the trade.

What made Wesley appealing to the older liberalism, with its emphasis on humanitarian reform in the context of a democratic, evolving, enlightened capitalism, makes him less than helpful in the eyes of those who see the results of that same capitalism in their own lands, where it has worked hand in glove with local power elites to enrich oligarchies and impoverish the masses. In his chapter "A Liberating *Pastoral* for the Rich," **Dow Kirkpatrick** writes out of his own encounter with Latin American realities. He undertakes the difficult task of interpreting to first-world Christians that, in all its well-intended charity and goodwill, the first world has not yet grasped the extent to which it is implicated in the third world's misery and that it has created situations not amenable to the traditional liberal approaches to problem solving. **José Míguez Bonino** states the issue clearly when he comments in a previous work,

> The liberal ideology under which the liberal project was launched in Latin America, however excellent its intentions may have been, and whatever value it may have had at a point in our history—as a means of breaking the stranglehold of feudal society—proves to be for us *today* an instrument of domination, an ally of neocolonialism and imperialism.[18]

Even the church's missionary efforts are implicated, he charges in chapter 2. "For us in the Third World at least, Methodism as a social force is part of history—and in some ways part of the history of our domination and exploitation."

If this is the case, the older social liberalism, which produced among other things an impressive body of Wesley scholarship, is no longer able to interpret Wesley convincingly in a world that has been sensitized by the Marxist critique of liberalism. The response to this dilemma, however, may be not to jettison Wesley, but to discover a hermeneutic that opens up his theology in a way that applies to the new situation.

## Challenge and Response in Wesley Scholarship

Confrontations such as the one posed by Latin American liberation theology are not to be feared or avoided. Indeed, judging from recent history, research and reflection in the Methodist tradition have been spurred by just such challenges. The two most creative periods of Wesley scholarship in this century were called forth by cultural and theological changes that provoked questions about the conventional images of Wesley and Methodism. After World War I, the rise of the social gospel confronted scholars with the necessity of demonstrating that Wesley had more to offer than the pietism, revivalism, and individualism popularly associated with his name. The spate of research and publication on the social implications of Methodism is evidenced by the bibliography appended to this book. From the series by Wearmouth and Edwards and the studies by Wellman, MacArthur, and Bready, down to the recent works by Schneeberger and Marquardt, this has proved to be a rich lode. It speaks directly to the concerns of black theology and feminist theology. The fact that it cannot, for the most part, answer as directly the Latin American situation by no means discredits its contribution.

When liberalism was challenged in Europe by dialectical theology and in North America by neo-orthodoxy, a new critique of Wesleyanism arose. As neo-Reformation thought became the norm in the Protestant ecumenical movement, the Methodist interest in religious experience was labeled "Schleiermachian" *(horribile dictu!)*, and the doctrine of Christian perfection was viewed as superficial and overly optimistic, in the light of the tragedies of World War II and its aftermath. In this period when continental Protestant theology was dominant, Methodists were regarded as not having a theology—at least not one that could contribute significantly to the ecumenical discussion.

Rising to the challenge, studies appeared that reappraised Wesley's thought in continuity with the Reformation tradition, beginning with Cell's early study of Calvinist elements in Wesley. This was followed by Cannon's treatment of the classical soteriological doctrines, Deschner's analysis of Wesley's Christology from a Barthian perspective, and Hildebrandt's examination of Wesley's continuity with Luther. Flew, Sangster, Peters, and Lindstrom all reinterpreted sanctification; and the works of Davies, Outler, Rupp, Williams, and others related Wesley more or less consciously to the mainstream of the Reformation tradition. The role of original sin was rediscovered, and the qualifications with which Wesley hedged Christian perfections were reiterated.

All of which is to say that each generation approaches the study of Wesley—or of any major figure in the past—with the questions and issues that demand attention in that generation's own time. If humanistic Marxism appears the most viable option to a significant segment of the world's population today, it is not surprising that the scholars of a world movement like Methodism begin to approach Wesley with questions generated by their encounter with Marxism. It can be argued, of course, that in the case of Marxism we are dealing with atheistic thought-forms inimical to any theological discussion. The long-standing Christian/Marxist dialogue would seem to indicate, however, that this is not entirely the case. Latin American liberation theology has consciously appropriated Marxist methodology and found it a useful tool for both biblical and historical reflection, much as Thomas Aquinas converted pagan Aristotelianism, which posed no inconsiderable threat in his time, to Christian use.

If the Marxist critical component in Latin American theology tends to discredit the older liberal interpretaion of Wesley, it treats the continential Reformation influence in contemporary theology in no more kindly fashion. Latin Americans fault their European Roman Catholic colleagues for allowing protestantizing concerns to dominate their rethinking of Catholicism after Vatican II. The doctrine of justification by faith alone has had fateful historical consequences, they warn. "The disappearance of the notion of *merit* from Protestant theology," says Juan Luis Segundo, " . . . seems to have undermined the possibility of any theology of history." The Catholic doctrine of merit, for all its shortcomings, gave eternal worth to human effort and right intention. But the exclusive emphasis upon justification by faith alone puts human beings in a completely passive position and turns the determination of history over to the secular powers. Segundo detects vestiges of this heritage even in today's Protestant liberation theologians, such as Moltmann and Alves, and in their Catholic allies, such as Metz, when they view the kingdom of God as so radically different from this world as to negate any human effort to approximate it. This is Luther's "two realms" doctrine *redivivus* in the thin disguise of political theology, Segundo suspects. "The 'revolution' it talks about seems to be more like a Kantian revolution than an historical revolution. It merely revolutionizes the way we formulate our problems." A theology of hope of the European variety, which speaks of a radical future but is unwilling to take responsibility for the concrete and ambiguous steps that lead from here to there, is no theology of hope—at least not of hope for our history. Segundo sees the continuing grip of the Reformation doctrine as the fundamental debilitating element responsible for this impotence. If the theology of hope "remains consistent with itself and its fonts," he claims, "the revolution it speaks about is transformed into faith and hope in something metahistorical and a disgusted turning-away from real-life history." Segundo does not favor a return to the Catholic doctrine of merit in its medieval form. That would reintroduce the legalism from which the Reformation revolted. Rather, he seeks an approach combining the freedom *from*, experienced in justification, with freedom *for* human responsibility.[19] What is needed, say the Latin Americans, is a holistic, critical, transformationist theology, one that understands salvation not only as a process that changes the individual, but as a historical process moving toward a divine goal—one in which the God of the Bible has a stake and takes sides—a process in which human efforts count for something and in which God enlists those efforts and brings them to fulfillment through their incorporation into the divine enterprise.

What happens when we approach Wesley with these Latin American concerns in mind? Because of the limits of this introduction, we can focus on only one example, but one that nonetheless is central enough to demonstrate the usefulness of the method. We shall focus on the role of *work* in the basic anthropologies of Wesley and Marx. In Wesley's case this will inevitably lead to a comparison with Reformation and quietist views on the relation of work to justification and sanctification, which in turn will open up parallels with Marx's criticisms of Feuerbach.

## Wesley and Marx on Work

What is the role of human work in Wesley's soteriology? This has been a continuing conundrum to those who wish to view Wesley as standing solidly within the Reformation tradition. He himself maintains that the Methodists espouse and proclaim nothing other than the Reformers' doctrine—justification by faith, without works of the law. At the same time he claims that "one who preaches justification by faith [and] goes no farther than this, [and] does not insist upon . . . all the fruits of faith, upon universal holiness, does not declare the whole counsel of God, and consequently is not a Gospel Minister." Introducing a distinction between "present" and "final" salvation, Wesley declares that "faith alone is the condition of present salvation," but that holiness and obedience are "the ordinary condition of final salvation."[20] As he explains, "Good works . . . cannot be the conditions of justification, because it is impossible to do any good work before we are justified. And yet, notwithstanding, good works may be and are conditions of final salvation."[21]

These and similar statements have led Cell and Peters to conclude that Wesley provides a "synthesis of the Protestant ethic of grace with the Catholic ethic of holiness.[22] Rupp and Williams find this "synthesis" less than helpful and, for their part, cannot believe that Wesley is guilty of adding a Catholic doctrine of works to a Protestant foundation. "The Catholic view of holiness [with its ladder of merit] cannot be molded onto the Protestant view of grace," they object.[23] And if Wesley actually has done this he must perforce have abandoned his essential Protestantism.[24]

But is it not possible that Wesley is operating out of an understanding of the nature and function of works that fits neither a traditional Protestant or a traditional Catholic position? Against the Catholic position as he understands it, he contends that human merit is *never* the basis for justification, whether initial or final; and against the Reformers, he argues that final justification is not apart from works. In terse form, this reduces to: We are not accepted for our works; and we are not saved apart from our works.[25]

If we bring to Wesley a Marxist understanding of the relation of work to human nature, however, we discover some intriguing parallels that may illuminate Wesley's underlying anthropology and in turn may clarify his notion of final justification.

The early Marx—the left-wing Hegelian humanist—has a special appeal for the advocates of liberation theology, in that he writes out of a deep compassion for the human plight. He wrestles to find categories not only to express that plight but to change it. During this early period he develops his basic understanding of human existence, as to both its nature and its implicit teleology.[26] For Marx, humans achieve their true being and come to self-consciousness through action.[27] Through our labor we take the empirical (*sinnlich*[28]) world outside ourselves and shape it into the authentic expression of our own being. In this process humans produce something that is objective and apart from themselves and that yet is their own product and the genuine expression of their own creativity, through which they find pleasure and a sense of fulfillment.[29] The artist is the paradigm of this process. The sculptor takes the empirical world of clay, stone, or metal and creates something that has an independent reality and is therefore "objective," but that also embodies the inner creativity and subjectivity of the artist.

We must add that what is expressed is not only individual but *social*, in the most profound sense. The sculptor is inextricably linked with the world that provides the material substance that interacts with subjectivity. The result is the product, not just of a single individual, but of the social, cultural, and natural context with which the individual interrelates and is in turn shaped. Thus "productive life is the life of the species. It is life-engendering life. . . . In creating a world of objects by his practical activity, in his work upon inorganic nature, man proves himself a conscious species being [*Gattungswesen*]," one

24

whose product is the result of social interaction in community. "The object of labor is, therefore, the objectification of man's species life." (The term *Gattungswesen* carries overtones of linkage and interrelatedness, as well as of sexual creativity, that are missing in the English "species.") The human thus "duplicates himself not only in consciousness, intellectually, but also actively in reality."[30] This creation of the "other," which is at the same time the expression of the self in its interrelatedness, is the basic model of human fulfillment for Marx and describes humanity in its ideal state or, so to speak, before the Fall.

Marx introduces the term "alienation" (*Entfremdung*) to show how "the relationship of the worker to the objects of his production" has become distorted in industrialized, capitalist society. Industrialization produces more goods, but relegates workers to the condition of cogs in a machine. Work no longer can function as the creative objectivizing of the self; it becomes instead the constant loss and deprivation of the self as one's life is poured out. Not only is the *product* alien and no longer the authentic expression of the self, but the mode of production—the *labor expended* to produce it—is alienating. "In the very act of production [the worker] is estranging himself from himself." In his labor the worker "does not affirm himself but denies himself." The proof of this, according to Marx, is seen in the fact "that as soon as no physical or other compulsion exists, labor is shunned like the plague. . . . The worker therefore only feels himself outside his work, and in his work feels outside himself. He is at home when he is not working, and when he is working he is not at home." His labor is in effect forced labor. It does not fulfill the intended function of satisfying his humanity but "is merely a *means* to satisfy needs external to it." The worker is enslaved to the production process because he must have the necessities of life for himself and his family, but the way he spends most of his waking hours alienates him from his essential humanity.

Work ceases to be a means of genuine life and becomes a means of subsistance.[31]

Moreover, the loss is not just that of the individual. "In tearing away from man the object of production, [alienating] labor tears from him his species life"—his contribution as a social being whose interrelatedness must come to expression.[32] The products made by alienated workers give objective form to that alienation and to the system that produces it—a system with goals in contradiction to humanity as such.

Though one may quarrel with Marx's "romanticizing" of labor, his analysis of what happens when work is alienating cannot be ignored. For our purposes, however, this brief summary of Marx's notion of humanity as coming to expression through work is included for the light it may shed on the essential differences between Wesley and the Reformers in their understandings of the relation of work to salvation. It also may enable us to see more clearly the nature of the change that occurred in Wesley at Aldersgate—an issue of perennial interest and speculation.

## Wesley and the Reformers

The medieval preoccupation with the certainty of one's salvation was not substantially altered by the Reformation, although the way in which that certainty was provided did change. For both Luther and Calvin, the certainty of salvation was best guaranteed by lodging it with God. Divine mercy, in Luther, and divine election, in Calvin, functioned to ensure that human salvation would be accomplished in a way that could not be subject to institutional control or—equally important—to the foibles of the human will, the waverings of the human heart, or the inadequacies of human deeds. Only in this way could the Reformers spring free from the medieval church's monopoly on the means of grace and from the necessity of constantly examining the state of one's soul and one's works to determine whether one is indeed saved or not. With a single sweeping move they removed salvation from the realm of dependence on human action and placed it in the realm of divine promise and faithfulness. The Christian looks not to self or to an institution for assurance, but to divine steadfastness. God has elected us from eternity (Calvin) or declared himself for us in Christ Jesus (Luther). Therefore our salvation is where God is—in eternity; or where the Son is—in heaven; and our fate cannot be determined by what we do or do not accomplish.

The price paid for this way of grounding security is a shift in the location of *essential* humanity, however. Our true being is to be found in God, in his election, or in his forensic declaration of our justification through Christ, rather than in our existence in this world. The result is the split to which Segundo refers—between the transcendent realm, in which our salvation is actually occurring, and this world, which is in effect bracketed out of salvation history.

Lest this be thought a peculiarly Catholic reading of the Reformation, Reformed theologian Otto Weber comments on these same developments in Protestant orthodoxy. He notes that a nonbiblical distinction was introduced. The "person" was separated from his or her "works." This distinction was first made in order to explain that sinners are justified, whereas their sinful deeds are not. But then, to guarantee that the justified would not rely on their good works, it was insisted that all good works must be attributed to the divine Spirit who instigates them. The work was "no longer a work of the person but an event independent of the person." The result was a kind of "pneumatological docetism," says Weber.[33] When action is no longer understood as the expression of the person who acts, it becomes difficult to show how the person is accountable for deeds that are extrinsic to him or her. Life in the world loses its cruciality and significance, leading historically to the twin reactions of antinomianism and otherworldliness. The Lutheran doctrine of "vocation" seeks to counteract these tendencies, but it cannot finally succeed if work must be viewed as extrinsic to the relationship that saves.

Although Wesley's early preoccupation with his own salvation and the certainty of heaven is reminiscent of Luther's search for a gracious God, when the assurance of divine love finally comes to Wesley, it is placed in the service of a grander scheme of the renewal of the world and the race.[34] Essential humanity becomes a *project,* to be realized not only in heaven but in this world. And the renewal of the race is an undertaking in which humans have their indispensable role; God enlists human beings in this redemptive process. They labor, knowing that God is at work in and through them, "to will and to do of his good pleasure." This is Wesley's model of synergism—human partnership with the divine. It is not that certain tasks in the process of salvation are parceled out to human initiative and free will while others require divine grace. On the contrary, all that humans say and do is to be inspired by the Spirit and, consistent with the nature of the Spirit, leads toward the perfecting of the individual and the restoration of the race.

"We know 'Without me ye can do nothing.' But, on the other hand, we know 'I can do all things through Christ that strengtheneth me.' . . . God has joined these together in the experience of every believer; and therefore we must take care, not to imagine they are ever to be put asunder." Because he works in us, we *must* work. "You must be 'workers together with him.' . . . Even St. Augustine, who is generally supposed to favour the contrary doctrine, makes that just remark, . . . 'He that made us without ourselves, will not save us without ourselves.' " The power of the kingdom, which has come near in the Spirit, provides both the goal and the motivation to those who in sanctification have been taken into partnership with the divine. "Say with our blessed Lord, though in a somewhat different sense, 'My Father worketh hitherto, and I work.' "[35] Even God's own being is seen in his work, which takes the form not of divine fiat in the counsels of heaven but of the creative intervention of divine love, intent to restore a lost creation.

We note in Wesley's anthropology, therefore, some strong formal parallels with Marx. Human life is seen fundamentally as activity; as work which is teleological, always directed toward some purpose—in Wesley's case, toward the service of God or the service of self in pride, vanity, gain, or whatever. This anthropology may be traceable in part to Jeremy Taylor, whose influence on the young Wesley was strategic, and whose *Rule and Exercises of Holy Living* enjoined upon the would-be disciple the most stringent accounting of time and activities:

> We must remember that the life of every man may be so ordered (and indeed must) that it may be a perpetual serving of God. . . . We have a great work to do, many enemies to conquer, many evils to prevent, much danger to run through, many difficulties to be mastered, many necessities to serve, and much good to do. . . . We must give account to the great Judge of men and angels. . . . We must account for every idle word; not meaning that every word which is not designed to edification [is] . . . sin, but that the time which we spend in our idle talking and unprofitable discourses, that time which might and ought to have been employed to spiritual and useful purposes, that is to be accounted for.[36]

Because this theme of strenuous accountability is found in Wesley both before and after Aldersgate (cf. his instructions to his preachers not only never to be unemployed, but never to be "triflingly employed"), and because they detect little modification in Wesley's basic anthropology and soteriology after 1738, Maximim Piette and others have concluded that the decisiveness of

Aldersgate is more a matter of Methodist lore than historic fact.[37] As far as formal doctrine is concerned, they are correct. Wesley's *theory* of justification was already largely in place in his 1733 sermon, "The Circumcision of the Heart."[38] And formally, his anthropology does not change; work remains the expression of the committed person. But the foundation for that work, the spirit that informs it, and the nature of the goal toward which it is directed, are all decisively modified. The fastidious compulsiveness that drove the young Wesley is now more relaxed, though his intensity remains. His ministry breathes a freedom he previously had not known. And the agent of this transformation is the same Martin Luther from whom, up to this point, we have been attempting to distinguish Wesley.

Yet, in speaking of the role of Luther in Wesley's development, we have struck another of those perpetual puzzles in Wesley scholarship. How could the Luther whose "Preface to Romans" was the catalyst for Wesley's experience of justification be the object three years later of a broadside attack? After reading the Reformer's Galatians commentary, Wesley accuses him of being "muddy and confused. . . . How blasphemously does he speak of good works and of the law of God; constantly coupling the law with sin, death, hell, or the Devil! and teaching that Christ delivers us from them all alike."[39]

## The Change at Aldersgate

What many fail to notice is that Luther's "Preface to Romans," read that evening in May, 1738, in the conventicle on Aldersgate Street, did not question the place of work in the Christian life. Quite the opposite. It explicitly and repeatedly linked faith and works in a way that was atypical for later Lutheran orthodoxy. The Luther of that preface is more holistic in relating person and work and—dare we say it?—makes instead the more Marxist distinction between works as the product of an alienated being and works as the expression of a reconciled being—and with this he put his finger on Wesley's problem.

> For even though you keep the law outwardly, with works, from fear of punishment or love of reward, nevertheless, you do all this without willingness, under compulsion; and you would rather do otherwise, if the law were not there. The conclusion is that at the bottom of your heart you hate the law. . . . To fulfil the law, however, is to do its works with pleasure and love, and to live a godly and good life of one's own accord, without the compulsion of the law. . . . Hence it comes that faith alone makes righteous and fulfils the law; out of Christ's merit, it brings the Spirit, and the Spirit makes the heart glad and free, as the law requires that it shall be. Thus good works come out of faith. . . .

> Faith, however, is a divine work in us. It changes us and makes us to be born anew of God; it kills the old Adam and makes altogether different men, in heart and spirit and mind and powers, and it brings with it the Holy Ghost. O, it is a living, busy, active, mighty thing, this faith; and so it is impossible for it not to do good works incessantly. It does not ask whether there are good works to do, but before the question arises, it has already done them, and is always at the doing of them. He who does not those works is a faithless man. He gropes and looks about after faith and good works, and knows neither what faith is nor what good works are, though he talks and talks, with many words, about faith and good works.

> Faith is a living, daring confidence in God's grace, so sure and certain that a man would stake his life on it a thousand times. This confidence in God's grace and knowledge of it makes men glad and bold and happy in dealing with God and with all his creatures; and this is the work of the Holy Ghost in faith. Hence a man is ready and glad, without complusion, to do good to everyone, to serve everyone, to suffer everything, in love and praise of God, who has shown him this grace; and thus it is impossible to separate works from faith, quite as impossible as to separate heat and light from fire.[40]

In all likelihood that is the passage to which Wesley refers in his *Journal* as the word which overcame the alienation in his own life. "While he was describing the change which God works in the heart through faith in Christ, I felt my heart strangely warmed. I felt I did trust in Christ, Christ alone for salvation; and an assurance was given me that He had taken away *my* sins, even *mine*, and saved *me* from the law of sin and death."[41] The transformation that occurred at Aldersgate is not in Wesley's anthropology (the conviction that human life is fundamentally purposive activity), but in the relational *foundation* that undergirds that activity. As Wesley looks upon his pre-Aldersgate existence, he sees that what Marx would call his "species" life was alienated. His good works did not flow out of freedom; they were not the expression of positive relations but emerged from the compulsive effort to fashion a life in which every thought and action would be well pleasing in God's sight—and therefore worthy of salvation. "My chief motive, to which all the rest are subordinate, is the hope of saving my own soul," he had written to Dr. John Burton before setting sail for Georgia.[42] Toward this end he gave up all—"friends, reputation, ease, country; I have . . . given my body to be devoured by the deep, parched up with heat, consumed by toil and weariness, or whatsoever God should please to bring upon me."[43] But as he later recognized, all such efforts could bring no peace, for at their root was alienation. He could not serve freely the law he had imposed upon himself. Luther's words identified the basic difficulty: "At the bottom of your heart you hate the law." As Wesley later confessed, given this fundamental alienation, there was no way his works could be good, since they emerged as the expression of a species life that was basically distorted, in relation both to God and to his fellow creatures. All his efforts could not fulfill the law, because the foundation was wrong.

Into this vicious cycle of alienation came the good news of justification by faith—the new foundation laid by God in

Christ Jesus, who is the outworking of the Father's redemptive intervention to release humanity from bondage. The Son does the Father's work in the world; he is the self-expression of the divine heart. His work alone provides the basis for reconciliation; it eliminates all human efforts toward self-justification because it makes them unnecessary. The new basis for relationship is his love which "has been poured into our hearts through the Holy Spirit which has been given to us." The reception of this love overcomes estrangement and is marked by the sense of forgiveness and liberation to which Wesley testifies in his *Journal*.

Nothing may appear to have changed, in the sense that the same good works are done that were done before. Yet everything has changed, in that life is placed on a different foundation. In Marxist terms, the previous economic base with its alienated method of production has been replaced by a "substructure" that puts all relationships on a new footing. The actual job one does may be exactly the same after the revolution as it was before, but one's way of relating to the system has changed, and the result is a liberated worker whose work now expresses a free and co-responsible existence. Analogously for Wesley, the deeds may seem the same as before, but they issue forth from a new status and embody a fresh spirit. Nothing less than "new birth" will do to describe this change. It is the shift "from the faith of a *servant* to the faith of a *son*; from the spirit of bondage unto fear, to the spirit of childlike love . . . enabling [one] to testify, 'The life that I now live in the flesh, I live by faith in the Son of God who loved me, and gave himself for me.' "[44] "Justification" describes this foundation and context within which life is now placed; "regeneration" describes the transformation in the person, made possible by the new mode of being related; and "sanctification" is the reordering and reconstituting of all interrelationships in conformity with the base.

The species character of this whole salvific process now

becomes evident. New birth is a social event that brings divine love down into the human family to take effect here. The nature of Christ's love is that it turns us immediately and inevitably toward others. Love that is self-contained, or purely and simply between the soul and its God, is not "evangelical" love as Wesley understands it. It is not the intent of the love "which is shed abroad in our hearts" to draw human love to itself in the heavenly spheres but to spend itself in the world in outpoured service. It is, as it were, poured *through* our hearts into the world.

> In truth, whosoever loveth his brethren not in word only, but as Christ loved him, cannot but be zealous of good works. He feels in his soul a burning, restless desire of spending and being spent for them. . . . The Gospel of Christ knows of no religion, but social; no holiness, but social holiness. *Faith working by love* is the length and breadth and depth and height of Christian perfection.[45]

Sanctification—or Christian perfection—is not in the final analysis to be defined negatively, as the absence of sin, but positively, as the active presence of love expressed not only in word but in deed: from God to humanity, from humanity to God; from God through human beings, to their fellow human beings.[46] This is the power of the Kingdom that begins to exercise its humanizing impact in the present age. Hence Wesley opposes the desire of some Christians to "separate themselves from sinners" in order to avoid commerce with the world as much as possible. Were they to withdraw, how could they fulfill their calling to be "the salt of the earth," he asks. "It is your very nature to season whatever is round about you. . . . This is the great reason the providence of God has so mingled you together with other men, that whatever grace you have received of God may through you be communicated to others."[47] Sanctification is the enlisting of the individual in God's own work—the redemption of his creation.

Summarizing the effects of Aldersgate, we can say that (a) it did not change the anthropology of Wesley, insofar as both before and after the events of 1738 he understood genuine human existence as being brought to expression through work; but (b) it did expose the alienated nature of his previous works of self-justification; and (c) it did bring about a fundamental reconciliation with God and a genuine concern for others, growing out of the love introduced into Wesley's life by justification and the regenerative power of the Spirit; which in turn (d) placed a new foundation of grace under sanctification while linking justification to the continuing drive for the transformation of the individual and society.

Now we are in a position to see, in comparison with the Reformation, Wesley's unique understanding of the way justification and sanctification are united, and why he must insist both on "justification by faith without works" as the foundation, and on works as the condition for "final justification." He approvingly quotes Bishop Bull, who in his *Harmonica Apostolica,* "distinguishes our first from our final justification, and affirms both inward and outward good works to be the condition of the latter, though not the former."[48]

From the standpoint of the Reformers this notion of final justification seems to abandon the essential point of justification by faith, since it takes works into account. Even though he adds the proviso "Those fruits are only necessary *conditionally,* if there be time and opportunity for them,"[49] Wesley appears to undermine the security given with Calvin's understanding of divine election, and Luther's notion of the justification of the ungodly, putting the burden again on the creature to justify him- or herself by achievements in the world. The interpretations of Luther and Calvin offer security because justification by faith preempts final judgment by anticipating it in the present, facing its terror and invoking the mercy of God manifested in the love of Christ, which covers the accused and guarantees divine acceptance and eternal life. The "faith that justifies" is so important, in that through it, one grasps the indispensable condition of eternal life: reliance on divine mercy. For Luther, therefore, justification provides the substructure for heaven and our relationship with God—but not for life in this world, which is left to be dealt with on grounds other than faith. To suggest the possibility of a second justification would seem to question the sufficiency and certainty of the initial divine act.

Wesley disagrees. Like the Reformers, he insists on the sole sufficiency of divine mercy. Faith is the trust that allows God's own mercy in Christ to define and provide the basis of the relationship. This is the kind of trust the Spirit quickens within a heart that is confronted by the love of God in Christ. Reconciliation is therefore not without work. But the work is God's. *Our* works are excluded—not because they are of no value, but because, in strict adherence to the Reformation insight, at no point are they the source of our certainty or security, either initially or finally. When Wesley uses the term "final justification," therefore, he is not speaking of a justification on a basis different from the first. Justification by grace through faith remains the only foundation for the divine human relationship throughout the whole course of sanctification. What is new is a modification of the *telos*—the inherent goal and purpose of justification. No longer is it directed primarily toward heaven. This is not to say that Wesley does not have the traditional concern for heaven.[50] But the direction is reversed. Heaven is brought to earth—not in utopian, humanistic fashion, but in the way that justification provides the substructure for refashioning life in this world through sanctification. Typically, Protestants see justification, or conversion, as the decisive, revolutionary event. Wesley would agree. But then, just as typically, the revolution becomes the maypole around which the rest of life is danced, rather than a bench mark that sets the course of the future that is to be built.

Accountability cannot end with justification, therefore. To eliminate further accountability is to make justification the equivalent of the eschaton and to collapse history into insignificance. But the process of sanctification is the purification of history, overcoming the elements of society and in the life of the individual that cannot stand at the latter day. Accountability must continue, for justification, though it is the revolution that provides a different base, does not mean that the struggle is over. An analogy may help to elucidate this: In Marxism the new economic substructure does not exist for its own sake but for the sake of the superstructure that is built upon it. The purpose of the revolution is not merely to defeat the sources of alienation in the previous system but to enable a new society and culture to be erected. Those revolutionaries who believe that everything has been completed when the revolution is successful constitute one of the main obstacles to further progress. The revolution, and the new economic base which it makes possible, are requisite to everything that follows. In that sense, the revolution never grows obsolete, since it is taken up and expressed in everything built upon it. But the foundation is laid in order that the superstructure might be built.

This analogy shows that Jürgen Weissbach is incorrect when he suggests that for Wesley justification is "only a temporary stage in the process of salvation"—a stage that is superseded.[51] On the contrary, justification is taken up and incorporated into everything that proceeds from it. The motto "the substructure is reflected in the superstructure" is as applicable to soteriology as it is to economics.

In evaluating a Marxist society, one would need to take into account not only the revolutionary efforts that brought it into existence but the extent to which the goals of the revolution were being effected. In the same way, justification does not stand by itself apart from the history it initiates. When the God who justifies has a stake in this history, it means, as Wesley knew, "A charge to keep I have." The fact that there is "a strict account to give," does not result in legalism or fear, however, because in final justification, one stands before the same God with whom one is reconciled in initial justification. Wesley's *doctrine of assurance* makes certain that the radical love of God that is encountered at the cross remains the experiential content of sanctification, as well as of justification. His notion of final justification serves to preserve that accountability appropriate to the stewards of the good news of the kingdom.

Pursuing a line independent of the Reformation, Wesley is also conscious of the necessity to distinguish himself from a position on the other flank, which seeks to build the sanctified life on the old foundation, without benefit of justification and new birth. This is illustrated in his criticisms of his former spiritual guide, William Law, whom Wesley accuses of having a "philosophical religion," which answers all questions within the web of its own speculations and "inner light."[52] Thus Law is not open to the renewing grace associated with judgment, repentance, and justification.

Consequently, we find Wesley battling two forms of *mysticism* that are opposed in many respects: the "Lutheran" mysticism of the Moravian quietists, with their exclusive emphasis upon forensic grace; and the "rationalistic" mysticism of Law, with his virtual neglect of community and the means of grace. Neither has a place for works. These are two fronts against which he has to maintain his understanding of justification and sanctification. And this struggle provides us with a final comparison with Marx and Marx's criticism of Feuerbach's "mysticism."

## Wesley and Marx Versus the Mystics and Feuerbach

Wesley's controversy with the Moravians was really a dispute with Lutheran orthodoxy's forensic doctrine of sanctification and the quietist form of pietism that resulted from it. Advocates of "stillness" asserted that good works bring with them the temptation to trust in what one can do, rather than exclusively in Christ and the "alien righteousness" he bestows. In a conversation with Wesley, Moravian leader Count Nikolaus von Zinzendorf maintained, "From the moment one is justified he is entirely sanctified. . . . Till death he is neither more holy nor less holy." Zinzendorf understood both justification and sanctification to be entirely imputed, covering the saved person like a cloak of righteousness that God sees, rather than seeing the sinner beneath. Because righteousness is required for salvation, and because "the best of men are miserable sinners till death," the only righteousness that counts is that assigned to one from the merits of Christ. Zinzendorf continues, "I know of no such thing as inherent perfection in this life. This is the error of errors, I pursue it everywhere with fire and sword! . . . Christ is our only perfection. . . . Christian perfection_is entirely imputed, not inherent. We are perfect in Christ; never perfect in ourselves."[53]

While Wesley held no brief for the kind of inherent perfection Zinzendorf attacked, he did insist that righteousness is imparted as well as imputed. Christians are not just *declared* righteous, they are regenerated—endowed by the Spirit and nurtured through the means of grace actually to become what they are declared to be. According to the stillness doctrine, "one must *do nothing*, but quietly attend the voice of the Lord," avoiding reliance on any of the usual means of grace, such as the sacraments, prayer, and reading of the Scriptures, and one must not do any outward work, lest one be tempted to trust that which is of this world.[54] Wesley was no stranger to radical trust, but from his vantage point, the stillness doctrine could present only a truncated view of salvation. In effect, it collapsed sanctification into justification, though it did not understand the proper purpose of justification, and it left no room for the actualization of righteousness in the world and the fullness of salvation. For the quietists, justification sealed for heaven, sanctification purified for heaven, and both were accomplished extrinsically to the person, hence bracketing out actual existence in the world lest it contaminate the heavenly status of the saved soul. Wesley eventually withdrew from the Moravian influences at the Fetter Lane Society and formed a new society at the Foundery.[55]

The other mysticism with which Wesley broke was that of his onetime mentor, William Law, as Law came increasingly under the influence of the German mystic, Jacob Boehme. Law's *Christian Perfection* and *A Serious Call to a Devout and Holy Life* had made important contributions to Wesley's early development and, with Jeremy Taylor's theories, had formed him in the tradition of Anglican "practical mysticism." Now Law had come to espouse a withdrawal parallel to that of the quietists, reducing the Christian life to mystical devotion, and insisting that the mark of genuine faith can be tested by the following "infallible touchstone."

Abstain from all conversation for a month. Neither write, nor read, nor debate anything with yourself. Stop all the former workings of your heart and mind, and stand all this month in prayer to God. If your heart cannot give itself up in this manner to prayer, be fully assured you are an infidel. . . . Be retired, silent, passive and humbly attentive to the inward light.[56]

We may safely assume that this kind of mysticism held some attraction for Wesley, and certainly for his followers, for we find him writing,

> I think the rock on which I had nearest made shipwreck of the faith was the writings of the Mystics; under which term I comprehend all and only those who slight any of the means of grace.[57]

> All the other enemies of Christianity are triflers; the Mystics are the most dangerous of its enemies. They stab it in the vitals, and its most serious professors are most likely to fall by them.[58]

But he also grasped the essential inconsistency between these forms of piety and the understanding of Christian perfection he affirmed. The Moravians look to heaven; Law looks to the inner light; yet both fail to see that the existence given in faith is social and must therefore issue forth in action. A piety that does not result in works is alienated from its source in the redemptive activity of the God whose love toward all his creatures cannot remain within himself, but must be expressed.

> What is it to worship God, a Spirit, in spirit and truth? . . . To obey him . . . in thought, and word, and work . . . to glorify him, therefore, with our bodies, as well as with our spirits; to go through outward work with hearts lifted up to him; to make our daily employment a sacrifice to God; to buy and sell, to eat and drink, to his glory;—this is worshipping God in spirit and in truth, as much as praying to him in a wilderness.[59]

This is why

> Christianity is essentially a social religion; . . . to turn it into a solitary one is to destroy it. . . . 'Ye are the light of the world: A city set upon a hill cannot be hid.' . . . Love cannot be hid any more than light; and least of all, when it shines forth in action, when ye exercise yourselves in the labour of love. . . . It is not only impossible to conceal true

Christianity, but likewise absolutely contrary to the design of the great Author of it.[60]

When he calls Christianity a social religion, Wesley is of course not using the term in the full-blown, twentieth-century sense of the social gospel—that is, the application of the Christian message to social, political, and economic institutions and the structures of corporate life; he is arguing in his own eighteenth-century context, in opposition to Law and the quietists, whose views had infected the Methodist movement.

> If thou wilt be perfect, say they, "trouble not thyself about outward works. . . . He hath attained the true resignation, who hath estranged himself from all outward works, that God may work inwardly in him, without any turning to outward things . . . ." Directly opposite to this is the Gospel of Christ. Solitary religion is not to be found there. "Holy solitaries" is a phrase no more consistent with the Gospel than holy adulterers. The Gospel of Christ knows . . . no holiness, but social holiness.[61]

> When I say, [Christianity] is essentially a social religion, I mean not only that it cannot subsist so well, but that it cannot subsist at all, without society—without living and conversing with other men.[62]

And he attacks those who "have advised us 'to cease from all outward action;' wholly to withdraw from the world; to leave the body behind us; to *abstract ourselves from all sensible things.*"[63]

Wesley's differences with the mystics provide intriguing parallels to Marx's critique of Feuerbach—parallels that reinforce a basic contention of this introdution that the anthropology implicit in Marx's doctrine of alienated labor can provide a helpful perspective—in spite of the seeming contradictions—from which to view the anthropology implied in Wesley's doctrine of sanctification.

Feuerbach's critique of the alienating nature of religion

provided the basic model, which Marx then applied to the alienation of labor; and Marx remained indebted to his fellow left-wing Hegelian for this insight. Feuerbach is essentially correct, says Marx, in describing religion as an alienating process in which humans reify their inner life by projecting it onto a cosmic screen, from whence it is reflected as an alien and oppressive judgment upon their existence. According to Feuerbach,

> Religion . . . is abstraction from the world; it is essentially inward. The religious man leads a life withdrawn from the world, hidden in God, still, void of worldly joy . . . But he thus separates himself only because God is a being separate from the world, an extra and supramundane being. . . . God, as an extramundane being, is however nothing else than nature of man withdrawn from the world and concentrated in itself, freed from all worldly ties and entanglements, transporting itself above the world and positing itself in this condition as a real objective being. . . . Religion is the disuniting of man from himself; he sets God before him as the antithesis of himself. God is not what man is—man is not what God is. . . . God is the absolutely positive, the sum of all realities; man the absolutely negative, comprehending all negations. . . . To enrich God, man must become poor; that God may be all, man must be nothing.[64]

While agreeing with Feuerbach's analysis of religion as alienating, in his "Theses on Feuerbach," Marx claims that Feuerbach stops short of dealing with the real issue—Why do human beings engage in such self-deprecating projection?—because Feuerbach remains captive to his own kind of mysticism, even though he claims to be a materialist.

> [Feuerbach's] work consists in the dissolution of the religious world into its secular [substructure]. He overlooks the fact that after this work is completed the chief thing still remains to be done. For the fact that the secular foundation detaches itself from itself and establishes itself in the clouds as an independent realm is really only to be explained by the self-cleavage and self-contradictoriness of this secular basis. The latter must itself, therefore, first be understood in its

contradiction, and then revolutionized in practice by the removal of the contradiction.[65]

Marx claims that Feuerbach, in spite of his avowed materialism, sees the contradictions primarily as wrong ideas in the mind. His materialism is still an idea, a system of thought, not praxis. The correct view (*Anschauung*) of things will supposedly free human beings from the wrong notions that constitute their bondage. Feuerbach is still operating from a mentalism that does not realize that it is because humans are caught in economic deprivation that they engage in flights of fantasy and construct supernatural worlds of perfection, nor does he understand that a change in mental attitude is not enough. These material circumstances must be changed before alienation can be overcome effectively. The solution is to be found, therefore, at the level of *work,* not simply in the "contemplation" of material conditions (Theses 1, 5, and 9). Though an atheist, Feuerbach is still operating in an essentially pietistic framework. He has transposed the alienation from heaven to earth in order to "understand" it. But, as Marx adds in his familiar eleventh thesis, understanding and interpretation are insufficient. "The philosophers have only *interpreted* the world, in various ways; the point, however, is to *change* it." What is missing in Feuerbach is *praxis,* and without praxis, theory remains theory and never becomes incarnate; knowledge without practice is deficient and is not yet genuine knowledge. Genuine knowledge must include human activity to change circumstances and therefore "can be conceived and rationally understood only as *revolutionizing practice*" (Thesis 3).

I am suggesting that an important way to grasp what is involved in Wesley's doctrine of sanctification is to see it as "revolutionizing practice," which refuses to "abstract [itself] from all sensible things," but understands divine salvation to be working itself out in the relationships of this world. This is not to deny the deep divide between Wesley on one side, and Feuerbach and Marx on the other. But, given the fundamental differences, the fascinating parallels cannot be denied either. Like Feuerbach, Wesley accuses the Moravian quietists of projecting the work of God away from this world and into a doctrinal heaven, where it is abstracted from the "sensible world" and society—the very objects to be saved. But, like Marx, Wesley is not content with a description of an error in thinking; his concern is for actual transformation. Righteousness is not merely imputed; it is imparted in such a way as to bring about not only "a relative, but a real change" in the human condition.

Wesley was not unaware of the functions of ideology and the relations of theory to praxis. His impatience with the fine points of doctrinal dispute and his usual tolerance toward those with whom he had doctrinal differences "which do not reach to the marrow of Christian truth," was not because he was indifferent to the substance of doctrine, but because he knew that the substance can never be contained adequately in finite words, which are only the representation of the reality; the substance must be worked out in practice.[66] Therefore it was to the practice that he looked for the indication of adequacy of belief. Where he saw deficient practice—in the followers of Jacob Boehme, or in some of the Moravians, or in the antinomians within his own movement—his immediate concern was the doctrinal understanding that lay behind this deficiency. He would have found congenial the liberationist insistence that *orthopraxis* is a more reliable clue to faith than is *orthodoxy*.[67]

Wesley not only sides with Marx against Feuerbach's mentalism, he also turns Feuerbach's (and Marx's) notion of religion on its head. The God of Feuerbach absorbs all human labors and virtues into himself in heaven and dries them up on earth. According to Wesley, the reverse is the case: God pours himself into the world to renew the creature after his image and the creation after his will. The "design of the great Author" is that love "shine forth in action" until all things in the created order are restored to their glorious state.

> Suppose now the fulness of time to be come. . . . What a prospect is this! . . . Wars are ceased from the earth . . . no brother rising up against brother; no country or city divided against itself and tearing out its own bowels. . . . Here is no oppression to "make" even "the wise man mad;" no extortion to "grind the face of the poor;" no robbery or wrong; no rapine or injustice; for all are "content with such things as they possess." Thus "righteousness and peace have kissed each other;" . . . And with righteousness, or justice, mercy is also found. . . . And being filled with peace and joy in believing, and united in one body, by one Spirit, they all love as brethren, they are all of one heart, and of one soul. "Neither saith any of them, that aught of the things which he possesseth is his own." There is none among them that lacketh; for every man loveth his neighbour as himself.[68]

Hence, in contrast with the present order of things, Wesley envisions a society of economic justice, where, in striking anticipation of the Marxist formula, they "cannot suffer one among them to lack anything, but continually give to every man as he hath need."[69] Religion is not to be viewed, therefore, as alienated humanity's means of escape to a more tolerable, heavenly realm, but as participation in God's own redemptive enterprise, transforming alienated servants into liberated sons and daughters, whose works are at one and the same time the expression of their own life in the Spirit and the sign of the new age of justice and love that is to come.

This grand vision of the renewal of creation is the context within which Wesley's doctrine of Christian perfection, culminating in entire sanctification, must be understood. Unfortunately Wesley himself was responsible for much of the confusion surrounding this doctrine. His definitive statement, "A Plain Account of Christian Perfection," is not a closely reasoned, comprehensive presentation, but a series of polemical, largely defensive arguments, assembled over many years in reply to attacks and published under one cover, in which Wesley spends most of his time attempting to convince his readers of the plausibility of perfection in this life.[70] To do so, he is forced to hedge "perfection" with casuistic distinctions, carefully calculated to claim neither too little or too much. Too often in the past sanctification has been considered only within the parameters of "A Plain Account." As a result the doctrine has not been seen in the context of Wesley's larger scheme of the divine renewal of fallen creatures and creation, with entire sanctification (which Wesley espoused because it seemed to be a scriptural promise and because he believed he had seen empirical evidence of it in the lives of others—though he never claimed it for himself) as an eschatological sign, a kind of first fruits of the age that is to come and an indication of what God through his Spirit can do in the world, "working in you that which is wellpleasing in his sight" (Heb. 13:21).

Therefore, without denying Wesley's interest in the individual—which after all was the bright new discovery of Pietism and the Enlightenment in the eighteenth century—much of the foregoing would appear to argue against the common notion that Wesley's doctrine of sanctification is culture-bound to individualism and to his own time. This is not to say that Methodists have not interpreted it as such. What this introductory chapter seeks to demonstrate, however, is that when Wesley is approached from the vantage point of liberation theologies, and especially from the perspective of the Marxist critique, his theology not only can be freed from the confines of pietistic individualism, it can counteract that individualism and offer resources for the responsible rethinking of theology in a time when both neo-Reformation and liberal models no longer suffice. Like Marx, Wesley reminds us that a theory must lead to a new praxis. Only a theology that is transformationist can do justice to the Christian doctrine of sanctification and to the quality of salvation which that doctrine seeks to express.

In a sense, this book is an exercise in theory and praxis. In the chapters that follow, the theory of sanctification criticizes the practice; and the new context of practice raises questions as to the adequacy of previous formulations of the theory. If in this process the ambiguities and inconsistencies of the tradition come to light, so much the better. Those committed to sanctification cannot afford to be content with the past.

# Wesley's Doctrine of Sanctification From a Liberationist Perspective

## *José Míguez Bonino*

Using "liberation" as a transcription of the biblical concepts, which the theological tradition has usually rendered by "salvation" or "redemption," is not new and should not be startling. Nor is it new with regard to the Bible—though it may be new for a good part of theological tradition—to understand the meaning of such liberation not merely in transcendent (mystical or eschatological) terms or in subjective terms, but also in the politicohistorical context. What *is* perhaps new is the theological attempt to think through the totality of the faith from that perspective.

Such an attempt did not originate primarily in the sphere of academic theology. Its roots must be sought in the experience of a growing number of Christians from different traditions, geographical areas, and sectors of society, who have begun to rediscover their faith as active commitment to the struggle for human liberation—sociopolitical and economic, as well as cultural and spiritual. As this active faith "seeks understanding" in order to deepen and purify and strengthen its commitment, some theological issues are bound to emerge.

Most of these issues have a long tradition; again and again they have engaged the thought of theologians. We must, therefore, interrogate the theological tradition. But a radical process of reconception and reformulation is necessary if such a quest is to have real significance, since the nature of the theological questions is determined by the nature of the faith-commitment from which they emerge. For us, such commitment is lived in the area of politicohistorical processes that can be dealt with only in categories such as power, conflict, ideology, social formations and relations, and economic systems and processes, that are foreign to most of our theological tradition. A mere transposition from a totally different world of thought (the subjective/psychological, for most Protestant theology) could only hide or distort the issues. Consequently, in order to repossess the tradition, we must subject it to a thoroughgoing criticism, so as to lay bare not only its conceptual contents or its intention, but also its actual historical operation. Only then can the tradition be rethought and incorporated into our own theological response to the questions posed by our present faith-commitment.

One of the theological questions that has surfaced in this context relates to the old problem of understanding God's action—his saving historical deeds—both in its transcendent relation to our human actions, projects, ideologies, and conflicts, and in its immanence in them. If faith is to be lived in the realm of history, *as* history, we cannot imagine a "transcendental" self that would relate to God apart from a historical self that acts in history. Neither can we envisage a transcendental action of God that would operate in history outside of, or in the "gaps" between the chain of processes in which human beings are subjects.

Traditional Protestant theology—and much Roman Catholic post-Vatican II thought, which follows a parallel line—is so concerned with the prevention of any "sacralizing of human projects and ideologies" that it seems to some of us to result in emptying human action of all theological meaning. The God-reference seems to mean the relativization, the restriction, the limitation of any human project or achievement to the realm of the penultimate, and therefore, whether explicitly or implicitly, to that which is perhaps dispensable, optional, or at least not "ultimately" significant!

It has seemed to me that Wesley's struggle with the doctrine of sanctification is one of the points in the theological tradition where this issue was discerned and seriously faced. In fact, I feel tempted to reread Wesley's famous discussion with Zinzendorf in 1741 about "inherent" and "imputed" holiness, in terms of our present debate with some of our European colleagues concerning the ultimate eschatological significance of human historical achievement and to confess with Wesley, "I believe, the Spirit of Christ works Christian Perfection [brings in the kingdom] in true Christians [in human historical action]."[1] But the very substitution of terms may be a *metabasis eis allo genos* which we cannot simply assume. Therefore, we must pursue this problem more systematically.

## A Powerful Insight
## and an Ambiguous Achievement

I must disclaim any special competence in relation to early Methodist history and thought. The questions and suggestions I am about to offer are prompted by a very incomplete and amateurish reading of some material from and about Wesley and early Methodism. Each should perhaps be prefaced by the caveat, "If I have rightly read"! But it is possible that some conclusions might be valid and profitable even if "I have wrongly read." I feel somewhat protected by the fact that there is scarcely any point in Wesleyan interpretation on which respectable scholarship cannot be brought in as evidence for diametrically opposed points of view!

Biographers of Wesley have contended over the relationship between the struggles and resolutions of 1725 and the experience of 1738. It seems to me that the unity and convergence of the two, rather than their contrast or discontinuity, may be the clue to Wesley's ministry and theology. In 1725, Wesley was agonizing over the question of *the active Christian subject*—the true and suitable partner of God in the "covenant." In terms of the specific contents of such active Christian life, he does not seem to have invented a great deal, but rather has synthesized the ascetic, philanthropic, and devotional exercises that the best literature of his time could provide. He did not substantially alter those contents, which he bequeathed to future Methodist generations—both for their profit and for their misuse! But in 1738, a deeper and more decisive answer became existentially true for him—the old Pauline and Protestant insight that it is God himself who creates his true and suitable partner; that the active Christian subject is a gift.

It is, indeed, Luther's answer—but it is his answer to Wesley's quest. Wesley is not concerned with how "to please a wrathful God" but with how to be totally dedicated to him. Consequently—if I may be permitted a theological license —Wesley gained from Luther a doctrine of "sanctification by grace through faith." Holiness, for him, continues to be the goal both of redemption and of the Christian life. Faith must be preached because there is no other way to enter this realm of sanctification. This progression is present, as I see it, in all Wesley's great sermons.

It would not be difficult to document the intention of the Reformers to reject all dichotomies between justification and sanctification. One might quote Calvin: "As Christ cannot be divided, so these two blessings which we receive together in him, are also inseparable: righteousness and sanctification."[2] Although Luther was less consistent in formulation, he was equally convinced of this unity. But the Reformers were unable to build the defenses that could prevent a subsequent gliding, which by Wesley's time led to such a solifidianism that an unsuspected witness such as Karl Barth cannot help saying, precisely in relation to Zinzendorf, that "in this monism the necessity of good works may be maintained only lethargically and spasmodically, with little place for anything more than rather indefinite talk about a life of forgiveness."[3]

Barth himself raises the question of the nature of this unity and whether an "order"—a *prius* and *posterius*—can be established in this relationship, not in temporal terms, certainly, but in terms of theological correlation. His typical answer is that "in the *simul* of the one divine will and action justification is first as basis and second as presupposition, sanctification first as aim and second as consequence; and therefore both are superior and both subordinate."[4] This is excellent as theological formulation. Wesley could easily agree that justification is prior in the order of execution. But in the dialectics of his piety and his preaching, the all-consuming concern is with the grand plan—the order of intention. And here sanctification holds an undisputed primacy. God intends the creation of a holy people, and this intention becomes an actual, experienced, visible reality when men and women turn to him in faith. This is good news!

It was, indeed, good news for the poor of the land—the miserable masses of uprooted people crowding into the new industrial and mining centers, caught in the crises of the birth of modern industrial capitalism—helpless victims of social *anomia*. They were not merely accepted by God, but they could be made anew—given an intrinsic, measurable, effective worth and power. They could become the conscious and active subjects of a new life. Their works counted; their will was set free. In a society for which achievement was the meaning of life, here was a realm of the highest possible achievement, accessible to everyone through faith!

The exact weight and direction of the social consequences in English society of the Methodist awakening continues to be debated. A certain consensus, nevertheless, seems to be emerging from the discussion, and it can best be summarized in Semmel's words.

> Modern society requires the transformation of large masses of men from the relatively inert passivity which characterizes their state in a traditional society to one in which their personalities are sufficiently strong to enable them to emerge from a state of subordination to one of relative independence. . . . In the eighteenth century, England proved able to make this transformation relatively peacefully. . . . I shall examine how the special character of the "new man" envisioned and to some extent created by Wesley's evangelical Arminianism *might* have helped—that is all we can safely say—to bridge the gap between the traditional and the modern orders without tumultuous upheavals, *while at the same time promoting the ideals which would be most useful to the new society* [final italics mine].[5]

One may question the decisive role that Semmel gives to the peculiar Arminian tenets in this process. Moreover, one may be tempted to ask whether "counterrevolutionary" might not be a better description of the process than the "revolutionary" that Semmel uses. But the important fact remains that, at this symbolic level of (religious) ideology, ethical guidance, and form of expression, the Wesleyan revival seems to have played a significant role in the new social and political relations that were emerging in England with the consolidation of a new mode of production.

Once we have recognized the validity of Wesley's basic theological concern and the significance of his achievement, it seems necessary to point out that both are open to serious questioning. It is not important to pass judgment on Wesley's theology or to vindicate or deplore the social consequences of his movement, and it would be utterly unfair to blame him for ignoring theological or sociological insights that would emerge a century or more after his time. But it may be profitable to try to lay bare the limitations and weaknesses in his theology and in his general understanding of man and society, which may have led to such ambiquity.

Wesley seems to have read voluminously in the history of theology and piety. But his theological reflection remains captive of some rather rigid scholastic categories and logic dominant in post-Reformation theology. His thought moves, moreover, in the religious climate of the Pietist movement. Finally, his theology is dominated by the soteriological concentration of evangelical religiosity. These limitations operate in different areas of Wesley's theology, with distorting effects.

The first has to do with the understanding of the human subject. Wesley's anthropology seems to me incurably individualistic. This criticism may appear arbitrary in the light of his repeated assertions concerning the social character of the Christian life, his insistence on "a social holiness," his indictment of "a solitary religion," and his practical arrangements to ensure a corporate growth in faith and holiness. A careful exegesis of the contexts in which these expressions occur will show, I believe, that for Wesley, society is not an anthropological concept, but simply a convenient arrangement for the growth of the individual. It is the individual soul that finally is saved, sanctified, perfected. The fellowship is, in the last instance, an *externum subsidium*. The same external character applies to physical and objective existence: It is not to be despised or neglected (witness his concern for medicine, for instance). But still, man is a soul, in terms of both eschatological hope and religious experience. The drama of justification and sanctification takes place in the subjectivity of the inner life—although it seeks objective expression in works of love.

The inherited theological framework of the *ordo salutis* is a straitjacket that Wesley was unable to cast off. Whatever the original value and intention of that notion, in the hands of Protestant Scholasticism it had become a rigid sequence of moments which, rather than helping to deploy the richness of the one, yet manifold, grace of God, forced Christian experience into a preestablished pattern. Soon the *ordo* was psychologized into a series of "spiritual awakenings, and movements, and actions and states of a religious and moral type."[6] Wesley was caught in this web. Having left justification behind as a "moment," it was inevitable that he would fall into the trap of double justification—making a distinction between a "provisional" and a "final" salvation—thus endangering the very heart of faith. Justification, and even sanctification, in such a view becomes a series of almost disconnected moments, always precarious and threatened by sin. Both the unity of the human subject and the faithfulness and unity of God's grace are obscured and distorted. Wesley's formulation of sanctification and perfection becomes in this way psychologically untenable for us. Spiritually, it opens the way for either an unhealthful scrupulosity or an equally harmful petulance. That Wesley himself did not seem to fall into either simply proves that his spiritual life—as in the case of many other saints—was much better than his theology.

John Deschner has rendered an invaluable service in his study of Wesley's Christology. While he tries to read him "in the best sense he allows," and, although he largely presupposes, to prove that Christology is constitutive of Wesley's theology, Deschner points out several serious shortcomings. Two seem to me important for our subject. The first is Wesley's lack of interest in Christ's humanity as a concrete historical reality, reinforced by the rather abstract emphasis on law in relation to the prophetic office and by his difficulty in fully conceding the reality of his humiliation. The second (which for Deschner is not a weakness) is such a concentration on the priestly office that the prophetic and kingly offices are seen only in that light. This is reinforced, again, by an almost exclusive emphasis on Christ's passive obedience as the cause of our justification.[7]

It seems to me possible and necessary to bring together the remarks just outlined concerning Wesley's anthropology and Christology, inasmuch as they tend to reinforce one another in portraying the radical dualism of the theological framework and categories which condition Wesley's reflection on sanctification. There is a "spiritual human subject" that corresponds to Christ's divinity—a "soul" with a reality of its own—only externally and circumstantially related to an earthly, social, bodily life. This idealistic conception operates also in Wesley's understanding of holiness. Although with a sound biblical and theological instinct he gives "love" as his basic and only definition of holiness, when he seeks for the practical outward operation of love (conceived as "motivation"), he seeks the mediation of "law" rather than wrestling with actual historical conditions. To put it in caricature, sanctification becomes the operation of a moral and spiritual self through the mediation of a divine moral code. Again we can admit gladly that Wesley's pastoral dispositions and counseling and even his codification of rules are much more historically relevant—much more concerned with actual life and the condition of the people—than his theology would justify. He did not find a theology worthy of his practice.

For us today, the ideological freight carried in this theology and anthropology is suspect. It is the idealistic dichotomy that justifies and sacralizes social relations in the capitalist bourgeois order that was beginning to emerge in Wesley's England: a free "political subject" who moves in a realm distinct from his existence as an object in the labor market; an autonomous democratic state in which those who control economic power function as neutral umpires in conflicts that will affect their interests; a religion that operates in the individual inward life, without meddling with the corporate political and economic relations of the outward and social self.

Wesley's relation to this ideology is a complex and contradictory one. His dominant concern for "sanctification in concrete forms" led him inevitably into the consideration of existing social and moral conditions and even the economic realm.[8] His wide curiosity about political events, as well as his direct concern for social causes, has been amply attested and researched and need not be repeated here. Once this has been said, though, we must remind ourselves of the fact that, historically, Methodism seems to have served to incorporate significant sectors of the emerging British proletariat into the liberal bourgeois ideology that undergirded the consolidation of the capitalist system and reinforced its imperialistic expansion. Why?

Aside from the objective economic factors that led to this development (and which Wesley himself pointed out in warning of the temptations that accompany the upward mobility of people in his societies), two inadequacies in Wesley's own thinking may help to explain what happened. In the first place, he was not able to develop a theology of sanctification in which the unity of creation and redemption could be the center of articulation. Had he done so, his concern for human life in its entirety, and for social conditions, would have become integral and not subsidiary to his doctrine of sanctification. But the grip of a pietistic religion and an idealistic anthropology was too strong. It has thus been easy for Methodism—and its various offshoots—to seek refuge in a "spiritual," subjective, and otherworldly holiness, whenever their interests or the intractable realities of the outward world advised them to do so.

The other inadequacy is equally important but almost inevitable: Wesley was unable to see the structural nature of the social problems with which he was trying to grapple. "Thoughts on the Present Scarcity of Provisions," which has been much discussed recently, is a good illustration of this point.[9] Here Wesley makes an attempt to identify and relate the causes of the economic crisis that gripped England in the early 1770s. His vivid portrayal of the miserable condition of the poor reminds us of Engel's systematic description, less than a century later, of "the condition of the working class in England in 1844."[10] Wesley's prophetic tone of denunciation is at times arresting. His attempt to work with hard data—statistics, prices, and market conditions—is extraordinary for a religious leader. But when he attempts to find causes and remedies, he remains totally within the premises of the mercantilist system and completely unaware of the structural causes of the crisis. He cannot see in it the birthpangs of a new mode of production and organization of society, and consequently he cannot see that the poverty he describes and denounces as the "selling of flesh and blood" is the inevitable sacrifice that the gods of the new order demand.

It would be absurd to blame Wesley for this failure. Adam Smith was working on his *Wealth of Nations,* which would appear three years later. David Ricardo had been born the previous year. But the social class that would pay the initial price for the wealth of the nation was already gathering. Some of them entered Wesley's societies; many more were indirectly influenced by his movement; the religious factor would become part of their consciousness; some of their leaders would be shaped by it. And the fact that Methodism was unable to disclose for them the reality of their condition as a class, but rather led them to accept their role in society and to improve their lot without challenging the rules of the game, was one element in the domestication of the working class in Britain. In the last decades of the century, when mounting exploitation and repression kindled the fires of revolt in some sectors of the working class—enrolling some Methodists in the struggle—the official ideology and stance were already fixed: Methodism would be a force for order, acceptance, submission, and willing and responsible cooperation in the creation of the new society. Soon the human flesh and blood needed for the sacrifice would be bought abroad—the Empire was rapidly progressing—and the Methodists would be able to join in this new divine/human enterprise of spreading "not only our *merchandise,* but our *Missionaries;* not only our *bales* but our *blessings,"* as the great Watson, half a century later, would translate Wesley's concern "to spread Scriptural holiness."[11]

## The Theological Nuclei for a New Discussion

I have given most of my attention to the critical task because it would be very dangerous and misleading to lapse into an "enthusiastic" and "triumphalist" exposition of Wesleyan doctrine as the new social ideology for a supposedly Christian transformation of society. For us in the third world at least, Methodism as a social force is part of history—and in some ways part of the history of our domination and exploitation. The future belongs, under God, to the people—whether Methodists or Reformed or Catholic—of whom we are the servants, not the masters or manipulators. Whatever symbols, ideas, and representations will lead them in their struggle for liberation cannot be brought from outside (least of all from a foreign history), but must be begotten in the womb of the oppressed peoples. But this is not the only word that is needed. On the one hand, the consciousness of the people is not developed spontaneously and in isolation: It must be informed, challenged by theory, analysis, and interpretation. On the other hand, that consciousness has in many ways been shaped and conditioned by religion: *Its liberation also must involve a transformation of its religious awareness and self-understanding.*

It is at this point that the relationship between sanctification and liberation becomes meaningful, just as the relationship between sanctification and enslavement has been significant for the people's present condition. To clarify these relations is the main task that lies ahead of us. I do not intend to chart our way into it, but it seems to me that Wesley's concern for sanctification—frustrated and distorted as it may have been by some shortcomings—underlines a basic theological question. Some of the theological nuclei around which he centered his defense of holiness are significant.

1. Wesley's anthropology was worthy of human beings. Although he accepted in principle the inherited Protestant view of man, based on the perspective of original sin, his own experience and good British common sense led him to revise it by reviving the Augustinian idea of prevenient grace. Thus he could establish a responsible ethical and religious human subject, which could enter into a meaningful relationship with God. One century later, the Methodist theologian William B. Pope would begin to point out some of the anthropological and ethical consequences of this "optimism of grace," which later Barth would carry through in the affirmation of "the universal relevance of the existence of the man Jesus, of the sanctification of all men as it has been achieved in Him."[12] A christo-soteriologically founded anthropological optimism can help in an affirmation of human dignity that steers clear of the naïve populist acceptance of any *vox populi* as *vox dei*, and the manipulation that pretends to exalt the masses but actually despises them.

2. But we need to move beyond this level of generalization. Human beings—individually and collectively—engage in actions, conceive projects, give shape to history and to their own lives. Is this a merely human action, a sort of meaningless pantomime, while beyond and outside, another Actor writes and performs his own script until the day he finally sweeps clean the scene of history and inaugurates

a new, totally different drama? The terms of this question would seem to have been given a stock formulation, at least from the time of the Pelagian controversy: Whatever is granted to human initiative and achievement must be subtracted from God's, and vice versa—when God acts in his sovereignty and transcendence, man is excluded.

But Wesley sensed that this could not be the last word. He was not afraid of names. "By all I can pick up from ancient authors, I guess he [Pelagius] was both a wise and an holy man" who "very probably held no other heresy than you [Fletcher] and I do now."[13] In the heat of controversy, Wesley tended to oversimplify. He was driven to it because he still worked within the traditional framework of two competing energies, or causalities—monergism versus synergism. We have not yet been able to overcome this dilemma, but we are becoming increasingly aware that it falsifies both the biblical perspective and the nature of a true Christian active obedience. Is God a substitute subject for men in historical action, or is he the where-from and the where-to, the pro-vocation, the power, and the guarantee of an action that remains fully human and responsible? If he is a substitute subject—however much we may try to explain it away—history is a meaningless game and man's humanity a curious detour.

3. A further step must be taken, in which Wesley leads the way in spite of his limitations: the concreteness of action. Sanctification is not merely a spiritual state. Wesley does not hesitate to spell out its meaning in specific actions, although his moralism seriously affects his views at this point. The believer is not left to pure ambiguousness— "Perhaps I am doing God's will!" We may, in our careful dialectics, recoil from Wesley's claim that Christians "know in every circumstance of life what the Lord requireth of them."[14] But it is not boasting; it is faith's grateful acknowledgment (which somehow broke through an idealistic captivity) that we can confidently engage in a concrete

course of obedience as long as we faithfully seek to do God's will. It is only this conviction that can lend "enthusiasm" to the believer's life. Here works are not a concession that God allows us in spite of their present imperfection and their eschatological futility—they are needed for our salvation. Indeed, they are needed by God himself—they are the raw material of the new heaven and the new earth.

4. It is in this perspective that I would like to look at the Wesleyan doctrine of perfection. Our sanctification must not be measured by some idealistically conceived norm of perfection, or (this against Wesley) by some equally unreal purity of motivation, but by the concrete demand of the present kairos. There is an action, a project, an achievement that is required of us now; there is an action that embodies the service of love today, and in my condition: It is *perfection*—the mature, ripe form of obedience.

If I interpret him correctly, Wesley, at all these points, was not giving up the prior initiative of grace which had become the foundation of his existence since 1738; he was restoring the biblical perspective of a covenant. God cannot say "I am your God," as Barth points out, without at the same time saying, "You are my people." And this means also that we are given a specific task, without which the convenant would have no meaning and no purpose. We are constituted into valid, active partners. We are sanctified!

But Wesley's articulation in thought and practice of this insight lacked a deeper understanding of the nature of this human subject who is thus called and authorized and freed. The instruments with which he worked concealed the corporal and corporate nature of human life, and thus he was unable to see these dimensions as constitutive of the holy life and could only co-opt them in a peripheral and nonessential way. It is at this point that, in some ways, his effort miscarried. But the dynamic understanding of Christian life that he championed still challenges us in our task.

# Justification, Sanctification, and the Liberation of the Person

## *Rupert E. Davies*

This chapter will investigate the relationship between Wesley's teaching on justification and sanctification, and the modern theologies of liberation. Some of these theologies claim to have sprung out of one or another of the Methodist traditions, and this fact alone makes the present investigation important. But a deeper question, affecting our own integrity as Methodist preachers, theologians, and historians, lurks insistently beneath all our inquiries into this matter: Is it possible to claim for ourselves allegiance to the theology of John Wesley—as Methodist ministers in Britain and elsewhere are required each year to assert that they believe and preach "our doctrines"—while embracing a theology of liberation? Or is it necessary to make a decisive choice between two conflicting types of theology, while, of course, admitting that the later type may have been influenced in some ways by the earlier?

Certain preliminary remarks should be made concerning the nature of this investigation. It is evident that the social, cultural, and political context of Wesley's theology is vastly different from that of the liberation theologies; it is equally evident that the thought-forms and language of Wesley are quite different from those employed by the liberation theologians and are, indeed, perhaps quite unintelligible to the Christians among whom they have done their thinking and writing. Moreover, that Christian truth is most effectively expressed (in the sense of appealing in a persuasive way to the greatest number of people in a position to grasp its import) in the thought-forms of the prevalent culture, or at least in the thought-forms of the culture that is powerfully operative at the time.

From these facts two inferences are commonly drawn— one I reject; the other I accept. The first is that when the thought-forms and language disappear, or are so deeply eroded that they no longer appeal to any except a dyed-in-the-wool traditionalist or antiquarian, the truths they were intended to convey will collapse also—in fact, they will be seen by subsequent generations as no longer worthy of the title "truth" at all, except in the feeble and, I believe, meaningless sense of that which is true for *me*, or for hellenistic Jews, or for the men of the Middle Ages, or for Victorians. For instance, taking this view, since the orthodox doctrine of the Person of Christ is creedally expressed in the language of late Greek philosophy, and since that philosophy is now discountenanced, the doctrine no longer need be accepted, except as a historical and social phenomenon.

I reject this inference, in the first place, because it contradicts itself. It is asserting: It is true that nothing is true—or, at greater length—It is true that the Homoousios is *merely* a cultural phenomenon because all statements are determined by the culture in which they are made. But in this case, the inference itself is determined by the culture in which it is made and it, too, is *merely* a cultural phenomenon. So the inference is not credible.

I reject the first inference also because it misunderstands the function of language. Certainly the authors of the Creed believed they were expounding "the last word" in the matter of the Person of Christ. We know that they were wrong, since so many words have been uttered subsequently. In fact, thought and language exist, not to express truth completely and to encapsulate it forever in a verbal formula, but to *point toward* that which is in the last resort inexpressible and to do it in the best available way—that is, in the language of a prevailing culture. I suspect that this is the case even with everyday matters and with the natural sciences; I am sure that it is the case with the important issues of human existence—the more important the issue, probably, the more it is the case. There is no last word on Christology or justification or sanctification. But the Creeds and the theologians *have* illuminated and pointed toward the inexpressible and cannot be dismissed out of hand as culturally determined.

The second inference, which I accept, is that to "canonize" any particular thought-language—that is, to regard it as a complete and definitive expression of truth and to impose it, if it is theological, on the clergy of a church—is to condemn its content to ultimate and general neglect. This is a fate that has been avoided only very narrowly by both the Roman Catholic and the Calvinist traditions. The well-tried cultural language of the late Greco-Romans remained potent for a remarkably long time, and biblical language, even longer—in some parts of the world they are not dead yet. But Greco-Roman thought-language makes little sense today outside those circles of the west that are still aware of their classical heritage, and biblical terminology is becoming increasingly irrelevant over large areas of the first world, never having reached a high degree of general importance in the third world.

Logically, then, the abandonment of traditional language in no sense involves the abandonment of the truths that the language intended to express. We do not question the truth of the Bible by reexpressing its ideas; we do not deny the Catholic faith by rejecting the Sistine Chapel's ceiling imagery, which depicts the whole history of the universe in terms of biblical mythology, from creation to the final judgment, exquisitely brought to life and rendered unforgettable by the Renaissance art and technique of Michelangelo. Nor does the African or modern western repudiation of the metaphysics of the Fathers or of the Schoolmen invalidate the doctrines of the Creeds. But on the other hand, it remains a vital concern of the Christian church, which in a pluralistic age continues to be an evangelistic agency, to reexpress in the terms of each succeeding culture the truths that it believes to be committed to it forever.

The question before us therefore is: *Are the Wesley doctrines of justification and sanctification expressed by the liberation theologies in terms of the cultures in which those theologians originate?* Or, if we cannot give an unreserved affirmative answer to that question, is there a distinct similarity between them, or is there evidence of a legitimate development of one from the other? If the answer is yes to one or the other of these questions, then we can say that liberation theology is in tune with Wesley's thought. If the answer in all cases is no, then no doubt we shall have to choose one or the other and deal with our consciences accordingly.

## Wesley's Great Salvation

I will begin the investigation proper by reminding you of John Wesley's teaching about God's "grand design for the salvation of mankind," using Wesley's own language as far as possible. We have seen that language is very important in the comparison on which we are embarked, and I have found in the past that the too-ready translation of Wesley's words into modern theological terminology has often blurred the outlines of his theology, especially when it is distasteful to modern man, and thus has begged the very sort of question we are now asking.

Wesley, then, taught that humans in their present state are fallen creatures. The Fall of Adam and Eve corrupted the whole human race; and Adam fell by wrongly using his freedom of choice. Because of Adam, we lost the moral image of God, with the result that all our thoughts and desires are impure, and with the further result that he introduced all the pain and suffering that exist in the animal world and the human world, including disease and the pain of childbirth. The final consequence of the Fall is death, both spiritual and physical. We are all involved. Fallen humanity, however, has not entirely lost the law of God, though we are incapable of keeping it and though it has the chief effect of condemning us; by the use of conscience—often identified with the prevenient grace of God—we are able to recognize God's law. But conscience can be either tender (which is good), or scrupulous, or hard (either of which is bad). Fallen humanity has lost much, but not all the freedom that originally belonged to Adam. God's grace works within us to enable us to choose the right and reject the wrong, to perform our duty, and above all, to hear and receive the gospel. If persons are not saved, it is not because they are damned in advance by God, but because they do not *will* to be saved. Thus fallen humanity can move toward God, though we cannot, by any means, save ourselves. Our good deeds are done by God's grace, and therefore have no merit toward our salvation.

Salvation is due entirely to God's gracious, unbounded, undiscriminating, and undeserved love, which is absolutely free to all, without exception. God has provided the sacrament of baptism for the cleansing away of original sin, but since the effects of baptism are often—perhaps always—obliterated by subsequent sin, God has provided the "merits of Christ," in his death and resurrection, for our redemption. Without the work of Christ, there is no redemption. Redemption is offered to all, again without any exception, and it is received only with the help of God's grace, through faith in Christ. There are various kinds of faith, but "saving faith," in Wesley's terms, is a "sure trust and confidence that Christ died for *my* sins, that he loved *me* and gave himself for *me*."[1] Thus I am "justified"—and to

Wesley this means, in spite of all the preceding Protestant sophistication of the word, quite simply, "pardon for sins, original and actual." By justification, we are adopted as God's children, and we are born again. The new birth is an elemental change—a change in the very soul—so that we rise from the death of sin to the life of righteousness: Our evil passions turn into virtues, our sensual minds are changed into the mind that was in Christ Jesus, and the image of God is restored in us. Normally, but not invariably, we receive the witness of the Spirit that we are the children of God, and that witness is direct, immediate, and unmistakable.

Sanctification begins immediately after justification and is a growth into holiness, by the work of the Spirit, received only through faith. The justified person does not commit outward voluntary sin, but inward sin continues, and sanctification refers to its gradual conquest; the seeds of anger, lust, and pride are as powerful as those of any weed, though they do not involve guilt in themselves. Our persistence in sanctification—for we can fall from grace— leads to Christian perfection, or perfect love. And love is the important word.

Wesley does not teach, of course, that the "perfect" person is free from errors or temptations, or from the limitations of human ignorance, or from illness and death. But he does teach that one who has reached perfection loves God with the whole self, and the neighbor as self. Perfection can be reached in this present life, and has been by some; it follows a steady growth in love and goodness and is conferred instantaneously (Wesley is not always quite sure of this point). If it is not reached in this life, there is no ground for condemnation; it will be conferred by God at the moment of death. In one sense, "perfection" is not perfection; a perfect person still grows in grace—both in this life, if one is perfect here, and in all eternity. And perfection, even though granted in this life, can subsequently be lost.

This process is what Wesley calls the *great salvation,*

whereby we are "perfectly restored" in Christ and "changed from glory into glory."

We will complete this summary of Wesley's theology by noting that he claimed to derive it wholly and exclusively from Scripture. So much has been said about the Methodist appeal to experience—as if Wesley were a Schleiermacher born before his time—that it is necessary to emphasize this. Wesley, of course, highly valued his own and his followers' experience of God—experience certainly was not limited in his mind to what we call feeling (in fact, he did not lay much stress on this element)—it covered the whole of a personal relationship with God as Father. Wesley appealed, moreover, to the experience of the whole church, and to that of certain men and women of God in particular. But he based no doctrine upon it. Doctrine, for him, was derived only from Scripture, and was *confirmed* by experience; experience alone proved nothing. Wesley was thus a strictly biblical theologian.

## Theologies of Liberation

When we turn to the liberation theologians of today, we seem to enter an entirely different world. Whether it is essentially a different world, we have still to discover. It is necessary, as well as convenient, to divide the theologies of liberation into three main categories. The first consists of those related to the liberation of people and societies from economic exploitation and oppression. The outstanding example of this is the work of Latin American theologians, both Catholic and Protestant. The second category is made up of those related to the liberation of the female sex from personal, political, legal, social, and economic restrictions and dominations; here we speak of "feminist theology." The third comprises those related to the liberation of societies and individuals from racial discrimination and degradation; the chief example is the black theology of North America, with certain counterparts in Africa.

Obviously these three categories have much in common: (a) They all draw largely on the prolonged and bitter oppression and partial liberation that the people for whom they speak have experienced—the experience that their oppressors even yet have not recognized for the terrible thing it was—or have not acknowledged that it occurred at all; (b) They all see the Bible, either solely or chiefly, as the record of God's liberation of his people from oppression and injustice, both in the Old Testament, which speaks of God's ancient people, and the New Testament, which speaks of God's new Israel. The new Israel, like the old, is described by the Bible as entering a new life, in spite of its enemies, and finding final vindication and triumph; (c) They all hope—in the biblical sense of hope—for the individual's growth into true personhood, within a just and compassionate community that gives equality of treatment to all.

It is sometimes said that they also have in common the acceptance of Marxist theories of human motivation and historical development. I can find no solid evidence for this acceptance in any of the three categories, although Marxist analysis is from time to time employed; it is hardly possible to find the work of any realistic theologian, or indeed any serious writer on economics or politics, of which this is not true. But it is no more true here than in many other cases. Perhaps I might add that if a liberation theologian accepted any form of Marxist determinism, that would indeed disqualify that person from any claim to thinking with Wesley. Economic determinism is, after all, the modern equivalent of predestination. But there is no sign of this in any of them, so far as I can tell.

## Latin American Theology

I select Gustavo Gutiérrez as the representative and exponent of the Latin American theology of liberation, although there are many others. Gutiérrez is convinced that the people of Latin America are passing beyond the stage of development—which was, no doubt, a useful phase—to that of liberation, or to put it plainly, social revolution. He believes that it is the business of theology to reflect critically on what is actually happening in history (he calls this historical praxis); and what is happening in Latin America is liberation. This fact of liberation offers and requires a new way of doing theology—a way that begins in Latin America but is universal in its application. Theology in this context starts with reflection, but it goes on, he says, "to be part of the process through which the world is transformed. It is a theology which is open—in the protest against trampled human dignity, in the struggle against the plunder of the vast majority of people, in liberating love, and in the building of a new, just and fraternal society—to the gift of the Kingdom of God."[2]

Such theology must abandon the "Christendom concept" in which temporal realities lack autonomy; still more sharply, it must repudiate every form of pietism and any kind of concentration on the unworldly. It must come right down into the arena of political and social conflict, and the church that professes it must work toward the transformation of Latin American life. In this transformation every oppressed person must be helped to attain "conscientization" (as Paulo Freire has called it)—the state in which one not only becomes aware of one's situation but consciously protests the oppression in it and siezes responsibility for modifying that situation and shaping the future, becoming freer and less dependent in the process, and committing oneself to the transformation of society here and now, where one lives.

This transformation, says Gutiérrez, is God's work in our time, just as the Exodus was God's work in Moses' time. The work of Christ forms part of this work of God and brings it to complete fulfillment. Jesus was no mere religious teacher or holy man; he was deeply involved in the politics of his time, confronting the power groups among the Jewish people, and dying at the hands of the political authorities who were the oppressors and enemies of the people. The salvation that Christ offers is liberation not only from sin, but also from all the consequences of sin—despoliation, injustice, and hatred. It is in fact a new creation and a new person. Christian hope leads us to thrust into the future, which holds for us immense possibilities of human fulfillment within history, and indeed, of a glorious utopia. This is the true eschatology—the promise of the future drawing us into direct and hopeful action in the present. The church is called to proclaim all this in deed as well as in word. The class struggle is a fact; the church does not have the option to say whether it approves or not, but must take part in it on the side of justice. Yet since the church is called to announce the love of God for *all*, it is bound up inexorably in the need to fight for the poor and weak, and at the same time to do good to the oppressors. For the universal love, which requires solidarity with the oppressed, also requires the effort to liberate the oppressors from their ambition and selfishness; oppressors need liberation as much as do the oppressed.

## *Feminist Theology*

Feminist theology takes its point of departure from the oppression that Rosemary Reuther terms "the oldest subjection of all," which also is the most extensive of all, for it is the subjection of more than half the human race. Since it is concerned with a phenomenon to be found everywhere and relates to an aspiration and a hope common to vast numbers of people in every culture, it can be stated in general terms. Women have been subordinated by men throughout most of history, largely because of the physical limitations imposed by childbirth and childraising and the advantage that men have taken of this. Women have been conditioned by society, which rationalizes the innate desire of men to retain the power they have acquired, to accept this position of inferiority; and this position has been concretized by legislation and custom in all capitalist societies, as well as in others. It has been defended by male thinkers of all persuasions, religious and nonreligious—even by that great liberator of human feelings and enemy of human ignorance, Sigmund Freud. It was no small part of the work of Christ to abolish this subordination of women and to bring them to their true fulfillment. He was himself, by the standards of his time, a feminist. But more than that, the salvation he offers to all is intended equally for women and for men, and the growth into true personhood, which includes full development of God-given powers in the service of God and humanity, is made possible by the Holy Spirit for each man and each woman alike. The image of God is in woman as it is in man, and indeed it is also in the relationship between them. Damaged or destroyed by sin, it is restored by Christ.

In spite of this, most Christian theologians through the ages have applauded the subordination of woman, quoting some culture-conditioned words of Paul and have described her, obscenely, as the source of lust or as defective man. The time has come to reassert the dignity of woman in Christ—not only to reassert it, but to fight against the oppressive law and custom that deny it and to embody the equal dignity of woman and man in the structures of the church and of society.

## Black Theology

I chose James H. Cone as the representative of black theology, even though his brother, Cecil Wayne Cone, has criticized his views at various points.[3] James Cone begins with the conviction that blacks think of God differently than do whites and therefore must have a different thelogy, based on the Bible and on their own experience; and since the theme of the Bible is liberation, there is a natural harmony between it and the black experience. The terrible sufferings of the blacks in America, both before and after the Civil War and into the present age, inescapably form one primary source of black theology. Jesus Christ is the truth for all people and for all societies, and the Bible is the witness to him; the Bible therefore provides the other primary source of theology, but for blacks it must be interpreted in the light of black experience. The essence of this experience is the desire for liberation, political and otherwise—long frustrated, but now gradually taking place. Christ is shown in the Bible to be a liberator, and a Christology that leaves out this fact is a white theology—or rather, a white ideology. Christ is a historical reality as liberator; he is also present as suffering and risen, in the worship of black congregations, and he will come in glory to complete his liberating work. These statements are not to be taken as ideological justification for black politics, for Jesus Christ is above politics, and he is the absolute Lord—the captain who never lost a battle. The Bible is the story of liberation, and black theology is biblical theology.

The meaning of liberation for those who have been oppressed is first, to be free for God, but also to be free to liberate those who are still oppressed. In the setting free of the oppressed, according to Cone, the black Christian is not governed by Jesus' example of nonviolence. We live in a violent, racist society which must be destroyed, he says, and the issue between violence and nonviolence as ways of changing society is a nonquestion. The question is only *what* violence to use and to what extent. It is useless to talk of reconciliation between black and white; reconciliation is impossible unless and until whites are converted to the black viewpoint. Reconciliation can begin only when justice is achieved, says Cone.[4]

## Wesley and Liberation Theologies

As we turn to the question of the relation between these theologies and the theology of Wesley, a whole host of questions arise, fully armed. We must select a few. The first is whether Wesley would have countenanced such terms as *liberation* theology, *feminist* theology, *black* theology, at all. Almost certainly, no. For him there was only *Christian* theology, although it might be urged in mitigation of that blanket statement, that Wesley certainly believed some parts of the gospel to be especially necessary for the particular people he was addressing. But the Latin American theologians, probably, and the black theologians, certainly, are saying much more than that—very nearly that their theology is now the only true one for everyone, though it springs out of a particular historical context. Sometimes, on the other hand, they seem to say, "This is the true theology for us; we are not greatly interested in what is the true theology for you." The feminist theologians are much nearer Wesley's position, since they claim that what they say originates not out of a particular historical context, but from the gospel itself.

The next question concerns the theology of fallen, or as we may well say, enslaved humanity. Here there is greater harmony than at first might appear. It is true that the liberation theologians have no concern with the sin of Adam and its alleged historical results. But they are, in all cases, willing to trace the present condition of the human race to a train of historical events rooted in the greed, ambition, and pride common to all human beings. For them, as for Wesley, sin is universal. They do not claim any natural goodness for the oppressed, even when announcing their solidarity with them. The primal sin is no doubt that of the oppressors, but the oppressed have acquiesced in their own oppression until they have taken on a slave mentality; they need to be "conscientized"—that is, awakened and made personally aware of the state of slavery into which they have sunk. The oppressed are, of course, victims of systems more than of individual oppressors, and we do not find in Wesley indictments of evil political and economic systems. But he does ascribe to the Fall, and to the consequent reign of sin, disordered thinking as well as wrong action. Pain and disease are consequences of the Fall and affect the working of the mind, he says. "Let a musician be ever so skillful, he will make but poor music if his instrument be out of tune. From a disordered brain (such as is, more or less, that of every child of man) there will necessarily arise confusedness of apprehension . . . false judgments . . . and wrong inferences."[5] It would not have been difficult, surely, to persuade Wesley that political systems built by people with perverse desires, inordinate ambition, and disordered brains, have caused untold evil to their citizens and have corrupted the souls of those who built them.

The third question concerns the work of salvation. As we have seen, Wesley ascribes this solely and entirely to the grace of God operative in Christ. We do not cooperate in the work of salvation itself; our repentance before we have true faith is not displeasing to God, but it does nothing to deserve or to achieve salvation. Once we are pardoned and reborn, we put our salvation into practice with the help of the Holy Spirit. But our salvation is the work of God alone, and it has been carried out for us by Christ.

We do not find in the Latin American or in the black theologians the same emphasis on the initiative of God or the same concentration on the saving work of Christ. "Liberation," their word for salvation, is certainly the work of God active in history; but we, in an almost Pelagian way, bring it into effect by our deeds and sacrifices. For Gutiérrez, Christ indeed is part of the process of liberation, which continues from the first act of creation until the complete arrival of the kingdom of God, and Christ (in a sense not clearly defined) fulfills the process. But he is not the sole mediator and agent of salvation. For James Cone, Christ is the liberator par excellence. He is not only the center of a particular event in time—he is the eternal event of liberation in the divine person who makes freedom a constituent of human existence, for he is the image of the invisible God, who is the liberating God.[6] Thus he is present in every act of liberation. Yet there is still a discrepancy between Wesley's assertion of salvation through Christ alone by his once-for-all act, and even the highest attribution of praise to Christ offered by the black theologians.

Feminist theology, on the other hand, is willing to ascribe full saving power to Christ, by whose reconciling act in death and resurrection the distinction of status between men and women is obliterated.

This leads to a yet more basic question. Is the liberation of which the liberation theologians speak the same as the salvation of which Wesley speaks? We cannot summarily dispose of this question by saying that whereas Wesley's salvation is spiritual, liberation for Latin Americans, blacks, and women is political. Neither logic, nor the Bible, nor the theologians in question, nor John Wesley, would admit this disjunction. Politics, to them (and I hope, to us) as far as the word needs definition, is the art or science of living together in communities; salvation, to Wesley and the Bible—liberation, to the theologians who emphasize it—is of the whole self, which must include the self in relation to others. "Spiritual" and "political" are not mutually exclusive terms.

But it is almost beyond doubt in spite of this, that salvation for Wesley—remembering that in salvation he included justification and sanctification, which are distinct but follow one upon the other as day follows night—concerned an individual's *personal* life and *personal* relations, first with God and then with neighbors and friends and fellow Christians. This was as far as Wesley looked for the whole self. Liberation as it is expounded, on the other hand, is concerned with nations and races and classes and sexes; there is very little talk of God's forgiveness of the individual, or of personal relations with God and with neighbor, except insofar as the development of the individual is made possible and actual by the reordering of society.

It could be urged by the liberation theologians, and particularly by the feminists, that this is simply a difference of emphasis; that they also are concerned about personal, spiritual growth in grace, but that they have other things to do first—things that must be done first if that growth is even to be possible for the oppressed. There is force in this, but it is hard to read first Wesley, and then the others, without being convinced that the areas of real concern are very different.

Yet it may be suggested that in spite of what the theologians themselves say or fail to say, it is logically and theologically possible to be a Wesleyan and a liberation theologian at the same time, as far as the point under discussion is concerned. The Bible, in both Testaments, as the liberationists can rightly urge, is about the total salvation of humanity through the grace and power of God—and salvation is not total until the corporate as well as the personal life of human beings is redeemed. We are not wholly saved (and in token of this we groan within ourselves) until all are saved—until the whole universe enters upon the liberty and splendor of the children of God. So much Wesley needs to learn. Yet for us, as the liberationists need to learn, these are empty words unless as individual persons we receive the gifts of forgiveness and holiness and grow in grace as the children of God. So Wesley and the liberationists can be on speaking terms after all; the teaching of one complements the teaching of the others.

But next we ask, is the man or woman who has been justified and is in process of being sanctified, the same person as one who is liberated in the way we have been describing? The marks of justification and sanctification are clearly set out by Wesley: the fulfillment of the law of God in its inward meaning; abstention from sinful acts; the bringing forth of the fruits of the Spirit—that is, love, joy, peace, and the rest; the steady conquest of temptation and inbred sin; a deep and practical love for God and neighbor. Wesley said that he knew of no holiness that was not social holiness, but we must not take this to mean that it was a holiness devoted to changing the social order; Wesley's holiness was social in the narrow sense that it related to personal relations with other people, especially those in the fellowship of believers. Although we cannot legitimately criticize Wesley for not holding views that had not yet been propounded about the social order, or for not analysing society in ways that had not yet been suggested—not even Wesley could do everything!—it is wholly fair to say that he thought of Scriptural holiness as being practised within the existing order. Nor does his belief that Christian perfection is possible in this life really supply a bridge to the belief that *society* can and should be transformed within the present historical process.

The liberated man and woman, on the other hand, have been made aware of the chains that bound them and have thrown off those chains, to live in freedom the life their innate powers enable them to live. Being themselves liberated, they become in their turn liberators, fighting against injustice, by violent means if necessary—since injustice itself is a form of entrenched violence and can be removed only by violence and, at least according to James Cone, by spurning mere reform and all attempts at reconciliation with the oppressors.

The two pictures called up in the mind are thus very different from each other, and although individuals have sometimes claimed to be true to both, in spite of the tension between them, it cannot be said that a theological or ethical resolution of the issues has yet been offered—so to be a Wesleyan in a revolutionary situation means impalement upon the horns of a very uncomfortable dilemma. The most that can be said is that Wesley himself perhaps would have been somewhat more sympathetic with the exponents of feminist theology than with those of Latin American or black revolutionary theology, since he refrained from those aspersions on womankind that are part of the stock-in-trade of classical theology and plainly believed that the way of holiness was equally open to women and to men. But we cannot really say more than this.

The sixth and last question relates to the sources of theology. For Wesley there was only one source—the Bible—though he himself was, of course, unconsciously influenced by many traditions. Experience was secondary, intended only to confirm. For the liberationists, the nature and history of women and men, the dynamism of events in Latin America, and the black experience (in slavery and emancipation and second-class citizenship and discrimination, and found also in black worship—above all in the words and music of its songs) are also sources of theology, and primary sources at that. The Bible alone for Wesley; the Bible with other things, for the liberationists. This real discrepancy is diminished by the consideration that the Bible, as at least one of its main themes, speaks of the liberation of people and nations from oppression, but the discrepancy remains, nonetheless.

## Conclusion

It is by now apparent that Wesleyan theology and liberation theology do not, in most cases, mean the same thing even when they use the same or similar words. In some respects liberation theology indicates a proper development of Wesley's thought, as in the account of fallen humanity; in some instances—as in the description of salvation—Wesleyan theology can be held in conjunction and mutual complementation with liberation theology. But in other respects, such as the matter of the nature of holiness and the sources of theology, there is a conflict that cannot at the moment be resolved. Yet it is impossible to conclude, as some might be tempted to do, that Wesley's theology justifies the maintenance of the social and political status quo, with a few mild reforms, while liberation theology cannot defend anything except violent revolution. Wesley's theology, reinforced and communicated of course by his preaching, brought into existence a still-growing company of people, most of them from the oppressed classes and/or the subordinate sex, who, forgiven by God through Christ and empowered by the Spirit, have entered upon a new, free, and creative life. Such people are destined to change society—and some of them have done exactly that. And if, when confronted by a situation in which this new life they have received is violently withheld from others, they join in the fight for justice, I doubt very much if Wesley would frown down upon them in disapproval from his celestial seat—for he had an immense and not entirely nontheological sympathy with the oppressed and the deprived.

# Methodism and
# Social Change
# In Britain

## *John Kent*

This chapter is in two parts. The first, briefer section contains a rapid historical survey of the relationship between Methodism and social change in Britian from 1800 to the present. The second section attempts to interpret this material in a more theoretical fashion.

## I

I would like to dissent from, or at least to qualify, Bernard Semmel's fashionable thesis that in England, Wesleyanism was the theological form of the democratic revolution and that its doctrine was essentially a liberal and progressive ideology, confirming and helping to advance the movement from a traditional to a modern society.[1] This is yet another variation on the familiar but quite unprovable Halévy thesis which suggests that one should first suppose that English society was threatened with revolution between 1740 and 1840, and then assume that one will find in Wesleyan history the explanation to show why this revolution did not actually occur. For Halévy, as for many other writers of a variety of political persuasions, Methodism worked this superfluous miracle through its Tory sympathies and its conservative influence; for Semmel, as for Harold Perkin, Wesleyanism weakened the revolutionary impulse in its violent form by substituting a theological rationale, inherently nonviolent and creative and conducive to a more democratic and liberal society.[2] In fact, the trick is so simple, whichever way you work it, that the cautious historian will suspect that there is no trick at all. And I would indeed hold that there was in England, after the disastrous defeat of English liberalism in the American War of Independence, no intense revolutionary pressure; on the other hand, there was a ruling class, encouraged by its slow but total victory over Napoleon, which was prepared to share some authority with the bourgeoisie but was strong enough to cope with popular unrest by the use of force, as it did in the 1830s and 1840s. A few Wesleyan itinerants still preached the eighteenth-century doctrine of sanctification during the 1830s, and it was part of the stock-in-trade of visiting American revivalists such as Caughey and Finney; but there were no obvious social consequences.[3] Throughout the period between 1791 and 1848, the various Methodist Connexions usually supported law, social order, the monarchy, and nonviolent politics. Jabez Bunting supported Melbourne's government when it sent the Tolpuddle Martyrs to Australia, as he had supported Wellington's government when it granted emancipation to English Roman Catholics. If institutionalized Methodism had social consequences, as distinct from itself being a social consequence, it was because Wesleyanism played a part in the formation of the evangelical Protestant and pietist subculture that came to dominate mid-Victorian British society.

The importance of this pietist subculture has been realized only recently. It bequeathed to the later Victorian world its passion for teetotalism and its impulse to withdraw from contact with potentially hostile social groups. Politically, however, the pietist influence on Wesleyanism is less clear. The Connexion carried over from the eighteenth century a strong pro-Anglican party, but although many Wesleyans would have liked to identify with the establishment, they also wanted the civil liberties that could be legitimized only by joining the Nonconformist campaign against the establishment. This in turn meant some sort of political alliance with the Liberal party, for the Conservative party defended, though not enthusiastically, the privileges of the Church of England. It has been customary to interpret Wesleyan nineteenth-century political history in terms of a movement from conservatism to liberalism, but apart from the fact of a change of labels, this interpretation can be very misleading. The latent anti-Roman Catholicism of the pietist subculture, for example, reacted strongly to the growth of Irish nationalism and caused Wesleyanism to play an important role in the consequent division of the Liberal party in 1886; Rosebery's self-contradictory "liberal imperialism" similarly attracted significant Wesleyan support. A more definitely pietist—if not exactly Methodist—style of politics appeared in the late nineteenth century in the "social gospel," when the subculture's powerful impulse to restrictionism, which certainly involved more than obedience to a theological line, was embodied in demands for public legislation to impose pietist rules with regard to drinking, gambling, and sexual behavior, on the whole society. I know that theologians do not like social explanations, and I also know that sociology is under a cloud, but although the doctrine of sanctification may be said to have affected these concerns about human appetite, it is also true that similar attitudes could be found at the time among evangelical Baptists and Anglicans, who had been quite untouched by Wesleyan perfectionism and even were traditionally hostile to it. In England—I am not of course speaking about America—the social gospel expressed bourgeois values, especially the nontheological cult of respectability; this helped to set off and identify the pietist subculture as a whole from both the working-class and the aristocratic cultures, which were much less inclined to restrict behavior in the areas of alcohol, money, and sex. A cultural struggle took place, in which pietism and

Methodism were defeated in the long run, though never completely driven off the field, as witness recent attempts to revive the law forbidding blasphemy against the Christian religion.

Between 1800 and 1850, therefore, Methodism may have helped to preserve social stability and enabled the new urban industrial working classes to move from the eighteenth-century deference society to a nineteenth-century class society; if this were true—and Semmel and Perkin advocate this view—it would make an important contribution to our understanding of social change. On the other hand, E. J. Hobsbawm has denied that there were any substantial links between Methodism and the absence of an English revolution in the early nineteenth century.[4] There is no evidence that Methodism was widespread among the new factory workers. There was more contact in the older mining districts, but even there, in the tumultuous 1840s, stability was preserved less by religion than by the willingness of the owners to starve out the strikers and by the government's well-timed displays of force.

It is easier to see Methodism as an instrument for social change in the second half of the century, as the pietist subculture grew richer and more self-confident and longed for a political power it never obtained. It is precisely between 1880 and 1914, however, that observers tend to agree that Nonconformity, including Wesleyanism, failed to translate its religious traditions into practical and successful politics, perhaps because of an inherent inability to think of society as a whole. The most representative leaders of the pietist subculture in those years had no desire to influence and mold British society, but, still feeling themselves outside it, they wanted to conquer it, and that was something they could not do.

This failure helps to explain the sudden switch from the euphoria of Methodism in the Edwardian years to its depression in the 1920s. In that more modern period, social change was affecting Methodism more than Methodism was effecting social change. Methodist institutions were perhaps very important between 1800 and 1860 in a fluid social situation; they were a significant part of the religious subculture that flourished between 1860 and 1914; but they were of rapidly declining social and political value after 1918, when much energy was wasted on the ill-judged, American-prompted revival of teetotalism and on the forlorn hope of the League of Nations. A political movement needs a social base, and as a serious religious subculture, Nonconformity collapsed very rapidly in the 1920s and 30s. The political ideology of Methodism, insofar as one can speak of Methodism as socially cohesive, can only reflect the implications of that cohesion—this is what ministers, who tend to overestimate their influence upon their congregations, are prone to forget.

What seems to have survived most strongly is the Wesleyan feeling of always having been a special case as far as Anglicanism is concerned; hence the unsuccessful policy of pursuing unity with the Church of England, a policy that appealed more to some Methodists than it ever did to most other non-Anglicans. Otherwise, Methodism shares the political ethos of the latest form of religious subculture that links all the major denominations and that must find very broad political issues, such as South African racialism, when it wants to flex its muscles. I think that one is bound to call this a subculture because on issues such as abortion, it does draw on a popular constituency; at other times, however, it is no more than a pressure group. Methodism has been a healthy influence in these circles, to the extent that its representatives have refused to declare a religious war on the bare possibility of divorce, contraception, abortion, and the teaching of other religions than Christianity in schools. It is to be hoped that ecumenism does not finally obliterate these remnants of religious common sense. Methodism could perform a useful, limited political role as the focus of dissent within the religious subculture. Whether the image of holiness that such behavior would suggest has any connection with Wesley's teaching on perfection is another matter.

## II

Wesley's doctrine of sanctificaion was based on the assumption that one knew what holiness was; he was vulgarizing Fenelon's doctrine of *amour pur* and, in terms of method, substituting a rather crude concept of divine intervention for Fenelon's more finely balanced account of the relationship between the human and the divine. Wesley's approach appeared to be individualistic because he was teaching in the context of static social assumptions; there was no need to add an elaborate sociopolitical dimension to the idea of holiness, since in the mid-eighteenth century the political structure in England was largely taken for granted. It was generally agreed that seventeenth century attempts to change the nature of society had rightly failed and now stood as a warning against schemes for radical political change, as well as against what might be called eschatological politics—the politics of the end of the age and of imminent divine intervention. These typical politics of a religious sect could be found, for example, in early Quakerism or in the Fifth Monarchy Men. The English ruling class—aristocrats and new businessmen—rejected the implication of late eighteenth century revolutionary movements as far as England was concerned; major changes in English society, they thought, would mean the corruption of the goodness of the "given," which writers such as Wesley linked directly with the Christian God (the God of the American and French revolutions was the God of the Deist imagination, of course).

At any rate, if you ask for the relationship between the concepts of sanctification and revolution in the mind of Wesley, the answer is available: Wesley opposed the American Revolution as a breach of the divine order revealed in the Bible. He did not belong to the small, courageous, unsuccessful minority who not only supported the Americans in the 1770s but was willing—as Burke, for example, was not—to support the French when they also challenged that divine order. For Wesley, the *ancien régime* adequately contained, or was contained in, the divine order, and as long as men were politically free to become sanctified, further change hardly mattered. Hence the demand for the abolition of slavery.

The eighteenth century is a context that has been lost; western attitudes to time and change have altered. In the mid-eighteenth century there was a brief numbing of the sense of being caught up in historical change, but the American and French revolutions restored the sense of forward movement in time, while frightening many people when they saw what change might mean. There were intellectual efforts to impose a pattern on what seemed to be happening. On the conservative side, for example, Hegel rationalized change as the self-creation of the eternal Spirit, a process within which the individual had no absolute need to sanctifiy himself, because he could not effectively sin against the creative power that must be using him for its own purposes. Change was creative, but the creative power transcended man. For example, in the mind of Sarah Hennell, who brought together influences from Hegel, David Strauss, Feuerbach, and Herbert Spencer, the individual found blessedness by assuming that God was in control.

> During the Revelation-period, there existed for us the dominant phase of religion, which expressed itself in the idea that God does good to his creatures—[but] the form that it is

now acquiring . . . is that he has endued man with power to work out good for themselves. . . . Man's invention is nothing at all but God's way of making himself known to us: a way immensely different from that which we thought he ought to take, by sudden revelation, clear and express all at once—but which turns out to be infinitely gradual.[5]

One has moved from the seventeenth-century Pascalian religious view that human troubles have their source in our inability to refrain from activity, to a nineteenth century view that perfection is a social aim, to be sought through activity. There was no need, as far as Sarah Hennell was concerned, to doubt the essentially moral nature of what was developing through history. Nor was it a long step from her position to that of Marx, who denounced what was happening as morally intolerable because it involved the exploitation of one section of humanity by another. According to Marx, it was necessary for the human race to recover its freedom, which had been subtly destroyed— partly by complicated societies and productive processes that had alienated humanity from itself, and partly by religion, which enabled humanity to accept its alienation, either passively or painfully, rather than changing the society that caused it. Sanctification, in Wesley's sense or in any other, was not a cure for alienation, but only evidence of the alienated state. A secular, natural perfection would follow the revolution, and this would relieve human beings of the pressure of internalized religious goals, making sanctification superfluous—a sign that the reactionary forms of the previous society were reasserting themselves.

In other words, the western imaginative grasp of existence was transformed in the period between the Renaissance and the mid-nineteenth century. The concept of positive change—development, evolution, and revolution, understood from the end of the eighteenth century in a new, creative sense—began to dominate. The effect was not necessarily secularizing, but where the idea of divine action persisted, it was increasingly thought of (as Sarah Hennell said) as infinitely gradual, rather than sudden, "clear and express all at once." The idea of holiness (sanctification) changed from a desire to stand outside historical time and events (the political) to a need to recognize one's prior involvement in history and to become more, not less, publicly active.

There was, of course, an element in the western theological tradition—one that received renewed emphasis through the Anglo-Catholic movement in England—which declared that the Church, however described institutionally, was a supernatural entity, the eternal becoming temporal, the invisible becoming visible ("becomes" had much the same force as in the liturgical assertion that the bread and the wine "become" the body and blood of Christ). Nineteenth-century Wesleyans reacted against that revival, however; in its Anglo-Catholic dress, it inevitably reintroduced monasticism into the Church of England as the symbolic form of sanctification appropriate to the concept of a thoroughly supernatural ecclesia. Similarly, Anglo-Catholics rejected the state church view of Anglicanism because the true ecclesia was divinely given, and one had to identify with it; one could not form a local ecclesia on a faith-basis, as in the Dissenting tradition, or compact with the state. The Anglo-Catholic leadership had grasped the way events were moving. It was no accident that one leader, John Henry Newman, should have published *An Essay on the Development of Christian Doctrine* in 1845, in an effort to reconcile the new emphasis on historical change with a conservative belief in the essentially supernatural nature of the ecclesia. That Newman entered the Roman Catholic Church in the same year suggests a deep confusion in his thought, of which, one feels, he never became fully conscious. He was moving away from the ecclesiastical understanding of change at the very moment when the idea

*91*

of development was beginning to dominate him intellectually. If one had to choose between the *Essay on Development* and the *Syllabus Errorum* (1846), one might accept the *Syllabus*, conditioned though it undoubtedly was by Italian politics and Roman parochialism, as being a more accurate reflection of the traditionally eschatological politics of the ecclesia than was Newman's more optimistic view of the possibilities of change. That is, could sanctification be reconciled with progress, liberalism, and modern civilization, targets of the famous papal anathema? The Pope's rejection of any composition with modernity was instinctive, but steeped in tradition.

Wesleyanism was rather at sea here. As the Bunting correspondence shows us, a powerful section of the Wesleyan itinerancy was very slow to accept a non-Anglican status. It opposed the Dissenting Chapels Bill (1844), for example, partly out of loyalty to Anglican antagonism to Unitarianism and partly because it did not want, even by default, to be classified with Dissent. One finds Edward Walker, superintendent of the Birmingham Cherry Street Circuit in 1844, repeating what already had become a myth among the majority: "We have had the character hitherto of being conservative in ecclesiastical and, as far as we have at any time meddled, in our civil politics also"; and Hugh Hughes in the same year told Bunting, from Carmathen in Wales, "It is a pleasing thought to know that none of our members and but few of our hearers were with the Chartists, nor with the Rebecaites."[6] They were both still invoking the fixed, static society in which their founder had believed he lived.

Significantly, in the 1840s, Wesleyanism approached quite close to the evangelical pietist impulse to denounce adiaphorism: novel-reading, dancing, theater-going, traveling on Sunday trains, and drinking of spirits, wine, or beer—all became contentious issues. Teetotalism, especially, became a Methodist trademark, surviving the nineteenth century, when most other forms of cultural isolationism were gradually abandoned. In the early Victorian period a broad pietistic political style emerged, aimed at the imposition of specifically pietist rules of behavior on society at large. Social change was to be made illegal, law was to be used to prevent and prohibit change, and all of society (not just the church) was to be fixed in a specific form. In Victorian Wesleyanism, it is not surprising, therefore, that American revivalists should campaign for individual sanctification through faith—Finney and Caughey in the 1840s, Caughey and Phoebe Palmer in the 1860s, and the Pearsall Smiths in 1875—though over the whole period the scope of Wesleyan revivalism contracted. This was holiness in Wesley's own individualistic style.

There was a double process at work here, however. While many leading Wesleyans stuck to outmoded eighteenth century views of society as a static but providentially ordered hierarchy, in which sanctification meant at least a subjective breach with the order of the world, there was also, as we have seen, a growth in dynamic pictures of society, which prompted criticism of sanctification by withdrawal. Herbert Spencer expressed the mood in a secular form when he said, in *Social Statics*,

> The inference that as advancement has hitherto been the rule, it will be the rule henceforth, may be called a plausible speculation. But when it is shown that this advancement is due to the working of universal law; and that in virtue of that law it must continue until the state which we call perfection is reached, then the advent of such a state is removed out of the reign of probability into that of certainty.[7]

Spencer was appealing to the absoluteness of a secularized natural law of his own invention, and not to the providential intervention of a benevolent deity in response to faith in

Christ; the perfection to which he referred was social and objective.

In the second half of the nineteenth century, then, Wesleyan Methodism, making the most sustained bid in its history for political significance, tacked between the evangelical pietist restrictionism that had largely replaced Wesley's concept of holiness as the subjective faith-transformation of the individual, and a political liberalism that did not reflect an eighteenth-century Wesleyan ethos at all. This very temporary alliance depended on a growing Wesleyan irritation with the necessity of accepting the limits of Nonconformist second-class citizenship. That irritation weakened its traditional alliance with Anglicanism, and its leaders, lay as well as clergy, became more susceptible to a Liberal program conceived in terms of political freedom. But this program also failed to absorb fully the growth of a new political culture, to which Hegel, Marx, Nietzsche, Spencer, and Darwin were all powerful contributors, and which sought to organize social change so as to transform the pattern of a whole society—not just limited aspects of its activities. As far as these more radical attempts were to be successful—in Russia under Lenin and Stalin, in China under Mao, in Germany under Hitler— they constructed completely new contexts for any concept of sanctification. In the meantime, the brief political influence of Nonconformity in British politics, and the political power of the Liberal party, with which it associated, crumbled to nothing between 1906 and 1931; the Roman Catholic Church took the place of Nonconformity (including Methodism) as the natural form of dissent from Anglicanism, and the Labour party halfheartedly replaced the Liberal party as the instrument of organized social change. In such a period, whether in Bristol or Moscow, Wesley's idea of sanctification as an individual experience of the transforming power of Christ in a public social order, which could be taken for granted as the work of God, counted for almost nothing, and it would take a bold man to say that Anglo-Catholic monasticism counted for more.

The question inevitably arises: Is there still a useful myth of sanctification? Myths in general remain effective in society: Marxism, Maoism, and their right-wing mirror images are still powerful, if only because so many people cannot tolerate the thought that constant social change is both meaningless and uncontrollable. These political myths, however, have failed to impose more than a very temporary coherence on the terrifying realities of atomic power, whether military or industrial; on the restless psychology of the market; or on the recurrent conflicts of social and racial groups, and so they have failed to provide the kind of stable background against which private sanctification may flourish.

Nevertheless, there has been a twentieth-century revival of interest in religious myth, in the sense in which the poet W. B. Yeats understood it, as "stylistic arrangements of experience comparable to the cubes in a drawing by Wyndham Lewis"—or, as we might now say, Picasso.[8] Yeats meant, among other things, that myths are effective only when they develop imaginatively from experience; that they no longer work as "myths" when one is tempted to rearrange experience to suit them, or perhaps even to confirm them. Properly speaking, in fact, myths grant only an individual, and therefore a temporary sense of either personal or social coherence; myths are not absolutes, existing permanently outside human experience (as in a common Roman Catholic understanding of religious symbols). Experience, not simply language, must be reencountered and rearranged in each generation—an observation that lay at the root of Kierkegaard's assertion that Christianity, unlike Christendom, has no history. It is easy for theologians to assume, as Coleridge has encouraged too many of them to do, that some myths inhabit the human mind through supernatural agency and therefore reveal to us the absolute truth. In fact, religious myths seem to be testable in human experience and appear to wear out in time. It well may be, for example, as professors Hick, Nineham, and Wiles have recently suggested, that the original myth of the divine-human incarnation is quietly falling to pieces and is ready to be replaced with

> a story in which the protagonist's role belongs undividedly to God, though of course the story would tell how once he worked in a vitally important way—though not a way necessarily unique in principle—through the man Jesus to bring the Christian people into a relationship of reconciliation and oneness with himself.[9]

I have quoted this passage for two reasons. It illustrates the fact that there were theological, as well as social obstacles to redrawing the doctrine of sanctification. The passage also illustrates the fact that one cannot go on forever writing histories of theology based on a theory of doctrinal development. Rather, one should distinguish between a flexible myth-making, which enables the imagination to operate more fully and the moral agent to act more generously, and a rigidity (springing from the claim to have caught the Absolute in a myth, so to speak), which turns myth into dogma, ties the imagination down, and dries up charity. In an illuminating passage in *The Sense of an Ending,* Frank Kermode says that religious myths (the dogma of the incarnation, for example) characteristically become rigid and demand absolute assent because they presuppose total and adequate explanations for things as they are and as they were. He distinguishes them from "fictions" (such as Shakespeare's *King Lear*), which ask not for absolute, but for conditional assent, and which are, as he puts it, "for finding things out"—not for demonstrating that everything is already known.[10] Wesley believed his view of sanctification to be "revealed." One does not modernize his doctrine by adding a modern political theology, since Wesley was assuming that a viable political theology, equally absolute, already existed.

The myth of the holy life, which Wesley adopted and which depended upon a prior belief in the divinely given coherence of human society, did not usefully survive the collapse of the *ancien régime*. Indeed, as the framework of the modern state decayed in the nineteenth century, the social withdrawal that frequently became explicit in the pietism of the evangelical tradition was itself one source of the political collapse, because, as Hannah Arendt would have said, pietism educated another of those subcultures that refused to come to the aid of the republic.

If one takes Simone Weil as an instance of one who tried intensely to combine a self-annihilating version of the holiness myth with a public role, whatever the conflict involved between external commitment and internal self-abnegation, we are immediately struck by the problems she faced in relating her religious existence to her Jewishness, her middle-class origin, her Frenchness, and her position in the devastated history of western culture. She could not take her Jewishness for granted any more than could any other partly assimilated Jew, for she shared the anti-Jewishness (not anti-Semitism) of many Jewish intellectuals, and she also lived through one of the most savagely anti-Semitic periods of western history. She could not reconcile her bourgeois background with the myth of the holy individual, but her attempts in the 1930s to identify with workers and peasants were sentimental and threw her back into isolation. This, together with the Nazi defeat of France and its occupation in the early 1940s, made her an exile in the United States and England for the few remaining years of her life.

We can see why she abandoned the pacifism which, when

she was faced with violence at an earlier stage, had seemed the natural equivalent of holiness, and why she wanted so passionately to share in the Spanish Civil War and the Second World War. There had been no subtle, concealed, enriching development of meaning in what happened nationally and internationally between 1918 and 1945, and so war gave apparent coherence to this irrational political legacy. There was, in her whole career, the implication that contemporary holiness requires a total absorption of the self into suffering outside the self; in the classical mystical tradition, her instinct was to reject the sphere of the political, except as the scene of self-immolation. In this sense, war seemed to her more natural than peace. There was something suspicious, after all, in her enthusiasm for the annihilation of the self during such a period, for that aim ran close to the goal of the poisoned romanticism of the Nazis. And this illustrates once more that the problems of holiness arise from the historical conditioning of the holy.

This can be seen also in Simone Weil's inability to relate her myth of the holy life to the existing institutions of the western religious tradition in its Christian form. She rejected the fashionable 1930s theological image of the ecclesia as the organization that could supply the needed link between history and the suprahistorical—an image that itself had been conditioned to some extent by the organic, omni-competent, anti-human state of the period. In 1943, she wrote in her New York notebook, "When the Devil offered Christ the kingdom of this world he resisted the temptation. But his Bride, the Church, yielded to it. And have not the gates of Hell prevailed against her?" Nor was she any more impressed by a political appeal to eschatology. To her, as to so many of her generation, the Christian translation of the Jewish eschatological symbolism seemed implausible in the face of the actual events of the 1930s and 1940s; it seemed an illegitimate attempt to reintroduce the discredited idea of providence by invoking an essentially nonpolitical blessedness outside history, to offset the political misery of humanity in the historical present. This was an illegitimate attempt, since whatever force there ever had been in Jewish eschatology had been generated by the belief that the divinely appointed end of history was imminent. Of course, in the prayer of Jesus, one says, "Thy kingdom come," but since it is not God's will to reign in this world, one adds, "Thy will be done." "One asks for the disappearance of the universe and one consents to its presence." She added the epitaph of her generation, whose mass graves could be found in every revolution and counterrevolution all over Europe, in Russia, in China, and later in Vietnam: "One asks God's forgiveness for our existence, and one forgives him for causing us to exist."[11]

There seems, therefore, to be a certain levity about theologies of hope, joy, and liberation or revolution. Whether they come from Western Germany (Moltmann) or from South America (Gutiérrez), they come after Auschwitz; and after Auschwitz, as Primo Levi said, no rational person could believe in providence. Theodor Adorno said that "after the catastrophes that have happened, and in view of the catastrophes that are to come, it would be cynical to say that a plan for a better world is revealed in history and unites it. . . . History is the unity of discontinuity and continuity."[12] That was meant as a secular comment on the crude forms of Marxism, by a critical Marxist, but it is just as cynical for a theologian to say that the church has been supernaturally guided in the past or to claim that, starting from the visible ecclesia in the present (thought of as some kind of divine society), one can talk convincingly about a better world revealed in history and able to transform its apparent chaos into numinous order. To quote Simone Weil again, "The church as a society pronouncing opinion is a phenomenon of this world, conditioned."[13] It is too easy for

English people, ignorant of their own past interventions in that part of the world, to support (or to condemn) revolution in South America or South Africa, on the ground that such revolutions (or counterrevolutions) somehow cohere with the idea of the holy life, either Wesley's or Simone Weil's. We easily forget that on subjects about which its members really care deeply—abortion, religious education, sexual censorship—the English churches rapidly show themselves conditioned by a society whose divisions they reflect. Or again, it is tempting to criticize the nineteenth-century pietists for their socially conditioned political choices and to forget that the choices of the twentieth-century churches, in a hundred years' time, will be seen as equally the product of social conditioning.

What the ecclesia is conditioned by, moreover, is not a total process that makes sense, or that will be seen in the much longer run to have made sense, in terms of either a Hegelian self-expressing spirit or a Marxist dialectic that moves through revolution to liberation. Nor is the ecclesia conditioned by an absolute totality whose meaning will be revealed—to Pannenberg at any rate!—at the end of time. Historical necessity, as Adorno said, is just a metaphysical accident. Politics and holiness have pulled so far apart in the past seventy years that each has thrown doubt on the credibility of the other. Just as one can see no historical development that necessarily guarantees the ability of the political revolutionary, or the nonviolent social liberator, to deliver the better world they promise, so one can see as little evidence of a supernaturally guided development guaranteeing the direction of the visible ecclesia's alleged growth through time, either theologically or politically. It seems to me, therefore, that holiness—far from being the definable state of consciousness Wesley took it to be, and which he encouraged his itinerants to describe from their own experience, in the *Methodist Magazine*; and far from being a game of spiritual chess, in which the players, if they are like Simone Weil, are always combining to checkmate themselves—is a constant improvisation of charity out of ignorance and against the conditioning odds. Here, liberation, understood as the kind of self-awareness that is central to both black theology and feminist theology, seems to be a more hopeful guide than are scholastic revivals of sixteenth-to-eighteenth-century doctrines of sanctification.

# John Wesley on Economics

*Thomas W. Madron*

As with virtually all John Wesley's social thought, that which had to do with the realm of economics represented an ethical critique of problems rather than a theory of economic relations. England in the eighteenth century was a nation in economic transition. At the beginning of the period the country was largely agricultural, though commerce was a major factor. During the first half of the century, the English were feverishly accumulating "those great capital reserves which were destined to play so dominant a role in world history." The economic geography of England continued to be determined largely by the sea and by navigable rivers, with the result that financial control was passing to London.[1] In the rural areas, however, away from the few commercial centers where trade and manufacture were important, the peddler's pack afforded the people's only contact with the riches of commercial England. The seventeenth century, too, had bequeathed a variety of problems—the enclosure process in agriculture, transition from trade guilds to the system of domestic industries, monopolies and monopolistic practices, the expansion of colonial trade, and the Elizabethan Poor Law to take care of the increasing hordes of paupers.[2] The life of

A version of some of the material in this chapter appeared in *Methodist History* (October 1965), under the title "Some Economic Aspects of John Wesley's Thought Revisited."

the nation during the period was characterized and complicated by lack of economic unity.

Society in England was stratified, with a disproportionate number of people on the bottom. Local landlords and magistrates were both the political and the economic leaders of their communities. The boroughs in England and Wales were dominant in the political struggle, returning three-fourths of the members of Parliament. "In most boroughs the immediate control lay with a small urban oligarchy of attorneys, bankers, merchants and brewers entrenched in a self-electing corporation."[3] It was against these men and their power that Wesley often fulminated.

The unpropertied masses (by far the largest segment of the population) provided the labor force, the backbone of the industrial system that developed in the latter part of the eighteenth century. The whole social structure of the nation was upheld by and closely entwined with the Church of England. It might be said that on the level of political ideology, the Tories were oriented toward the Church of England, while dissenting opinion formed the main force of the Whig party.[4] This fact accounts in part for the success of Wesleyanism; it ministered primarily to the classes of people who were disfranchised politically, economically, and religiously. During the time when the working people in England were being dislocated and alienated (by the enclosure acts and by machine labor), the population also was increasing, and the situation made for an abundance of cheap labor. This factor, coupled with the accumulation of capital, set the stage for the advent of the Industrial Revolution. Then, as Kathleen Walker MacArthur points out, "Out of these conditions came hosts of problems centering around the psychological reconditioning of the people in character and morale."[5]

It was into these conditions that John Wesley came with his religious movement, and it was to these people that he addressed himself. While the specific economic order that confronted Wesley may have been peculiar to the eighteenth century, the way in which he dealt with it may be interpreted as a constant in the continuing evaluation of the ethical consequences of an economic system. In a very real sense, Wesley recovered the reform tradition of England. His was the approach of Wycliff, rather than that of the continental Reformation, and he brought it to some measure of fulfillment in the disinherited classes of England.[6]

Wesley's economic views, like all his social thought, were based on his ethics and theology. The two general concepts of greatest importance were his ideas of God and of humanity. To Wesley, God functions in two roles—as Sovereign (or Creator) and as Governor. God as Sovereign is omnipotent, but God as Governor imposes self-restrictions. From God's role as Sovereign comes all God's grace. This includes the whole of creation, both physical and social. Power and authority in such human institutions as church and state are grants made by God to his corporate representatives on earth.

In the concept of God's role as Governor, Wesley sought an answer to the problem of freedom. In order for God's revelation in Jesus to make sense, human beings need to be free, for without freedom they simply are not responsible. Thus human responsibility arises out of human freedom and conscience, which are functions of prevenient grace. In the human's ability to respond freely to God lay Wesley's synergism—that is, the cooperation between God and human beings—and this contributes the individualistic, subjective elements of Wesleyan theological and political thought. Prevenient grace is granted by God to humans, enabling them to differentiate between good and evil. If we can in reality distinguish between good and evil, this ability makes sense only if we can choose, or fail to choose, God. Thus, Wesley said, grace is resistible. Moreover, people can participate in God's love. We have this capacity because God first loved us. As a result of God's love, humans are able to love both God and their fellow human beings. Out of this conception of love arose (in part) Wesley's ideas of ethics, justice, and Christian perfection. The love concept itself was a social idea and was related to Wesley's thesis that Christianity is essentially a social religion.

The other major theological problem concerned human nature. Wesley's perspective was premised upon the Christian doctrine of original sin, which claims that human nature is corrupted as a result of Adam's Fall. All people are equally infected. The revelation of God gives to us all the possibility of salvation, though we are always capable of knowingly contravening the will of God. Sin, therefore, has a twofold character. It is, on the one hand, conceived in terms of the very depravity of human nature which originated in Adam; on the other hand, it is thought of as the transgression of divine law. The impulse to break God's law, however, comes partly as a result of the ongoing influence of original sin, even after justification. It is as a result of sin, in both senses, that the problem of evil arises; and Wesley found ample evidence of the reality of evil in war, class exploitation, and other social problems. Because of human sinfulness, government has the rather explicit ethical imperative to preserve order. Wesley's ethical assumptions rested upon the twin foundations of human responsibility and the creativity of divine and human love. Grounded in these is his conception of righteousness and an ethic that is inevitably both personal and social. Also related to the love concept were his ideas of social justice and Christian perfection.

The process through which perfection is realized is sanctification. Sanctification makes righteousness possible—not good and gracious acts themselves, but the operation of God in us produces these acts.

The goal of the process of sanctification is perfection in this life—that is, the perfect possession of the perfect motive—love of God and love of others. Thus Wesley stated that when a person is justified, "he is 'born from above,' born of the 'Spirit;' which, although it is not (as some suppose) the whole process of sanctification, is doubtless the gate of it." Wesley continued, indicating that this new birth implies "as great a change in the soul, in him that is 'born of the Spirit,' as was wrought in his body when he was born of a woman: Not an outward change only [though this is to be expected] . . . but an inward change from all unholy, to all holy tempers." In the final analysis, sanctification is God working in us to make us just and righteous. Therefore "nothing will avail without the whole mind that was in Christ, enabling you to walk as Christ walked."[7]

## The Social Ethics of Sanctification

In applying this position of Christian perfection to the relationship of the individual to society, Wesley insisted on the inseparable relationship between the love of God and the love of others. The love of which Wesley speaks is completely inclusive, extending to all classes and states of people. This love underwrites the fundamental egalitarianism implicit in Wesley's thought: "For [the perfected Christian] loves every soul that God has made; every child of man, of whatever place or nation."[8]

The doctrine of perfection was at once profoundly theological and ethical, which led his thinking into the problems of political and social reform. The love concept was first a social concept, rather than an individualistic one, and as such led to social and political criticism.

## Social Ethics and the Economic Order

How did Wesley translate the love ethic, as elaborated in the doctrine of sanctification, into a perspective on the economic system? In order to better understand Wesley's approach, we should consider several specific economic issues that were of concern to him, and which may be conveniently summarized in three categories—the nature of property, general economic problems, and issues of humanitarian reform.

## *Property*

A significant aspect of Wesley's political economy was his concept of property, which involved elements of his theology associated with both God and the human condition. Unlike John Locke, whose ideas dominated much of the eighteenth-century political and economic thought, Wesley refused to elaborate a theory for the absolute protection of property rights. Both Locke and Wesley agreed that God gave the earth to the whole of humankind in common. Locke sought to show, however, that persons "might come to have property in several parts of that which God gave to mankind in common, and that without any express compact of all the commoners." Locke argued that individuals mixed labor with the grant of nature that had been provided, and the product "excluded the common right of other men." The reason for this is that "labor being the unquestionable property of the laborer, no man but he can have a right to what [it] is once joined to, at least where there is enough and as good left in common for others."[9] As a result of these assumptions, for Locke, property became an inalienable right which must be defended.

For Wesley, on the other hand, property was never an inalienable right; any person holds property only as a steward of God, and God can at any time take the property away. Thus God, in his capacity as sovereign, makes the final choice as to the disposition of property. Because God is sovereign, "he must be the possessor of all that is," and because he holds title to all that is, he may resume his own property at any time.[10] People may use property only for those purposes that God has specified, and those who fail to use it as God directs have no moral right to it. It is possible, though by no means clear, that Wesley thought a person's legal right to property should be questioned if, in the use of the property, God's law is contravened. Thus, for Wesley, a person is not an owner, but rather a trustee or steward of property.[11]

The charge Wesley directed at the rich was, "Be ye 'ready to distribute' to every one, according to his necessity."[12] This is essentially what Wesley meant when he counseled that people should gain all they can, save all they can, and give all the can.[13] In its highest development, this concept of distribution according to need refers to what, in Wesley's thought, is the highest concept of economic organization— primitive communism, the kind of organization he thought existed among the earliest Christians.[14] The outcome of Christian love was to be a society in which all things would be held in common. Thus in the early church, "so long as that truly Christian love continued, they could not but have all things in common."[15]

Wesley went so far as to advocate the practice of a community of goods among Methodists. His objective was to bring them as close as possible to the practices of primitive Christianity. The evidence for this position is clear. Among the rules set down for the Select Societies by the first Conference (1744) was the following: "Every member, till we can have all things common, will bring once a week, bona fide, all he can toward a common stock."[16]

Apparently there was a good deal of opposition to the goal Wesley had in mind. One Richard Viney reported in his diary on February 22, 1744, that Wesley "told me of an intention he and some few have of beginning a Community of goods, but on a plan which I told him I doubted could not succeed."[17] According to Viney, the plan was to be carried out by the formula that later appeared in socialist thought—from each according to his ability, to each according to his need. The fact that Wesley did not seriously promote this scheme after 1744 suggests that the opposition was great enough to dissuade him. The three rules of gain, save, give, constituted a compromise developed after 1744, between what Wesley considered as ideal and what apparently was possible.[18]

This is not to argue that Wesley was an early English socialist; he did not try to force Methodists into the kind of framework he had once contemplated. The facts presented, however, do illustrate the lengths to which he thought the principle of the stewardship of property should go.

The attempt to read Wesley, therefore, in terms of the so-called Protestant ethic is not justified. Max Weber wrongly contends that Wesley's theology and ethics simply fostered the notion that the number of possessions a person has demonstrates the extent to which God's grace has fallen upon that individual.[19] Wesley objected to the "duty of getting a good estate."[20] Any interpretation of Wesley to the effect that the "presence of success indicates a state of moral soundness" is impossible to maintain, in the context of the totality of his writings.[21] In this sense Wesley represents an exception to the general Protestant ethic of Calvinism, which influenced the eighteenth century so greatly.[22]

The point is that Wesley did not accept the view of a sacred and inviolable right to property, but rather that the right to property was bound up with its proper use. His original notion that property is a gift of God, his contentions about its purposive use, and his rejection of the Protestant ethic, justify this interpretation. Wesley's concern with property led him to protest the monopolization of farms, and on one occasion he advocated, as a means of encouraging or compelling the redistribution of land, not allowing any farm to rent for more than one hundred pounds a year.[23] Apparently he was willing under some circumstances to accept governmental regulation of property.

The result of Wesley's view of property was a cooperative spirit in Methodism. As H. Richard Niebuhr noted, "Among the poor members of the societies it fostered, as all such movements have done, a high degree of mutual aid and cooperation and laid the foundations for popular education."[24] Wesley described one example of this kind of cooperation.

> I rode through one of the pleasantest parts of England to Hornby. Here the zealous landlord turned all the Methodists out of their houses. This proved a singular kindness: For they built some little houses at the end of the town, in which forty or fifty of them live together.[25]

Whether Wesley's three rules can be put to use in the twentieth century, or for that matter, whether they were realistic for his own time, is a moot question. Our objective is simply to demonstrate that Wesley did not hesitate to apply his theological and ethical principles to concrete political and economic circumstances, as will become even more evident as we turn to the issues of poverty, unemployment, inheritance, labor relations, and business ethics; and to Wesley's ventures to overcome human distress, such as work projects, lending stock, relief, and the Strangers' Friend Society.

## *General Economic Problems*

Poverty and unemployment are two sides of the same economic coin; one is usually found in the company of the other. In Wesley's day some thought poverty was the will of God or that it happened to some individuals because they had been unworthy. Rarely did the eighteenth century see poverty and unemployment as results of social inequity. In this sense it may be said that "Wesley discovered the poor," for he was able at least to see past these superficial analyses.[26] While he did not perceive all the social causes of economic distress, he declared that it was "wickedly, devilishly false" to say that people are poor only because they are idle. A more honest evaluation, he said, would recognize that people are in want "through scarcity of business."[27]

Perhaps the most extended analysis made by Wesley of the causes of poverty and unemployment at any particular period was in a letter to the editor of *Lloyd's Evening Post,* published in December, 1772, and brought out the next month in a slightly expanded form as a tract entitled *Thoughts on the Present Scarcity of Provisions.*[28] This period was characterized by war, high prices, bad harvests, and general distress. The letter opens with a description of the hardships Wesley had seen among the people of England, and it then asks, "Why is this? Why have all these nothing to eat? . . . They have no meat because they have no work." Employment was declining, said Wesley, because goods and services were not being purchased as a result of the increasing price of necessities, especially food. Due to reduced consumption, employers were not able to retain personnel, and "many who employed fifty men now scarce employ ten."[29]

Why were prices high and going higher? Here Wesley launches into an analysis that involves an oddly connected sequence of interrelated problems, including the misappropriation of grains, lands, and so forth. High taxes are major causes of high prices, according to Wesley, and these in turn are the result of war and the national debt. Therefore he advocates ridding the nation of the national debt (a plea similar to that of Jefferson in the United States). How are these evils to be remedied? First, people need to go back to work. By obtaining expanded markets for their goods, employers could hire more people. Second, the prices of food and other essential commodities must be lowered so that the people will be able to afford other goods and services.[30]

Wesley was always on the alert for indications of economic distress among the people. In a letter to the Earl of Dartmouth, Secretary of State for the Colonies, written in

August, 1775, Wesley detailed the woes of the people and pleaded for relief.[31]

A second problem to which Wesley gave attention was inheritance. Inherited wealth was a prime evil, he said, "for it will be certain to injure those who receive it."[32] "Have pity upon them and remove out of their way what you may easily foresee would increase their sins, and consequently plunge them deeper into everlasting perdition!" If a man had a considerable fortune to leave, Wesley said he should will to his family just enough to provide for them and "bestow all the rest in such a manner as would be most for the glory of God."[33]

Labor relations and business ethics, the two final examples of Wesley's attitude toward economic problems, are manifestly related, and Wesley was concerned with both. "Workers who migrated to centers where economic opportunity offered a livelihood constituted the "very social material Methodism was wont to lay hold upon."[34] Because of this attribute of Methodism, the employing classes were fearful lest Wesley should encourage a working-class movement, and some employers discharged workers for espousing or showing sympathy toward the Wesleyan movement, despite the fact that Methodism often made a person a more dependable worker.[35] For Wesley, the "labor relationship was an ethical one."[36] The other aspect of this situation was Wesley's attitude toward business integrity. His primary question was, "In what spirit do you go through your business? In the spirit of the world, or in the spirit of Christ?" And he added,

I am afraid thousands of those who are called good Christians do not understand the question. If you act in the spirit of Christ, you carry the end you at first proposed through all your work from first to last. You do everything in the spirit of sacrifice, giving up your will to the will of God; and continually aiming, not at ease, pleasure, or riches, not at anything "his short-enduring world can give," but merely at the glory of God. Now, can anyone deny, that this is the most excellent way of pursuing worldly business?[37]

Thus Wesley regarded the whole realm of business and labor as one in which the Christian ethic ought to be given an opportunity to function. If this were done, he believed society would be able to solve the problems posed by those elements of the economy. It should be noted that Wesley rejected here and elsewhere the concept of free enterprise, in the sense of unbridled competition.

## Humanitarian Reform

Wesley's desire to help the poor manifested itself in a variety of ways. Particularly important were those that today would be labeled as humanitarian reform measures.

Wesley's characteristic response to poverty was to find work for the unemployed. When that was not possible, he established work projects and cottage industries of various sorts. For example, he trained and employed several people in the processing of cotton and established others in a small knitting industry.[38]

Wesley also attempted to work out more long-range solutions to the economic problems that beset his people. He established a "lending stock "—a sort of credit union—from which people were able to borrow limited amounts of money without interest. This program was launched in 1747 and continued in operation for many years. Thus the old Foundery in London, for instance, became a veritable melting pot of projects—"a house of mercy for widows, a school for boys, a dispensary for the sick, a work shop and employment bureau, a loan office and savings bank, a bookroom, and a church."[39]

The normal mode of relief, however, was the outright collection of money, either for direct distribution or for the purchase of clothes, food, fuel, and other necessities. The usual procedure was for Wesley or his stewards to determine systematically the needs in each local society and the appropriate method of relief, and then to raise the necessary money.[40]

Another example of Wesley's attempt to relieve distress through humanitarian action was the formation of the Strangers' Friend Society. This organization was instituted in London in 1785 by a group of Methodists and was supported by Wesley. It was "wholly for the relief, not of our society, but for poor, sick, friendless strangers."[41] Such societies soon spread wherever Methodism was established.

Much of the foregoing is a commentary on Wesley's view of the role of government in the economy of the nation. He believed that at times governmental planning and control are necessary to alleviate conditions of distress. Most significant in this regard was the expression of surprise evoked from Wesley in 1776, after reading a book that contained "some observations which I never saw before . . . that to petition Parliament to alter [prices and fix money policies] is to put them upon impossibilities, and can answer no end but that of inflaming the people against their Governors."[42] Wesley did not name the book, but the view it set forth was typical of the laissez-faire philosophy of Adam Smith and Adam Ferguson. Smith's *Wealth of Nations* was published in that year, while Ferguson's *An Essay on the History of Civil Society* had appeared ten years earlier. In the realm of economics, both Ferguson and Smith advocated governmental nonintervention.[43]

Judging by the evidence, therefore, it would seem that Edwards' claim that nowhere in Wesley's works is there "an appeal for collectivist legislation" is too strong.[44] Clearly Wesley advocated governmental supervision, especially in times of economic crisis. He implicitly recognized that social institutions must be reformed through institutional and structural processes. Taken together, Wesley's concept of property and some of his specific proposals for alleviating unemployment, poverty, and other social inequities, remained consistently opposed to the laissez-faire philosophy that developed in England during the latter part of his life.

Wesley's economic ideas are interesting and important, not because of the remedies he suggested or because of the particular theories he set forth, but for the humanitarian spirit they exemplified—a spirit that well might be emulated by the church in the twentieth century. In historical perspective Wesley's economic ideas may be designated as preindustrial; indeed, in some respects they may have been more medieval than modern. Even so, they were founded on sympathy for human need, and they prompted imaginative attempts to do something about that need. In Wesley's thought, if the social ethic of love—as developed in his doctrine of sanctification—were systematically applied, then the social order itself might be perfectible.[45]

# Holiness and Radicalism in Nineteenth-Century America

## Timothy L. Smith

The year 1835 was the *annus mirabilis* of both liberation theology and the doctrine of sanctification in the United States. Phoebe Palmer professed the experience of perfect love at a weekly ladies' prayer meeting held at her sister's home in New York City that year, and for the next four decades she made the New York Tuesday Meeting for the Promotion of Holiness the center of Methodist perfectionism and spiritual feminism, and the source of much of its social concern.[1] That year also, Orange Scott, presiding elder in Springfield, Massachusetts, won a majority of the New England Methodist ministers over to abolitionism by sending each a three-month subscription to William Lloyd Garrison's *The Liberator*. Scott's subsequent agitation of this issue, in defiance of the bishops, led to the secession, eight years later, of the Wesleyan Methodists in western New York and, in a move to prevent New England from joining them, to the division of the Methodist Church, north and south, at the General Conference of 1844.[2]

Methodists scarcely dominated the scene, however. Evangelicals of New England Congregationalist backgrounds, when they resided west of the Hudson River and were required by the terms of the plan of union of 1801 to

Versions of the material in this chapter appeared in the *Wesleyan Theological Journal,* vol. 13 (Spring 1978) [© Timothy L. Smith, 1978], and in the *American Quarterly* (Spring 1979) [© the University of Pennsylvania]. Used by permission.

become Presbyterians, moved in parallel directions in the year 1835. In January of that year, John J. Shipherd and Asa Mahan came to New York City to persuade Arthur Tappan to consider Oberlin, Ohio, as the location of the college he planned to support for the students who had withdrawn from Presbyterian Lane Theological Seminary in Cincinnati when the trustees forbade their antislavery activities the year before. Tappan, who had been a mainstay of Lane and had supported the students during much of the year of feverish antislavery activity that followed their withdrawal, agreed to the plan, and named Mahan, a Cincinnati Presbyterian pastor who had sustained the students against the trustees, to be president at Oberlin. The conditions were, however, that evangelist Charles G. Finney, recently pastor of the congregation of revivalists and reformers that Arthur and his brother Lewis Tappan had helped organize in New York City, should spend half of each year in Oberlin as professor of theology; that the faculty, not the trustees, should be in control of the college; and that it should be committed to "the broad ground of moral reform in all its departments."[3]

Oberlin immediately became the vital center of Christian reflection and action aimed at the liberation of black people from slavery and racism; of women from male oppression that excluded them from the higher professions but exploited them in the oldest; of the poor from ignorance, alcohol, and the greed of merchants and land speculators; and of American society generally from all those forms of institutionalized evil that stood in the way of Christ's coming kingdom.[4] Theodore Dwight Weld, whose perfectionist view of Christian faith underlay his recent emergence as the most prominent evangelical abolitionist in the country, appeared at Oberlin in the fall of 1835 to give a series of lectures on abolition and to train students as antislavery agents, just as Finney completed his first half year as professor there.[5] That autumn, Finney, whose New

York congregation meanwhile had erected the Broadway Tabernacle as his church and revival center, began the *Lectures to Professing Christians,* signaling his growing involvement with the doctrine of the sanctification of believers, which he thought crucial to further progress in Christendom's march toward the millennium.[6] The widespread merging of Christian perfection with moral reform, in a theology no longer Calvinist, though professedly Puritan, was too much for the more conservative of the Scotch-Irish preachers in the Presbyterian Church, U.S.A., and certainly too much for the Princeton Seminary faculty. Within two years, that denomination also had divided, ostensibly over theological, but in fact over social issues as well.[7]

The broader significance of these events has been obscured by the tendency of historians—a tendency now in the process of being reversed—to view perfectionists and abolitionists as representing eccentric, if not lunatic strains in American theology. Another series of events in 1835 suggests instead, that Christian radicalism was for the moment in the mainstream. Nathaniel W. Taylor, professor of theology at Yale and the chief architect with Lyman Beecher of the New Divinity, or the New England theology as it was called, published in his journal, *The Christian Spectator,* four essays which placed him firmly in the camp of those to whom sanctification had become the crucial issue. By grafting onto covenant theology the doctrine of the moral nature of divine government, which required the consent of the human will to all that God provided or demanded; by locating depravity not in our natures, as had Jonathan Edwards, but in our dispositions—our selfish wills; and by adopting Samuel Hopkins' idea that disinterested benevolence, or unselfish love toward God and other humans, was the sum of the Christian's duty, Taylor and Beecher transformed Calvinist dogma into a practical Arminianism, without having to jet-

tison Calvinist verbiage.[8] Meanwhile, Lyman Beecher's son
Edward, who joined the famous "Yale band" to become the
first president of Illinois College, spoke for many of the
young New Englanders sent out by Yale and Andover
seminaries as missionaries to the Midwest in the 1830s.[9] In
1825 he called for "the immediate production of an elevated
standard of personal holiness throughout the universal
church—such a standard . . . as God requires, and the
present exigencies of the world demand." With Finney,
Edward Beecher believed that on the creation of this
standard depended all hopes for the establishment of the
kingdom of God on earth.[10]

The ethical seriousness of the New Divinity equaled that
of the Methodists on the one hand, or the Unitarians on the
other. The title of the first of the four articles Taylor
published indicated its content: "The Absolute Necessity of
the Divine Influence for Holiness of Heart and Life." The
second article began with refreshing directness:

> The promised agency of the Holy Spirit, for the conversion of
> sinners and the sanctification of saints, is the rock of safety to
> the church, and the hope to the world. All preaching and
> prayer which dispenses with the necessity of this divine
> influence . . . tends to drive revivals of religion, and religion
> itself, from the earth.

This divine influence, however, Taylor went on to say,
"never violates the great laws of moral action or contra-
venes the freedom of the subject." It does not leave the
human being "the mere creature of passive impressions or a
machine operated upon by compulsory force."[11] As such
radical moralism became the central expression of evangelical piety, Boston's Unitarians could no longer claim a
monopoly on ethical concern. In the years 1834 and 1835
their most honored leader, William Ellery Channing,
brought to a climax his series of twelve sermons on *The
Perfect Life,* which closely paralleled the radical ethics of

the New Divinity. In each, he insisted that absolute personal righteousness, attained by obedience to the commands of Jesus and by the imitation of his character, was the only standard of Christian virtue and the only assurance of everlasting life.[12]

Finally, the year 1835 was crucial in the history of the movement to free the slaves. Lewis Tappan assisted William Lloyd Garrison in outmaneuvering Arthur and two other Tappan brothers, both Unitarians living in Boston, who wanted to moderate the abolitionist crusade for a moment in search of broader popular support. Arthur then joined Lewis in financing an immense expansion of abolitionist propaganda through four monthly journals, scheduled so that one appeared in each week. They flooded the country in the twelve months following July, 1835, with a million pieces of abolitionist literature. The antislavery movement, having mounted this radical and public challenge to the South, never again could unite moderate Christians in a genteel moral consensus.[13]

That year also, Garrison embraced radically perfectionist piety as the only means of motivating the nation to free the slaves, liberate women, renounce warfare, and substitute love for force in the administration of justice. A company of able scholars have recently underlined the essentially evangelical commitments that governed the abolitionist crusade, not only in its earliest years, but during and after the year 1835, when Garrison began to advocate a platform of "universal reform." He aimed to overthrow "the empire of sin" by an agitation whose only weapons were truth and love.[14] Aileen Kraditor has shown that biblical ideas of righteousness dominated his thought until 1843, when he began to question the authority of the Scriptures, and 1845, when he discovered Thomas Paine. That before those dates Garrison's position paralleled that of Finney, Weld, and Orange Scott, is evident from an editorial entitled "Perfection," which he published in *The Liberator* on October 15, 1841. "Whether this or that individual has attained to the state of 'sinless perfection' " is not the issue, the unsigned editorial began. What matters is "whether human beings, in this life, may and ought to serve God with all their mind and strength, and to love their neighbors as themselves!" Rather than assailing the doctrine "be ye perfect," Garrison continued, believers who were "not wholly clean, not yet entirely reconciled to God, not yet filled with perfect love," should acknowledge that "freedom from sin is a Christian's duty and privilege" and should obey St. Paul's injunction to "put on the whole armor of God."[15]

It is tempting, now, to a Nazarene like myself, to devote the rest of this chapter to Wesleyan aspects of the movement "to reform the nation, and spread scriptural holiness over the land." Since my days in graduate school, when I wrote *Revivalism and Social Reform,* evidence has multiplied to indicate that holiness preaching has been an important catalyst to Methodist participation in movements for social justice, from Francis Asbury's time onward. Philip Bruce, a preacher stationed in Portsmouth, Virginia, wrote Bishop Thomas Coke on March 25, 1788, telling of immense revivals among African slaves as well as among free whites in Isle of Wight County. "Here liberty prevails," he wrote. "The conversion of the poor Blacks gives huge offense to the rich and great. I suppose if they dared, they would tear us in pieces: but through the grace of GOD, we regard them not, and had rather offend one half of the world to save the other, than let them all go quietly to hell together." On one preacher's circuit, in nearby Sussex and Brunswick Counties, Bruce continued, between twelve and fifteen hundred whites and a great number of blacks had been converted; and a friend had informed him that at the February court in Sussex, Methodists had filed deeds of manumission setting free more than one hundred slaves.[16] By the 1830s, Wesley's followers in New England had established a reputation of commitment to the popular side in such political issues as universal white manhood sufferage, workingmen's rights, and a tax-supported system of free public schools. They generally endorsed the crusade for total abstinence sooner than others, in response not only to Wesley's influence, but to the cries of their American Indian converts and the free blacks and working-class whites in northern cities, who insisted that liquor was a tragic curse for their people.[17] And at the end of the century, Norris Magnuson has shown, such Wesleyan organizations as the Salvation Army and the Door of Hope Mission learned from the poor they served the necessity for a moral reconstitution of those social and legal structures that allowed exploitation of the indigent. Evangelicals of many persuasions, including Methodist William Arthur, author of the famous holiness tract *The Tongue of Fire,* came by the same route to a similar conclusion during the 1850s.[18]

But on the American scene, at least, the denominational approach is myopic, as indeed I find it to be, to some extent, in Bernard Semmel's study of what he calls *The Methodist Revolution* in England. I have briefly examined the reports of Moravian missionaries in Antigua in the years between 1800 and 1833, and have compared them with those of the Methodists, who were equally effective on that island. I find little difference between the efforts of the two missions to liberate black people from the molds in which their African past and their American enslavement had imprisoned them. An immensely detailed plan of personal interviews and moral instruction for individual converts kept Moravian missionaries busy from dawn to dark of every day. True, they scorned the preaching of academic theology, being convinced that to tell the simple story of the cross of Jesus was the surest way to awaken the hearts and minds of the Africans. Once awakened, however, the converts found that biblical teachings about purity, honesty, unselfishness, loyalty to marital bonds, and a forgiving spirit—in short, the life of holiness—defined the character of a Moravian, despite what Methodists complained (and Semmel argues) was the antinomian character of the Moravian doctrine of justification.[19]

The same is true for the home-missionary movement that swept American Congregationalism in the early decades of the nineteenth century. Whether at Yale College or along the advancing frontier of Yankee settlement in New York, Pennsylvania, and the upper Midwest, revivalists and home missionaries whose doctrines were still cast in Calvinist language displayed the same purpose as the Methodists: to produce, through a free response to the gracious truth of the gospel, the sanctification of disorganized and demoralized persons.[20] The rising expectations of the millennium, which both home and overseas missions inspired, did not initially glorify nationalism or westward expansion, but demanded repentance. The millennial vision seems to have been at least as ecumenical as Wesley's and Coke's view of the world parish. Those who shared it proclaimed the judgment of God upon all laws, governments, and social institutions, whether in the United States or elsewhere, that stood in the way of hope for a just and holy future for all humankind.[21]

Spokesmen for the New Divinity were never able to see, or at least to admit, what their critics readily perceived—their adoption of many Methodist doctrines.[22] In the same year—1835—when the columns of Nathaniel Taylor's *Christian Spectator* made the sanctifying work of the Holy Spirit the central issue in New England theology, Taylor published an attack on Wesley's doctrine of the witness of the Spirit, which represented the founder of Methodism as teaching that a subjective and personal revelation from God, rather than a transformed ethical life, attested one's conversion. Nathan Bangs remonstrated, but Taylor stuck to his charge. Methodists were only partially dismayed to hear themselves denounced by Congregationalism's greatest intellectual leader for not making personal holiness the only assurance of saving grace.[23]

For these reasons, then, the story of Charles G. Finney and how, in the crucible of Oberlin's social activism, he forged a theology of liberation in which the Arminianized Calvinism of the New Divinity was the chief element, and his doctrine of "perfect sanctification" through the baptism of the Holy Spirit was the catalyst, seems to me to illuminate best the history of radical Christian social thought in nineteenth-century America. Among "new school" Congregationalists and Presbyterians generally, the notion of Christian perfection was radically new and therefore almost impossible to associate with a traditional order. Methodists, however, tended to link that doctrine as much with loyalty to their Wesleyan past as with concern for a revolutionary future. Some of them preached and wrote about Christian holiness without any reference at all to the social crisis of the 1830's, for which their message was newly relevant. Any such antiquarian or individualistic views were not possible for preachers whose roots lay in New England Calvinism. At Oberlin especially, the interaction of theological reflection and spiritual experience with revolutionary ideology and political action was evident in all parties, especially in the evangelist whom Arthur Tappan had made a professor of theology, Charles G. Finney.

Finney had consented, after some initial reluctance, to accept the appointment at Oberlin because he had become convinced that the church could not save the nation unless its members found a way to translate the doctrine of sanctification into concrete experience. He had carried his evangelistic crusade from western New York to Philadelphia, to New York City, Providence, and Boston; and then had become pastor of Arthur Tappan's circle of revivalist and antislavery radicals in New York City. There, however, the institutionalized evil evident in urban culture, the optimism with which, in preceding years, he had anticipated the early onset of the millennium, was harder to sustain. Reform crusades—even one mounted to liberate "fallen women"—encountered withering opposition, some from less aggressive "new school" Calvinists. In the invitation to Oberlin, Finney saw an opportunity to train a company of leaders who would make the idea of Christian holiness the center of a renewed campaign to subject American society to the rule of Christ.[24] In agreement with the Tappans, Garrison, Beecher, and Weld, he thought the times demanded a widespread raising of public consciousness that the old order was in crisis and that justice and love were destined to prevail in the new. Equally necessary was a believable plan for socializing the dispositions of individuals. Oberlin College could supply a trained corps of revivalists, ready to declare judgment upon all institutions that ran counter to the law of God and to affirm the dawn of a new day; but only the sanctifying power of the Holy Spirit could transform both them and the Christian public into God's instruments so that the dawn might become a reality.[25]

Finney's role, as he conceived it, was not to agitate for particular reforms so much as to provide spiritual inspiration and a Christian ideology for them all. When Arthur Tappan guaranteed that the Oberlin faculty and students would be free from the interference of trustees or other outsiders, and then guaranteed not only Finney's salary but whatever might become necessary to maintain the solvency of the school, the evangelist agreed to plant himself for half of each year at what he thought were the two arenas where America's moral destiny would be decided—New York City and the upper Midwest. The Oberlin venture did not in any sense, therefore, isolate him from the main currents of American social idealism. Rather, the college and community furnished him with a laboratory of both spirituality and radical social action, in which the idea of Christian perfection soon reigned supreme.[26]

Both Finney and Mahan left behind autobiographies, written in their later years, which recounted, with some improvement from hindsight, the events at Oberlin between 1835 and 1840. Far from fitting the image of a backwoods evangelist, Mahan was a moral philosopher of great sophistication. His textbook, asserting an absolute standard of righteousness and directly challenging the increasingly popular utilitarian views of Jeremy Bentham and John Stuart Mill, was the second most widely used in the standard course taught by college presidents to their senior classes in nineteenth-century America. Both Mahan and Finney, moreover, were very astute students of the English Bible; their study aimed not only at understanding theology but at cultivating their own spiritual life. They freely acknowledged that during Oberlin's first five years a deep hunger for the highest personal achievements of piety and righteousness was their primary motivation. Mahan wrote that though he had been an effective evangelist and had preached often at Methodist camp meetings, he found in St. Paul's writings evidence of a personal relationship with Christ that he did not know and for which he continually prayed.[27] Never, since Luther and Wesley, had theology and experience been so closely intertwined.

In September 1836, in the middle of the revival with which the college opened its second year, a student asked whether there were biblical grounds for Christians to anticipate a relationship with Christ that would enable them to live without committing sins that produced guilt and condemnation—in short, to live a morally sanctified life. President Mahan answered passionately, "Yes," though acknowledging he had not yet attained such a relationship. During that evening and the following day, however, he broke through to what he saw as the way to the experience of Christian perfection: faith in Christ's atonement. "When I thought of my guilt, and the need of justification," he recalled, "I had looked at Christ exclusively, as I ought to have done; for sanctification, on the other hand, to overcome the world, the flesh, and the devil, I had depended mainly on my own resolution."[28]

The next evening he preached to the revival congregation on the text "The love of Christ constraineth us," declaring that both from Scripture and from his own experience, "We are to be sanctified by faith, just as we are justified by faith." Although he did not use the phrase "baptism of the Holy Spirit" in the sermon, as he remembered having done when he wrote his autobiography more than thirty years later, the version of the sermon that appeared in print in 1839 declared that "the appropriate office of the Holy Spirit" is to reveal the love of Christ so powerfully that it will enable Christians to consecrate themselves fully to him.[29] Later, in a thoughtful discourse entitled "The Divine Teacher," Mahan explained that the Holy Spirit "enlightens the intellect, and carries on the work of sanctification in the heart," presenting Christ to our minds "in such a manner, that we are transformed into His image" and freed from forlorn reliance upon "our own natural powers as moral agents."[30]

Finney was not present that second evening and probably did not yet approve Mahan's decisive turn toward the idea that a "second crisis" of Christian experience was necessary for a life of sanctity. But he began immediately what proved to be a three-year process of working his way through the teachings of the Bible concerning the covenant of holiness. As always, it was necessary that his head precede his heart. That fall and winter, which proved to be his last in New York City, Finney included in the second series of his *Lectures to Professing Christians* one entitled "Sanctification by Faith," two on the subject of "Christian Perfection," another declaring "Love is the Whole of Religion," and a final one titled "Rest of the Saints." This last lecture defined faith as "yielding up all our powers and interests to Christ, in confidence, to be led, and sanctified, and saved by Him." All these lectures had as their starting point the general outlines of the New Divinity.[31]

In the fall of 1838, when ill health prevented his spending the winter traveling in evangelistic work, Finney undertook to deliver a series of lectures on Christian perfection and published them in *The Oberlin Evangelist,* the faculty's new organ of religious and social reformation. In a letter to readers printed with the third lecture, he explained that in the years before 1835, he had been wholly and, he believed in retrospect, wisely committed to revival preaching aimed at securing the conversion of sinners. During his years in New York City, however, he became "fully convinced, that converts would die" and "that revivals would become more and more superficial, and finally cease, unless something effectual was done to elevate the standard of holiness in the church." He subsequently realized that he had known Christ "almost exclusively as an atoning and justifying Savior," but not as a sanctifying one. In the last two or three years, he continued,

> I have felt as strongly and unequivocally pressed by the Spirit of God to labor for the sanctification of the Church, as I once did for the conversion of sinners. . . . God has been continually dealing with me in mercy. . . . How often I have longed to unburden myself, and pour out my whole heart to the dear souls, that were converted in those powerful revivals.

Through these lectures, then, he hoped to correct the deficiencies of his earlier ministry.[32]

The suggestion some scholars have made, following William McLoughlin, that such high-blown spirituality indicated a turning away from the movement to reform society, will not fit the facts. The years of 1839 and 1840 were vintage ones for Christian revolutionary ideology at Oberlin. Finney's *Skeletons of a Course of Theological Lectures*, published in the latter year, included several on human government in which he declared that

> when one form of government fails to meet any longer the necessities of the people, it is the duty of the people to revolutionize. . . . In such cases it is vain to oppose revolution; for in some way the benevolence of God will bring it about. . . . God always allows His children as much liberty as they are prepared to enjoy.[33]

Finney claimed, in a passage cut from his *Memoirs* before their publication in 1876, that he led the faculty in resistance to racism. He reported that when students from the South questioned the propriety of eating at the same tables with black students, the faculty adopted his proposal that separate tables be set up where any who did not wish to eat with the blacks might take their meals; the historic arrangements thus being reversed, the separate tables remained empty.[34] Moreover, the lectures on sanctification themselves contained a radical attack on prevailing legal standards of business ethics and left little room for the profit motive.[35]

When in 1839, the Ohio legislature adopted a statute which seemed to extend the jurisdiction of Kentucky law over fugitive slaves to all of Ohio, Finney introduced a resolution at the next meeting of the Ohio Anti-slavery Society declaring the statute "a palpable violation of the Constitution of this state, and of the United States, of the common law and of the law of God," and announced that it was "a well-settled principle of both common and constitutional law that no human legislation can annul or set aside the law or authority of God."[36] At the commencement exercises in September 1839, Jonathan Blanchard presented his famous address, "A Perfect State of Society," to the Oberlin Society of Inquiry. More than a thousand persons attended a meeting of the Lorain County Anti-slavery Society on commencement evening, denounced "the disgraceful 'Black laws' of Ohio," and resolved that the membership would "not support any man for the legislature" who did not favor the repeal of all Ohio laws "founded on a distinction of color."[37] The announcement of these events in the *Evangelist* accompanied a stirring account of schools for the children of fugitive slaves, which Oberlin graduates were maintaining in Canada, and a denunciation of the "blood-thirsty and land-coveting whites" of Florida who had waged a three-year war against the Seminole Indians and now were resisting the Indians' permanent settlement in the southern part of that state because runaway slaves would find protection among them.[38]

The development of Finney's doctrine of Christian perfection, then, reflected and reinforced his own revolutionary interest, and that of the Oberlin community generally, in reforming society. The lectures of 1838 and 1839, which we shall examine in a moment, demonstrate the essentially religious basis of this concern and help to explain why Oberlin's political radicalism won such widespread attention: It was rooted in the central theme of Old and New Testament Scriptures. The God of eternity had bound himself in covenant with those who would be his people, making them morally responsible to him and to one another in helping his kingdom come, as Jesus put it, and his will to be done on earth as it was in heaven. Unlike John Wesley, Finney drew deeply upon Moses and the prophets and upon the long tradition of Puritan, or covenant, theology. Moreover, his starting point in New Testament studies was not Moravian pietism, but Samuel Hopkins' distillation of the ethical teachings of Jesus and Paul into the law of disinterested benevolence—Wesley's "perfect love." When Finney discovered, apparently from his own study of the English Bible, the logical and historical links between the covenant and promise in the Old Testament, and that of Jesus' covenant in the New—the promise of his continuing presence through the sanctifying comforter, the Holy Spirit—the circle was complete. He then proclaimed, as Wesley refused to authorize his preachers to say, that the entire sanctification of the believer's moral will is achieved through the baptism of the Holy Spirit. That proclamation did not reduce, but in fact radicalized, Christian concerns for social justice, for it offered to Calvinist, Pietist, and Arminian alike a way of repossessing the doctrine of the sovereignty of God over individuals as well as over the structures of society.

The result, Finney recognized, was a radical reshaping of what he called the "science of theology." Like other branches of knowledge, he declared, theology must be open to "new truth" and ministers of the gospel should cast aside the fear of changing their opinions about the teachings of the Scriptures.

> I was to a wonderful extent blind to my profound ignorance of the word of God, till about three years past. Since that time I have been able to read it with a degree of astonishment in respect to my former ignorance which I cannot express. . . . I pray the Lord to deliver me, and to deliver the ministry, from the absurd prejudice that chains them and the Church to a set of stereotyped opinions on all religious subjects.[39]

Finney began the lectures, then, with one which, based on a text from the fifth chapter of I John, equated eternal life with the present experience of sanctity, rather than with a future experience of blessedness. True faith, he said, is "receiving Christ as indwelling Savior," who becomes "*the eternal life* of the soul." God's presence does not alter human nature, but enables the Christian to begin a life of complete obedience.[40] The second lecture, based on Jesus' response to those who asked him, What shall we do? insisted that

Calvinists and Arminians alike were attempting to produce faith by obedience, despite God's directive that holiness flows from "faith which works by love." Finney declared that in his earlier *Lectures on Revivals* he had erred in not showing "that the exercise of faith is the first thing to be done." The key element in that faith, he wrote, is "the consent of the heart or will" to the truth of God's faithful love, as "perceived by the intellect." Trust stems from "confidence in the character of God."[41] The third in this trilogy on hope, faith, and love was titled "Devotion," which Finney defined with characteristic concreteness as "that state of the will in which the mind is swallowed up in God, as the object of supreme affection." In such a life of devotedness, "We not only live and move *in* God, but *for* God." He renounced the tendency to separate devotion from duty, including faithfulness in the ordinary duties of business life. And he rebuked those who forget that "devotion belongs to the will," not to the "ever-varying states of emotion," which some "are prone to call religion."[42]

For the fourth in the series, Finney revised one of his earlier *Lectures to Professing Christians* entitled "True and False Religion," based on Galatians 5:1. True religion, he said, is the opposite of slavery: It is genuine liberty permitting one to act out of love. "The true Christian never yields to the will of God by constraint" but is drawn and persuaded, engaged and committed by joyous awareness that "infinite wisdom and love" make Christ the soul's "supreme, eternal choice."[43] Slavery consists of being obliged to choose between two evils. The slaves in the American South were not, strictly speaking, in a state of involuntary servitude, he said, for they "prefer being as they are, to being in a worse condition—to being imprisoned or whipped for attempting to escape." Though the religion of many persons is analagous to such slavery, he said, true faith brings genuine liberty.[44]

Finney then turned to two lectures on the law of God. Its demands were wholly fulfilled, he said, following the commands of both Moses and Jesus, to love God with all your heart, soul, and mind, and to love your neighbor as yourself. Drawing upon but expanding Samuel Hopkins' idea of disinterested benevolence, he made a crucial distinction between loving oneself as an act of benevolence, and mere self-indulgence. Even more important, however, was Finney's explanation that by "love of the heart" he did not mean simply an emotional attachment.

> By the heart I mean the will. Emotions, or what are generally termed feelings, are often involuntary states of mind . . . and of course do not govern the conduct. Love, in the form of an emotion, may exist in opposition to the will. . . . [Since] the will controls the conduct, it is, therefore, of course, the love of the heart or will that God requires.[45]

The second talk on divine law set forth the doctrine that behind the American Constitution stood a higher law—disinterested benevolence, or pure love—which Hopkins had declared was defined by the nature of God and the sum of human duty.

> In the light of this law [Finney wrote] how perfectly obvious is it, that slavery is from hell. Is it possible that we are to be told that slavery is a divine institution? What! Such a barefaced, shameless, and palpable violation of the law of God authorized by God himself? And even religious teachers, gravely contending that *the Bible santions this hell-begotten system?* "Oh shame where is thy blush?" What! Make a man a slave—set aside his moral agency—treat him as a mere piece of property . . . and then contend that this is in keeping with the law of God?[46]

The two lectures came to a climax, characteristically, in a concrete application of the law of radical love to the ethics of conducting businss. Every violation of the rule of disinterested benevolence, or perfect love, "is fraud and injustice," not only toward God but "toward every individual in the universe." To transact business merely upon the "principles of commercial justice" that are upheld by courts of law is "rebellion against God"; in a Christian, such behavior is "real apostasy," for which restitution must be made in all cases possible, "or there is no forgiveness." Fiercely denouncing on this ground not only slaveholders and merchants who priced goods beyond their real value, but speculators in western lands, Finney declared that such offenders must "give back their illgotten gains" or suffer damnation. He then outlined the proper Christian attitude toward wealth in terms that differed from John Wesley's popular formula, "Gain/save/give all you can." "The law of love," he said, "requires that we should afford everything as cheap as we can, instead of getting as much as we can. The requirement is that we do all the good we can do to others, and not that we get all we can ourselves. The law of God is, sell as cheap as you can—the business maxim, as dear as you can." Not content to leave the matter there, Finney added a third lecture titled "Glorifying God," which defined holiness as faith in practice, decried the love of money,and praised simplicity of life, particularly in clothing and food; then it returned grandly, to link the idea of holiness to the first question of the Westminister catechism.[47]

The eighth lecture, on "True and False Peace," followed a letter to readers of the *Evangelist*, which had revealed that Finney's doctrine of "sin in believers" was very close to Wesley's, as was his appeal to converts to have faith in Christ, the sanctifying Savior. The lecture itself dealt with the psychic dimension of choice. When conscience and will unite in holy commitment to God, peace is complete. But to yield one's will to conscience or to persuasion, without a deep conviction that God is trustworthy—that is, without a motive rooted in the assurance of his love—is to paper over cracks in the wall.[48]

By late April, both Finney's lectures and his accompany-
ing letters revealed the results of his deepening personal
quest for biblical understanding. The scriptural promise of a
renewed covenant of grace, taken from the prophecy of
Jeremiah as well as from the Epistle to the Hebrews, laid a
basis in logic for the subject that preoccupied him in the
succeeding months—the work of the Holy Spirit. And his
dawning awareness that the Christian needs divine help
beyond the mere illumination of the intellect was evident in
his thoroughly Wesleyan exposition of chapters 7 and 8 of
the Epistle to the Romans.[49]

Five lectures on "The Promises," printed from May
through the middle of July, bore the fruits of his study of the
old and new covenants. "We never keep the commandments,
only as we take hold of the promises," Finney began. "By
this I mean that grace alone enables us, from the heart, to
obey the commandments of God." In a vastly complex
recitation of Old Testament promises that "belong emphati-
cally to the Christian church," with special emphasis on
God's pledge recorded in Jeremiah 31 and Ezekiel 36, to put
a "new heart" within his people—passages that he quoted at
length three or four times in the first lecture—Finney burst
through to an assertion that holiness consists in partaking
of the divine moral nature. This did not mean that God had
promised "to change our constitution—to destroy our
personal identity—and make our spiritual existence iden-
tical" with his. Rather, Christians were invited to become
"partakers of the moral nature, or attributes or perfections
of God," which are "by the Spirit, through the promises,
begotten in our minds." This assertion, though couched in
the language of God's moral government, was staggering to
anyone not teethed on the apostle Paul. It clearly made the
work of the Holy Spirit central to the new covenant. And
that covenant, Finney now saw, was not the promise itself or
an "outward precept" or "any outward thing whatever, but

an inward holiness brought about by the Spirit of God—the very substance and spirit of the law written in the heart by the Holy Ghost."[50]

This study of the promises inspired Finney's decisive turn to the language of Pentecost in order to expound the covenant of grace. On further examination of the Scriptures, he concluded that "the blessing of Abraham," which Paul wrote had "come on the Gentiles through Jesus Christ," was not simply Christ himself, but the Holy Spirit. The promises of the Spirit's coming formed "one unbroken chain from Abraham to Christ," completed when the risen Lord pledged to his disciples that they should be baptized with the Spirit. Finney declared that Christians must receive this "blessing of Abraham" which, though it begins in "perception of the truth," is complete only when their wills are yielded to "the guidance, instruction, influences, and government of the Holy Spirit."[51] It was now clear to him, he said, that Christ and the apostles regarded the day of Pentecost "as the commencement of a new dispensation," in which the old covenant was set aside only in the sense that it was fulfilled in the new.[52]

In this rich context of scriptural and covenant theology, Finney finally was able to declare the doctrine of sanctification through the baptism of the Holy Spirit. "Every individual Christian may receive and is bound to receive this gift of the Holy Ghost at the present moment," he proclaimed. Christians who have been born again do not have that gift "in such a sense as it is promised in these passages of the Holy Scripture, or in a higher sense than [the Spirit] was received by the Old Testament saints, . . . of whom it was said that 'they all died in the faith, not having received the promise.' "[53]

In 1840, Finney's "Letters to Ministers of the Gospel" urged them to preach earnestly the doctrine he had so recently come to understand himself. They should spare no pains to help new converts realize their need of the experience of entire sanctification. He acknowledged again that his instruction to converts had in former times "been very defective," for he had not seen clearly "that the baptism of the Holy Ghost is a thing universally promised . . . to Christians under this dispensation, and that this blessing is to be sought and received after conversion." Baptism in the Holy Spirit "is the secret of the stability of Christian character," he declared; new converts need "to be baptized into the very death of Christ, and by this baptism to be slain, and buried, and planted, and crucified, and raised to a life of holiness in Christ."[54]

Throughout all their lectures and letters of those years, Finney and Mahan consistently declared that the only assurance that God was accomplishing his purpose in human lives was ethical: the righteousness that showed itself in radical rejection of all sin, whether individual or structural, through faith in Jesus Christ. Again and again, they and other members of the Oberlin faculty rang the changes on this theme, renouncing what they alleged to be the antinomianism of the Oneida "perfectionists" on one hand and, on the other, the unwillingness of conservative Calvinists to trust the promises of God.[55]

Here was a theology cradled in experience and nurtured in the Scriptures, just as Wesley's had been. And the experience was that of persons ready to organize their lives around the pursuit of a right relationship with God, attested to by just and loving relationships with their fellow human beings and by a holy war on the corrupt structures of society. The immediate background, however, was that of the revitalized Calvinist ethics of Samuel Hopkins, rather than the Anglican moralism that had launched Wesley on his quest or the pietism that had enabled him, at a crucial juncture, to see that he could realize that quest only through trust in Christ. The social context, moreover, was that of the optimism of a new nation, where hopes were blossoming for a social order hallowed by divine grace and hence characterized by justice and love.

Finney's earlier preaching had so stressed the freedom of human beings and their responsibility to repent and make new lives, as to allow the charge that he ignored the role of God's grace in sanctification. Now, however, he was affirming that divine grace, poured out in the baptism of the Holy Spirit, was indispensable to the sanctification both of persons and of the institutions of society. Individual Christians must receive that divine gift by a faith so reasonable and a consecration so deliberate as to leave their moral responsibility fully intact to help build a righteous society and a holy character. Never a Pelagian, I think Finney had found a way to reclaim the doctrine of God's sovereignty without becoming a Calvinist, either. He had discovered in Scripture, he believed, a pentecostal version of covenant theology, which brought within reach the evangelical unity that Wesley and Whitefield had pursued but never were able to grasp. Rooting the experience of the baptism of the Spirit in the Old Testament covenant of holiness also insulated it against the anti-intellectual and mystical corruptions that Wesley had feared and that, alas, forgetting Finney, twentieth-century Pentecostals often seem to have embraced.

In conclusion, my commitment to open communication prompts me to try to say plainly what I conceive a theology of liberation requires, when grounded in the religion of Moses and Jesus and addressed to the circumstances of humanity's present varied enslavements.

It demands first an awakening among the oppressors and the oppressed of a consciousness of the presence of the eternal God in history and therefore of the continuing truthfulness, both within and outside history, of the commandment to love him with all our hearts and minds and to love our fellow human beings as, by his grace, we are rightly enabled to respect ourselves.

Second, it requires a full commitment—of which we are entirely capable by the power inherent in the story of Jesus, as it is proclaimed in the Gospels—to follow his example, the only model we have of the holy person. As dying and risen Lord, he gives himself in holiness that we might be sanctified in the truth and that we might, in that continuing gift of sanctity, rejoice also for his ready forgiveness of the daily imperfections and the frequent folly of our efforts to follow him.

Finally, a Christian thelogy of liberation anticipates that only in the power of the Holy Spirit, as a strength but not as a substitute for our responsible choice and action, can we do what is true—that is, be both loving and just. Only in this way can Christians sustain that continuing revolution in persons and institutions that the church is called to foment, in order that Christ's kingdom might come and his will might be done, both in and beyond this present world.

What the Scriptures, Old and New, say with authority to those who will make this trinity of holy commitments, is that love, defined in God's own mighty acts as loyalty—as faithfulness in covenanted relationships—offers both prophetic judgment and redemptive healing to the human community. This principle of faithful love is intensely personal, insistently social, and never static. It stands at the center of biblical revelation and unfailingly emerges at the apex of humane aspirations in every age and in every cultural setting. Jesus made it the touchstone of his strategy to overpower the structures of racism, male chauvinism, and economic oppression, which were the major strongholds of injustice in his time, as in ours. His pacifism, like that of his modern follower Martin Luther King, was no idyllic or sentimental escape from pain and violence, for it brought down violence upon his own head and upon the leaders of the early church. The Christian *shalom,* the peace through grace which he breathed upon his hurting and angry disciples on the evening of Easter day and into their lives on the morning of Pentecost, sustained a passionately realistic strategy. He offers it to us in preference to the violent options that have been available to deal with inequality, jealousy, anger, and shame, since the first encounter of the sons of Adam, just east of Eden.

Being free and responsible, then, the Christian community is to expect no blueprint for the new society from the hands of God, but is to rejoice in the use of our common intelligence to deal with social realities as we find them. In this freedom that God has bestowed, I believe we are called to improvise creatively the structures of custom and of law that seem to us to promise fulfillment, in our times and places, of the covenants and promises of a holy community. There are many forms and acts that may embody beauty, purity, and love, and hence many ways to build a life and to reconstruct a society. Our heavenly Father, who rejoiced in his own works, rejoices also in ours. His government, as any proper Arminian should realize, is a moral one, and its chief glory is the moral response his faithfulness inspires in those who willingly participate in it.

That the moral freedom of the Christian community, like that of the Christian individual, is always constrained within the bonds of social and psychic reality on the one hand and, on the other, by the authority of the truth that is revealed in Jesus and, fragmentarily, in our own consciences, creates the tension that makes acts of liberation and social reform so complete a challenge to Christian intelligence. Freedom without constraint would bore us; its expression would require no exercise of mind or will. For from our mothers' arms, the constraints have given our freedom its meaning and value.[56]

Finney's doctrine of freedom under grace, and the Wesleyan and Puritan sources from which it drew much of its biblical basis, sustained just such a theology of liberation, I think. It united human wills with God's will, in free and loving choice.

# Whither Evangelicalism?

*Donald W. Dayton*

One of the most discussed and analyzed of recent North American religious phenomena has been the resurgence and growth of evangelicalism. *Newsweek,* for example, proclaimed with a cover story that 1976 was the "Year of the Evangelicals."[1] Shortly thereafter, Jimmy Carter, a Southern Baptist deacon who made open profession of his evangelical faith, was elected president of the United States. Though Presidents Richard Nixon and Gerald Ford (as well as candidate George McGovern) had each in his own way claimed "evangelical" roots, something in 1976 enabled a submerged evangelical presence to break into the media spotlight as news that merited analysis and discussion.

There is still no agreement about what is happening. Optimistic triumphalist claims abound from a variety of evangelical sources. Some sober analysts discern the signs of a coming revival not unlike earlier "awakenings." Even pollster George Gallup comments that "evidence is mounting that the US may be in an early stage of a profound religious revival, with the Evangelical movement providing a powerful thrust."[2] Other more cynical voices perceive the trend as a retreat from the activism of the 1960s—more like a fascination with the occult and esoteric. Still others claim to see the spiritual and intellectual fruition of the work of a post-World War II generation of postfundamentalist evangelicals, who gave themselves to building up such movements as the Billy Graham Association, Youth for Christ, and Intervarsity Christian Fellowship. It is difficult to deny the cold statistics of one such as Dean Kelley, who shows that highly disciplined "conservative" churches are growing to the detriment of others because, as he suggests, they succeed in giving meaning to life, in his view the appropriate task of the church.[3]

Whatever we should decide about the validity of all or any of these suggestions, evangelical currents are a major cultural phenomenon in contemporary American life, generating forces that will determine the future shape of the church. Nor are they a matter of merely provincial concern to North Americans. For good or ill, the United States not only has exported to much of the world its politics, its economics, its media culture, its consumerism, and its technology, but also its churches, and its varieties of religious life with their divisions and squabbles. For this reason it is not out of place in the context of an international theological consultation to probe certain distinctive features of the North American Christian experience. And so into these tangled thickets we go!

## The Meaning of the Word "Evangelical"

One way into these thickets is to consider the meaning of the word. In spite of the warning of Ralph Winter to the effect that one can no more describe evangelicalism "purely theologically than one can eat soup with a fork," we shall seek to give particular attention to the varieties of theological meaning that can be conveyed by the word.[4] Though there exists an honorable history of the use of the word evangelical from New Testament times through the Middle Ages, it has more often been adopted by a variety of Protestant parties for their own purposes. With regard to our own analysis, we would draw attention to three periods in the history of Protestantism when the word has come particularly to the fore.

The first would be, of course, the Reformation—"evangelical" is used to designate the emergent Protestant movement, especially its Lutheran wing, over against what has come to be known as the Roman Catholic Church. Here the word evokes the themes of the great "solas" of the Reformation— *sola scriptura, sola Christe, sola gratia,* and *sola fide*—and seems intended to convey a bibliocentric and Christocentric expression of faith, with special emphasis on such themes as an Augustinian anthropology (or some other variety of the doctrine of "bondage of the will"), an "objective" view of Christ's atonement, a forensic concept of grace, and especially the doctrine of justification by faith.[5] In this context, evangelical means, roughly, "Protestant," and so it is used in much of the world. In Germany, *evangelisch* means Protestant, especially Lutheran. And in Latin America, *evangelico* carries a similar meaning, perhaps in part because the Protestant population is so small as to render finer distinctions superfluous.

But in the English-speaking world, the word has added connotations that arise from its use in two additional historical periods. The first is the era of the Great Awakenings and the evangelical revival of the eighteenth century, with its outworking in the revivalism of the nineteenth. Here the emphasis is on conversion and the process of personal appropriation of grace. In this sense, we might agree with Ian Bradley that "Evangelicalism was never really a theological system as much as a way of life."[6] But at the same time it is possible to point to certain theological themes, and concern narrows to those related most directly to the "plan of salvation"—human sinfulness, the need for conversion, the appropriation of justifying grace, and the outworking of this in the sanctified life. It is also possible to discern a generally "low church" orientation and hints of innovations that pitted this understanding of evangelicalism against orthodoxy and traditionalism. These themes are present in varying degrees, whether one speaks of Methodism, the Anglican evangelicals, or American revivalism.

Here of course we are close to the heart of the topic of our consultation and are speaking generally of Methodism and related movements. These currents are so important for developments within the United States that one may speak of the nineteenth century in North America as the "age of Methodism," a term used by Baptists and Presbyterians as well as by chauvinistic Methodists.[7] From its small beginnings about the time of the American Revolution, by the 1860s, Methodism had grown to be the largest denomination in the United States. In addition, one may interpret the emergence of "new measures" revivalism, (associated with evangelist Charles G. Finney) as in many ways the "Methodistizing" of American Calvinism. At any rate, during this period a form of evangelicalism—consisting of an intermingled mixture of Methodists, Baptists, and revivalist Presbyterians and Congregationalists—emerged to become the dominant form of religious life in North America. And this form of evangelicalism was permeated with distinctively Methodist themes.

But this common ethos was soon to break up under the impact of modernity in a controversy that would produce a third meaning of the word evangelical. This was, of course, the fundamentalist/modernist controversy that peaked in the United States in the 1920s and 30s. This experience is closer to our times and lies behind the meaning most often given to the word today. In the mid-nineteenth century the rise of Darwinism and the results of geological study began to shake traditional interpretations of the early chapters of Genesis. When combined with the new biblical criticism being imported from Europe, these questions opened a split in North American Protestantism between a liberal party which attempted to reexpress the Christian faith in terms of these new intellectual developments, and a conservative, or fundamentalist, party which resisted these new currents, fearing that accommodation to them would ultimately destroy the faith itself. "Evangelical" has, since World War II, been used increasingly to designate the conservative party in this great struggle within the churches.

As we shall see shortly, the story is much more complicated than this simple division between liberal and conservative indicates, but we have said enough to suggest the basic connotations given to the word evangelical in this third paradigm. Here the word means basically orthodox, or conservative, and opposed to the rethinking that liberals find necessary in response to "modern" questions of science, historical consciousness, and biblical criticism. The fact that evangelicalism in this sense has been primarily reactionary has tended to undercut the innovative side of an earlier evangelicalism that was in many ways opposed to traditional patterns of life and thought. Evangelicalism in this third sense has usually represented a cluster of conservative values, politically and socially as well as theologically.

This third and widely accepted meaning obscures some important theological differences between the second and third paradigms of evangelicalism, which for our purposes, require a fuller explication in order to illuminate the contemporary situation. These differences are often ignored, as illustrated by a recent anthology entitled *The Evangelicals,*[8] a much-discussed attempt to analyze and interpret North American evangelicalism. In a preface, the editors, David F.Wells and John D. Woodbridge of Trinity Evangelical Divinity School, lament the decline of impact on American culture of evangelicalism as it found expression in the nineteenth century, and they express hope for a twentieth-century recovery. They do this with little recognition that the two evangelicalisms are significantly different and that theologically they are divergent in ways that relate to the varying social impact they have had. This may be seen at two points.

The first difference is that nineteenth-century evangelicalism found its most characteristic expression in a form of *Arminianism,* while twentieth-century evangelicalism has been dominated by a very conservative form of *Calvinism.* This in effect reversed the transition brought about by the Great Awakening of the eighteenth-century, which Martin Marty has described as the "hinge from Calvinist to Arminian America."[9] Much American revivalism incarnated an anti-Calvinist animus that gave extra impulse to the Arminian side of the rising tide of imported Methodism in the wake of the British evangelical revivals.[10] Timothy Smith's essay on *Revivalism and Social Reform* has demonstrated how extensively, on the eve of the Civil War, revivalism in America was permeated by Methodistic themes.[11] By contrast, twentieth-century fundamentalism was most acrimoniously present in Baptist and Presbyterian contexts. The dominant theology of this movement was the old "Princeton theology," represented especially by Charles Hodge and B. B. Warfield, defenders of the "old school" Calvinism that consistently opposed the "new school" revivalistic Calvinists of nineteenth-century evangelicalism. Though in some ways distinctively American, this theology is best understood as a repristination of Reformed Scholasticism of the post-Reformation era. Until Hodge finished his three volumes of theology, early Princeton students worked from the Latin text of the *Institutes* of Francois Turretin. Determinative for the self-understanding of the modern expressions of this theology was the struggle at Princeton which led to the founding of Westminster Theological Seminary, an effort to maintain intact the old Princeton theology, especially against its erosion in the face of the rise of modern biblical criticism and related currents. Most characteristic of this tradition of theology has been a doctrine of "biblical inerrancy," formulated especially by B. B. Warfield. As

Claude Welch has put it, the Princeton theology became "a haven sought (properly or not) by all sorts of conservative revivalists and fundamentalists in the face of the threats of biology and biblical criticism."[12]

In addition to this contrast between Calvinism and Arminianism, we must notice another contrast between the evangelicalisms of the nineteenth and those of the twentieth century—one of *eschatology*. The dominant, though not exclusive, eschatology of the pre-Civil War era was postmillennialism, a view that was so confident of the efficacy of God's transforming grace that it saw itself on the edge of being ushered into the utopia of God's millennial reign. This was in a sense the social correlate of the Wesleyan doctrine of Christian perfection—a doctrine of social sanctification or a form of realized eschatology, in which God would universally manifest his will. By contrast, the dominant, though again not exclusive eschatology of fundamentalism was a form of premillennialism that forsook any sense of continuity between this life and the next and despaired of social transformation, looking instead to the return of Christ before the millennium as a way of being rescued out of this evil age. It does not take too much penetration into these two eschatologies to recognize fundamentally different worldviews and contrasting solutions to the perennial problem of "Christ and culture," which would have major implications for the shape of any social witness—or its lack. And there is a sense in which the transition between those two evangelical eschatologies represents as well the shift from Arminianism to Calvinism described in the preceding paragraphs. Robert Whalen has analyzed these eschatologies to reveal the Arminian tendencies of the first and Calvinist tendencies of the second.[13] This is a shift toward what has come to be known as fundamentalism. Ernest Sandeen has argued that fundamentalism must be understood primarily as the culmination of a long history of premillennialism that, in the later part of the nineteenth century, coalesced with the

Princeton theology to form an uneasy theological coalition on the basis of a common commitment to biblical literalism.[14] Our analysis confirms this, emphasizing in addition that these two traditions also have in common the rejection of the pre-Civil War optimistic Arminianism.

Understanding these distinctions is crucial to any discussion of the meaning of evangelicalism. Only by attention to them can we realize that what is at stake is not just a struggle between orthodoxy and liberalism, but a much more complicated matter, involving issues of eschatology, varying thelogical frameworks, and so on. One also may see how "American" some of the issues are—even though many of them have been exported abroad. Moreover, such distinctions are crucial for understanding the vicissitudes of evangelical social witness. The transforming impulse of pre-Civil War revivalism was in part related to its distinctive eschatology and its Arminian affirmation of the role of human ability and effort in the process of personal and social reconstruction, though other factors obviously were at work as well.

It is no accident that contemporary, postfundamentalist evangelicalism, for the most part, has not been marked by a strong impulse toward social witness and reconstruction.

## The Holiness Movement Among These Currents

Within this analysis we turn now to the special focus of our interest, *the holiness movement,* a form of Wesleyanism too often ignored and lost between the Methodistic currents of nineteenth-century evangelicalism and modern Calvinistic, postfundamentalist evangelicalism. The movement emerged in the pre-Civil War intermingling of Methodism and "new measures" revivalism and especially incarnated the revival of the doctrine of Christian perfection that took place in that era, in part in response to the sense of perfectionistic optimism that pervaded the culture. Early intimations of the movement may be seen in the Boston

*Guide to Christian Perfection* of the late 1830s, the turn to Methodist themes in revivalist Oberlin College at about the same time, the emergence of the abolitionist Wesleyan Methodist denomination in the early 1840s (this movement became, I believe, the first denomination to add a statement of Christian Perfection to its Articles of Religion), and related currents. All these movements were radically reformist in character, expressing and even carrying to an extreme the reform impulse carried by the broader forms of revivalism of the era. In addition, these movements reflected some differences from classical Wesleyanism, as a result of the American context and the impact of anti-Calvinist revivalism. They were generally more Arminian, more self-consciously postmillennial in eschatology, more oriented to the moral law and the possibility of its fulfillment (and therefore perhaps more "legalistic"), and in general more likely to affirm the broader perfectability of human life. These themes were in part distortion and in part intensification of classical Wesleyanism.

More determinitive for the events that would follow was a parallel variation of these currents that developed within Methodism, especially around circles associated with lay evangelist Phoebe Palmer of New York City. Her parlor meetings for the promotion of holiness advocated a more experientially based and less socially radical form of Wesleyanism, in a style somewhat akin to the modern charismatic movement (though without any sign of the experience of glossolalia). Reinterpreting the Wesleyan doctrine of entire sanctification in terms of Finneyite new measures revivalism, Phoeby Palmer emphasized its universal and immediate availability to all who would cast themselves on the "altar" of "consecration." Her emphases contributed to a holiness variation on Wesleyan theology— one that tended to narrow the focus to the *experience* of sanctification, which had the effect of diluting the teleological orientation of Wesley's formulation by moving sanctification from the goal, to an earlier point in Christian experience, and of giving greater attention to the mechanics of achieving the "second blessing." At about 1867, the National Campmeeting Association emerged, and proved to be the major institutional carrier of this renewal of the Wesleyan emphasis upon sanctification. The late nineteenth century was to see a proliferation of these currents, which, with the collapse of central control, produced a variety of movements and denominations. Among these was the more classically Wesleyan denomination, the Church of the Nazarene, and the more radical Pilgrim Holiness Church, as well as a number of other bodies and such missionary movements as the Oriental Missionary Society and what has come to be known as the World Gospel Mission. In the process, these currents broke through the confines of Methodism and generated an interdenominational holiness movement which swept others into its orbit and left a lasting impact on non-Methodist bodies as well.

Another factor in the emergence of the holiness movement was the reaction to what might be called the *embourgeoisement* of Methodism. As a result of the upward social mobility among Methodists that gradually had taken place in the nineteenth century, the denomination was becoming farther removed from its origins in the lower classes and its commitment to simplicity. The National Campmeeting Association expressed concern about this alienation of Methodism from the masses. The Free Methodist Church, founded in 1860, fought for simple churches and free pews, in the face of Methodist affluence and rented pews. The Wesleyan Methodists were protesting Methodism's compromise on the question of slavery, calling for primitive standards and earlier disciplines. Even evangelist Finney's churches in New York City were called free churches because of their identification with the "free pews" slogan and thus with the lower classes. And similar themes were expressed by early Nazarenes and Pilgrims who boasted of their commitment to the poor of the inner cities and castigated the "steeple churches," which seemed to ignore those masses. The full meaning of this reaction against *embourgeoisement* is not yet clear to me, but it is a factor that deserves further research and must be taken into account in any full analysis of the emergence of the holiness movement.

At any rate, out of all this has flowed a church tradition with a distinctive Wesleyan character and shape that was in some ways conservative, though in other ways radical, and therefore is not to be confused with reactionary fundamentalism or Calvinistically inspired orthodoxy. It consists of a variety of subgroups: pre-Civil War perfectionist and abolitionist movements such as the Wesleyan Methodists and the Free Methodists; certain currents that remained as a self-conscious holiness wing within Methodism, as exemplified in Asbury College and Theological Seminary; products of the post-Civil War sect formation—the Pilgrim Holiness Church, the Church of the Nazarene, the Church of God (Anderson, Indiana), and others; various Quaker and Mennonite movements, deeply shaped by the impact of the holiness teaching; and the Salvation Army, originating in England, in part under American influence and later imported into the States, where the distinctively holiness orientation deepened. In addition, one may trace a radiating circle of impact in such related movements as the Keswick Conventions, various European movements, sister bodies such as the Christian and Missionary Alliance, and ultimately, pentecostalism—though the sibling relationship to the latter is resisted by those in the orthodox holiness tradition.

The study of this holiness tradition has recently come into its own. There is now a burst of secondary scholarship and efforts to rethink and reinterpret it.[15] Such reflection comes at an opportune time because this tradition may provide not only important keys for understanding contemporary evangelicalism, but also paradigms and models that could offer a more satisfactory solution to some of the theological issues bedeviling recent evangelicalism.

For example, Robert Mapes Anderson comments that "any analysis of the Fundamentalist movement should take the Pentecostal and Holiness movements into consideration, but this has hardly been the case." He goes on to say that "when this is done, however, the inadequacies of existing historical interpretations of Fundamentalism will be readily apparent."[16] Anderson's comments raise certain questions of methodology, especially as to whether it would be better to understand the holiness movement and fundamentalism as distinct but related, or whether it would be better, as Anderson seems to suggest, to expand one's analysis of fundamentalism by the incorporation of data from holiness and pentecostal traditions. I am inclined to take the route of distinguishing the movements and tracing interaction; but whatever option is chosen, it is clear that contemporary evangelicalism cannot be understood apart from study and analysis of the holiness tradition.

This may be seen on several levels. Contemporary evangelicalism in the United States (and probably also beyond) is built, to a surprising extent, on institutions and movements that are products of the holiness tradition. About a third of the membership of the National Association of Evangelicals consists of holiness denominations or closely related bodies. Of the colleges recommended recently in the pages of *Christianity Today,* about the same percentage is rooted in the holiness movement, and this percentage is increased when one turns to the more visible Christian College Consortium that is a major force in contemporary North American evangelicalism. The significance of this force in American church life is also illustrated by another statistic, in comparison with the

United Methodist Church. United Methodism, now with somewhat fewer than ten million members, has about one-third of its membership in church on any given Sunday. By contrast, the holiness churches, with membership somewhere between one and two million, often have a larger Sunday attendance than their membership—sometimes double, especially when the large Sunday school attendance is taken into account. What we have then in the holiness traditions is a major force within evangelicalism—a force that can claim impact approaching the classical Methodist tradition, but that usually is interpreted today, within and outside evangelicalism, by using categories drawn from traditions alien and even antithetical to the spirit of Wesleyanism.

What therefore emerges when this holiness tradition is taken into account? On the more technical historiographical level, one could follow the vicissitudes of popular evangelical movements in the crucial decades of the nineteenth century by tracing the development of the institutions they spawned. One might look, for example, at Wheaton College, perhaps the most prestigious of the evangelical Christian colleges, and trace its founding by the Wesleyan Methodists as a center of perfectionist reform, its movement in a more Calvinistic direction under the influence of Congregational leadership, the impact of the rising tide of premillennialism and the consequent dampening of the earlier social witness, the increasing influence of the Princeton theology, the emergence of non-evangelicalism in the post-World War II era, and so forth. Or one could study the movement by focusing on the literature it has produced; as a popular movement, less anchored to confessional and academic constraints, the holiness movement provides a literature more in touch with the subliminal feelings of the people. There one can easily trace the significance of the shift from postmillennialism to premillennialism or chart the popular religious response to industrialization and urbanization. Study of these neglected aspects of nineteenth- and twentieth-century religious currents also would fill important gaps in our understanding of the broader culture.

More to the point, however, is the possible future impact of the holiness tradition in providing paradigms that may indicate ways out of current evangelical impasses.

To understand the contemporary evangelical scene, we must sketch the developments since the fundamentalist/ modernist controversy. The generation of the 1940s reached toward the label "evangelical" to project a more positive image and a new style, centering on several themes that were in reaction to the stances of the preceding generation, especially earlier separatism.[17] The move back into the mainstream denominations was an effort to recover an apologetic offensive by entering into dialogue with the dominant theological culture and by recovering a social dimension to the gospel. Westminster Theological Seminary played a major role in mediating the themes of the old Princeton theology to this movement, and the basic concern and badge of evangelical authenticity came to be adherence to the doctrine of the inerrancy of the Scriptures. This concern is obvious in the variety of institutions spawned by this movement: The National Association of Evangelicals, *Christianity Today*, Fuller Theological Seminary and related institutions, and others. Holiness groups, just beginning at that time to emerge from cultural isolation, were attracted to this movement as a part of their push toward respectability. In the process they lost many of their distinctive Wesleyan characteristics and become largely indistinguishable from the more Calvinistically inclined general movement.

But the 1960s have seen a further development within this postfundamentalist evangelical tradition, that in some ways is a reaction to the earlier ethos and in other ways is in continuity with it. The members of this new generation have been variously labeled "young evangelicals," "new evangelicals," and even "radical evangelicals." If they have a manifesto, it is to be found in a book by Richard Quebedeaux, *The Young Evangelicals,* in which the following themes seem to be especially important: a more ecumenical stance, replacing the earlier antiecumenicity of the preceding "conservative evangelicals"; a greater willingness to draw upon the insights of the charismatic movement and its nondogmatic style of life in the Spirit; a reaction against older premillennialism, especially in its dispensationalist forms; a greater openness to biblical criticism and critical theological scholarship; a renewed emphasis on sanctification, particularly in the search for a new shape of the Christian life and a recovery of social witness; and a broader cultural affirmation than was permitted by the taboos of an earlier form of evangelicalism.[18] The ironic aspect of Quebedeaux's book is the fact that it speaks so exclusively out of the self-understanding of contemporary evangelicals that it shows little awareness of the earlier styles of nineteenth-century revivalism. One well might argue that the Wesleyan/holiness tradition is better able to incorporate these themes than are the dominant forms of Calvinistic evangelicalism. If so, the time is ripe for a resurgence of Wesleyan thought that could reshape contemporary evangelicalism toward Wesleyanism, just as the Princeton theology of a generation or two ago led the evangelicalism of that day toward Calvinism.

This could be illustrated on a number of levels, although one can only hint at most of them. The turn to sanctification on the part of the young evangelicals provides obvious opportunity—if the Wesleyan/holiness themes can be restated, leaving behind some of the shibboleths of the holiness theology. Similarly, the holiness tradition provides paradigms for a nondogmatic vision of the work of the Spirit that emphasizes ethical and social outworking rather than ecstatic experience. Holiness eschatology has been more resistant to dispensational premillennialism, and this fact makes it easier than in some other contexts to oppose this influence. One might even find bases for certain cultural affimation, especially in some liturgical traditions from Anglicanism that have been preserved in at least parts of the holiness movement. There is also an important basis in the holiness tradition for a broader ecumenism. The *Discipline* of the Wesleyan Methodist Church, which was among the most deeply influenced by modern fundamentalism of the various holiness denominations, recognized in the preamble to its "Articles of Religion" that their purpose is not only to define belief but also to "prepare the way for more effective cooperation with other branches of the Church of Christ in all that makes for the advancement of God's Kingdom among men." And there is among the holiness churches a pattern of recent mergers that rivals better-known illustrations of organic union. There also has been an ambivalence about the National Association of Evangelicals that has kept some holiness churches out, and has pushed others to a variety of ecumenical contacts, even in some cases to relationships with conciliar movements. These contacts and orientations well might become the basis of new arrangements and configurations that could make a major contribution to the ecumenical stance of modern evangelicalism.

But let us focus more closely on the remaining questions. One is the most controversial issue among modern postfundamentalist evangelicals—the doctrine of Scripture; the other is the recovery of the social witness of earlier evangelicalism.

One has only to look at the study by Harold Lindsell entitled *The Battle for the Bible* and the various responses that it has engendered, to sense both the acrimony of this debate and the theological stalemate to which the Princeton formulation of biblical inerrancy has led.[19] The emerging new evangelical critique of this doctrine points in two significant directions. There is first the suggestion that the

Princeton formulation is at root docetic, in that it does not attach enough inportance to the human aspect of the Scriptures; and second, that it fails to account for the fact that the classical Christian teaching has been more interested in its teleological purpose—that of effecting salvation—than in historical and cosmological detail. At both points the Wesleyan tradition provides paradigms superior to those of the older Calvinism so influential in contemporary evangelicalism. Surely the docetic tendencies of the Princeton formulation are at least partially rooted in the high Calvinism of that tradition and its tendency to undervalue the role of the cooperating human will. Are there not resources in the Wesleyan/holiness interpretation of grace for developing more adequate understandings of the role of the human in the production of the Scriptures? Similarly, the growing emphasis on the teleological and transformational function of the Scriptures fits more naturally into the Wesleyan vision of them as being given for our salvation and sanctification. From these starting points it would be possible to articulate fuller doctrines of Scripture that would avoid the postfundamentalist fixation on inerrancy and propositional revelation, without denying valid aspects of these concerns. And such a concern for the transformational intention of Scripture also would provide a point of contact for discussion with the liberation theologies.

Even more pertinent, however, is the young evangelical push toward recovery of their lost social witness. Here the Wesleyan/holiness tradition provides a rich fund of historical models. On one level, my own book is an effort to project into a wide evangelical audience the styles from the Wesleyan tradition that counteract the fundamentalist tradition's denial of the importance of social aspects of the gospel.[20] Here the relationship with the preceding generation of evangelicalism is particularly ironic and poignant. It was Carl Henry who first called evangelicals to "kingdom preaching" and to the recovery of an evangelical social witness in his book *The Uneasy Conscience of Modern Fundamentalism*.[21] But it was also Henry who was editor of *Christianity Today* during the 1960s, when the older evangelical social vision so clearly revealed itself to be limited and hopelessly reactionary.[22]

For many, the experience of the 1960s broke the spell of the older evangelical theology and set up a search for new models, socially as well as theologically. The first indications came from a series of new periodicals, which attempted to sort out the relationship of evangelicalism to a variety of liberation movements that were emerging in the culture. The civil rights movements produced an evangelical journal, *Freedom Now,* which since has evolved into *The Other Side* (the title is significant in its identification with the poor and oppressed), "a magazine for radical Christian discipleship." Concern for urban ghettos found expression in a magazine titled *Inside,* now a newsletter for political action in the legislative arena. The Jesus Movement produced *Right On* (now *Rādix*), which has developed into a politically conscious countercultural expression of Christian life. Perhaps most significant was the emergence of *The Post-American* in the antiwar protest movements of the late 1960s. That journal has become *Sojourners,* an important force today for forging both new visions of the social outreach of the church and new ecumenical channels of contact and interaction. Most recently, *Daughters of Sarah* has attempted to find a standpoint of Christian feminism rooted in the Scriptures in such a way as to chart a path between post-Christian feminism and evangelical traditionalism.

In all this turmoil there has been a discernible tendency to reach toward the Wesleyan tradition for paradigms that can be used as evangelical theologies of liberation. Looking to the nineteenth century for examples of social involvement, significant interconnections are being uncovered between evangelical faith, abolitionism, and feminism.

Roger Anstey has recently critiqued some economic analyses of the collapse of slavery and indicates that its decline was dependent at least in part upon the rise of the evangelical world-view.[23] Anne C. Loveland has argued for a fundamental congruence between the evangelical vision and that of immediate abolition, emphasizing such themes as repentance, human ability, and benevolence.[24] And John Hammond has analyzed Ohio voting records by computer, to demonstrate a close connection between revival religion and antislavery politics.[25] Hammond emphasizes the significance of the collapse of Calvinism and the rise of doctrines of "free will" and "human agency." His analysis is given impressionistic support by the fact that Arminian Wesley was a more active critic of slavery than was his Calvinist contemporary, George Whitefield. At any rate, it would seem safe to presuppose at least some connection between abolitionism and Arminian evangelicalism.

This evangelically grounded abolitionism gave an extra impulse to the emergence of feminism—by extending the egalitarianism another step toward full human freedom; by raising up a generation of professional reformers who expanded the range of issues being agitated; by forcing women engaged in benevolent work for the slaves to defend their work in the face of biblically based objections; but most important, by providing a hermeneutic that permitted the reinterpretation of the Scriptures. Feminists found that "the Bible argument against slavery" provided a method for dealing with the Scriptures. The *magna carta* of Galatians 3:28 seemed to permit a relativizing of the prohibitions against women's speaking and teaching (especially in face of the fact that women in the New Testament seemed to have engaged in such practices). And the *Haustafeln* passages about women were to be handled as were the parallel passages on slaves. Out of all this came an extension of the egalitarian impulse that was transmuted into feminism and carried especially by the perfectionist traditions in American revivalism.

With this background, we more easily may understand phenomena of the period. Early Oberlin College, deeply under the influence of the evangelical abolitionism of Charles G. Finney, was a natural place for women to find new roles, even though it remained more conservative than might have been wished by the many feminists of the era who attended. We are not surprised to discover that the Seneca Falls meeting of the first women's rights convention was held in a Wesleyan Methodist church, though most historians of feminism are insufficiently attuned to Methodist distinctions to be aware of the significance of the location. Nor are we astonished to learn that Antoinette Brown, usually celebrated as the first woman fully ordained as a minister, was a disciple of Finney and a graduate of Oberlin; and that the minister who preached her ordination sermon was Luther Lee, one of the founders of the Wesleyan Methodist Church.[26] In addition, B. T. Roberts, founder of the Free Methodist Church, was an ardent feminist who defended the ministry of women and the concept of "egalitarian marriage" in a book titled *Ordaining Women.*[27]

This pre-Civil War egalitarian feminism, carried by perfectionistic revivalism, is in many ways parallel to modern forms—though it was to some extent grounded in the postmillennial eschatology of the era. Some of the liberature of that period seemed to view the gospel as a sort of time bomb, dropped into history and set to go off with the unfolding of providence, successively eradicating slavery, the subordination of women, and so forth, in ever-widening circles of the influence of its transforming power. This vision supported to a great extent the reformist dynamic of the era, and as the underlying eschatologial vision fell into disrepute, the reforms also declined.

Holiness feminism, however, was something of an

exception to this pattern and was continued in the movement and given a different grounding. It was linked with the premillennialism and the rise of pentecostal imagery (not yet "pentecostalism") that became dominant by the end of the century and was taken up by the Church of the Nazarene and the Pilgrim Holiness Church. In the latter the mix of themes was forcefully stated by Seth Cook Rees, who insisted that the ideal church made no distinction with regard to the sexes. In his view, "as the grace of God and the light of Gospel are shed abroad . . . woman is elevated until at Pentecost she stands, a second Eve, by the side of her husband."[28] Some writers in the *Guide to Holiness* were able to bend this argument in an even more distinctly feminist direction, to claim, for example, that "Pentecost laid the axe at the root of the tree of social injustice."[29] Similarly, Catherine Booth, called to the ministry under the influence of Phoebe Palmer, carried a feminist thrust into the creation of the Salvation Army to help create one of the few Christian movements committed from its beginning to the equality of women. And perhaps the most radically consistently feminist of Christian bodies is one of the most esoteric and sectarian of the holiness groups, the Pillar of Fire, founded at the turn of the century by Alma White. For years this body fought for suffrage and other reforms through a periodical called *Woman's Chains*. Other similar currents could be traced, but these hints indicate a massive amount of Christian feminist sentiment largely obscured from the rest of the church, as well as from feminist scholars, by its unexpected location.

The purpose of this chapter has been to demonstrate the debt of contemporary evangelicalism to the holiness movements of the last century, and to point to the impoverishment that has occurred as evangelicals have lost contact with that Arminian heritage and have been co-opted by fundamentalism, premillenialism, and biblical literalism. The creative alternative to reactionary versions of Calvinism is to be found, I believe, in those Wesleyan sources. And the challenge to Methodist theologians of an evangelical persuasion today is to make the evangelical world aware of that alternative.

# The Wesleyan Movement and Women's Liberation

*Nancy A. Hardesty*

The mention of "John Wesley and women" most often conjures up fragmentary images of his bungled romance with Sophy Hopkey of Georgia, his abortive engagement to Grace Murray, and his miserable marriage to Mary Vazeille.

However, when one looks more closely at Wesley's life and the history of Methodism, one is impressed with the depth and the extent of Wesley's relationships with women and with the impact women have had on the movement. In a wealth of correspondence with women, Wesley displayed deep affection, sincere respect for them as colleagues, appreciation for their spiritual guidance, and also offered them thoughtful advice. Historian Robert Wearmouth goes so far as to suggest that "the emancipation of womanhood began with [Wesley]."[1] Abel Stevens declares, "It may be doubted whether any section of ecclesiastical history since Mary, 'the mother of Jesus,' is richer in female characters" than Methodism.[2] While such claims may seem a bit grandiose, one can trace themes and currents in Wesley's own thought and practice that led Methodism to greater sympathy for women and their ministries.

Wesley's high regard for women undoubtedly stemmed from his close relationship with his mother Susanna. Popular Methodist lore long has pictured her as the epitome of Christian motherhood. She found opportunity and energy in an impoverished household to spend quality time each week in nurturing the intellectual and spiritual lives of each of her thirteen surviving children. Susanna was also a woman of very independent mind. Her political sympathies provoked her husband Samuel to declare, "You and I must part; for if we have two kings, we must have two beds." Thereupon, he left Epworth for London and stayed away for a year. After the coronation of a new monarch, Queen Anne, he returned, and John, born in June, 1703, was the child of their reconciliation. Until her death in 1742, Susanna remained her son's closest spiritual advisor.

Other women functioned in similar roles throughout Wesley's life. Sally Kirkham ("Varanese") was his first "religious friend." She played a crucial role in guiding his spiritual development during the years around 1725, when he was ordained deacon. Later he would find more such friends in Grace Murray, Mary Bosanquet Fletcher, Hester Ann Rogers, and others.[3]

The stories of the lives of these women had a great effect in turn upon North American Methodists, who received their original organizational impetus from another woman, Barbara Heck.[4] In the mid-nineteenth century Phoebe Palmer transformed Wesley's distinctive doctrine of Christian perfection into fuel for a revival that swept both North America and the British Isles, eventually giving birth to such denominations as the Church of God, the Church of the Nazarene, the Pilgrim Holiness Church, and the Salvation Army, all of which encourage the ministry of women.

A wealth of factors combine in Wesley and in the Methodist tradition to create a climate conducive to women's spiritual growth and empowerment.

1. The first of these factors is the emphasis upon experience. Wesley's own definition is that a Methodist is one who experiences the love of God in his or her heart. Methodists speak of four sources of authority: experience, Scripture, reason, and tradition. Ideally, all function in a check-and-balance system; yet for Wesley and for many of

his followers the primary question has been simply, Is "thy heart . . . right, as my heart is with thy heart?"[5]

Wesley was a man of tradition—the Anglican, catholic tradition, which still is not noted for its openness to women. Yet he also drew heavily upon the mystical tradition, in which women such as Catherine of Siena, Teresa of Avila, and Madame Guyon appear almost as frequently as do men.[6] In addition he stood in a line of Puritan dissenters and was nurtured by Moravian pietism; both of these traditions stress experience.

His own spiritual search was for assurance—the confidence he received at Aldersgate that Christ "had taken away *my* sins, even *mine,* and saved *me* from the law of sin and death."[7] That experience empowered him to step outside the walls of Oxford and the Church of England pulpits to preach in fields, prisons, and market crosses. It gave him courage to stand up to mobs and bishops.

Experience, rather than history, biblical interpretation, or ecclesiastical sanction, became the hermeneutical key of Methodism. As Wesley said, in giving his approval to the preaching ministry of Mary Bosanquet,

> I think the case rests here, in *your* having an extraordinary call. So I am persuaded has every one of our lay preachers; otherwise I could not countenance his preaching at all. It is plain to me, that the whole work of God termed Methodism is an extraordinary dispensation of his providence; therefore, I do not wonder if several things occur therein which do not fall under ordinary rules of discipline.[8]

An emphasis on experience also entailed a commitment to growth, and so he encouraged another early preacher, Sarah Crosby, in this manner: "Look to the anointing which you have of God, being willing to follow where he leads, and it shall teach you of all things."[9] Obedience to God's call was central. One Sarah Mallet resisted God's call to preach, which came to her through dreams, and for several years she suffered recurring seizures which ceased only after she consented to obey. At the conference in Manchester in 1787, Wesley gave her a preaching license. "We give the right hand of fellowship to Sarah Mallet, and have no objection to her being a preacher in our connection, so long as she preaches the Methodist doctrine, and attends to our discipline."[10]

American women have grounded repeated defenses of their expanding ministries in the belief that it is imperative for those who have experienced justification and sanctification to give testimony to that experience. Phoebe Palmer said that her *Promise of the Father,* an argument for women's ministry, was written after she had heard the anguished testimony of a woman who felt compelled to speak and yet was rebuked by the elders of her church. Books such as *Forty Witnesses* tell of women like Osee Fitzgerald, who could not receive the "blessing" until she agreed to speak publicly, and Frances Willard, who missed the joy of that experience as long as she followed the counsel of men and kept quiet. An emphasis on experience simply required more freedom of expression for women.

2. Scripture, for Welsey and for Methodists, has always been authoritative, but not authoritarian—not an oppressive dead hand from the past but a living, helping hand. Wesley called himself *homo unius libri,* but he was not afraid to try to understand the Bible anew in the light of the questions of his day. As he wrote to Bosanquet, "St. Paul's ordinary rule was, 'I permit not a woman to speak in the congregation.' Yet, in extraordinary cases, he made a few exceptions."[11] Bosanquet was to be one of Wesley's exceptions! Adam Clarke, an early Methodist Bible commentator, laid the foundation for women's rights when he asserted, concerning Galatians 3:28, "Under the blessed spirit of Christianity, [women] have equal rights, equal privileges, and equal blessings, and let me add, they are equally useful."[12]

Nineteenth-century American Methodists produced a shelf full of biblical reinterpretations on the relationship between the sexes and on the role of women in ministry.[13] In addition to earlier arguments grounded in creation, the *imago dei,* and equality in Christ, further arguments were developed based in the promise of Pentecost: "And it shall come to pass in the last days, saith God, I will pour out of my Spirit upon all flesh: and your sons and your daughters shall prophesy" (Acts 2:17, quoting Joel 2:28). Equality of the sexes was to be one of the visible marks of God's coming kingdom.

3. Because it has interpreted the Scriptures according to their spirit rather than their letter, Methodism has not been encumbered by a legalistic reading of culturally conditioned biblical restrictions on women. All persons are endowed by God with reason, said Wesley—with the ability and the responsibility for making choices. Although reason cannot supply faith, hope, or love, Wesley encouraged his followers to "let reason do all that reason can: Employ it as far as it will go."[14] This led to a practical, pragmatic, innovative style; it permitted a freedom, almost a responsibility, to be experimental.

Thus, for example, Wesley, the Anglican priest and Oxford don, allowed lay preaching. Susanna encouraged him at the inception of the practice, "Beware what you do; for [lay preacher] Thomas Maxfield is as much called to preach the gospel as ever you were!"[15] Since she herself was the one who had encouraged Wesley's own ordination, this statement carried weight. She also may have been speaking from her personal experience, for when John was about ten years old and his father was off to London again, Susanna began to read devotional books and sermons to her household, in addition to the regular family prayers on Sunday nights. Before long some two hundred people were "dropping by." When Samuel heard the news and objected, in part because she was a woman, she replied,

As I am a woman, so I am also mistress of a large family. And though the superior charge of the souls contained in it lies upon you, as head of the family, and as their minister; yet in your absence I cannot but look upon every soul you leave under my care as a talent committed to me, under a trust, by the great Lord of all the families of heaven and earth.[16]

After an exchange of letters, Susanna finally reached the bottom line.

If you do, after all, think fit to dissolve this assembly, do not tell me that you desire me to do it, for that will not satisfy my conscience; but send me your positive command, in such full and express terms as may absolve me from all guilt and punishment, for neglecting this opportunity of doing good, when you and I shall appear before the great and awful tribunal of our LORD JESUS CHRIST.[17]

No further correspondence or any other record that the Sunday evening services were discontinued has been found.

As early as 1739, Wesley appointed women as class leaders in Bristol, and they were soon prominent at every level of Methodist work, including the intineracy. In the United States women were not circuit riders, as far as we know (although women such as United Brethren preacher Lydia Sexton and evangelist Eunice "Mother" Cobb did itinerate in local areas), yet holiness women, in particular, developed their own creative vehicles for ministry in Tuesday meetings, Bible readings, camp meetings, and the like.

It was evident that women had the gifts and graces; therefore Wesley did not refuse them the leadership roles in the movement through which those gifts could be employed to God's glory and for the blessing of others.

4. Women were especially prominent among those who professed entire sanctification—something Wesley taught but never testified to having experienced himself. The

stories of Mary Bosanquet Fletcher and Hester Ann Rogers became legendary.

In 1835 Sarah Lankford experienced the assurance of entire sanctification; two years later her sister Phoebe Palmer had a similar crisis experience, and together they founded the Tuesday Meeting for the Promotion of Holiness. In the beginning, they studied and taught the process spoken of in Wesley's *Plain Account of Christian Perfection,* but Palmer was repeatedly asked, "Is there not a shorter way?" She outlined her affirmative reply in *The Way of Holiness* (1846), buildng on the logic of revivalist Charles G. Finney, who preached that "religion is something to *do,* not something to *wait for.*" He argued that "when God commands us to do a thing, it is the highest possible evidence that we can do it." The problem is not one of "cannot" but "will not." As Finney said, "It is not a question of *feeling* but of *willing* and *acting.*"[18] Both friends and foes termed this theory "immediatism," as opposed to "gradualism"—and it applied to conversion, sanctification, and reform.

Palmer began with the premise that "God requires *present* holiness." Since God does not command us to do a thing without providing a way for us to accomplish it, Palmer declared that the first step is to consecrate all to God. Volumes of subsequent testimony show that "all" usually included material possessions, children, and spouse. For women, there were usually two more questions from God: Will you risk your reputation? and, Will you speak publicly? Using rather dubious biblical exegesis, Palmer termed this consecration "laying all upon the altar" and declared that "whatever *touched* the altar became holy, virtually the *Lord's property, sanctified to His use.*" Since God has declared this to be true, Palmer asserted, persons who consecrate everything to God may then simply claim the "blessing" and testify publicly to sanctification, whether or not they receive any inner assurance from the Holy Spirit. One claims God's promise by faith, not by feeling.[19]

Thus holiness for Palmer was not the culmination of a lifelong process but an initial experience. Rather than seeing sanctification as growing "unto the measure of the stature of the fulness of Christ" (Eph. 4:13), she saw it in terms of Pentecost—"And they were all filled with the Holy Ghost" (Acts 2:4). As she declared repeatedly, "HOLINESS is POWER."[20] "Holiness is a gift of power, and, when understandingly received by either old or young disciples, nerves for holy achievement."[21] Holiness or perfection thus implies both a critique of the status quo and the moral power to challenge and change it. It is a call to transformation of the individual and also of the society.

5. Power for this transformation is universally available by God's grace and through the gift of the Holy Spirit. While Wesley believed in original sin, he argued that it was total in its pervasiveness but not in its destructiveness. All have sinned and do sin, yet all are also the recipients of prevenient grace—a consciousness of good and evil and the ability to choose the good. Sin is not a nature but a disease. Holiness is wholeness and health. Healing grace is freely and abundantly available to all. Thus Wesley and his followers seldom are bogged down in pessimistic contemplation of sin. Rather, to cite an inclusive translation of Oral Roberts' favorite verse, Wesleyans are confident that "greater is God who is in you, than the god of this world!" (I John 4:4—author's translation). Genesis 3 is not the last word; nor even is the earthly life of Jesus, for he said, "Greater works than these shall [you] do; because I go unto my Father" (John 14:12).

Both within Wesley's life and within later Methodism there was a growing emphasis on the work of the Holy Spirit. Donald W. Dayton has traced a shift from Wesley's more Christocentric formulation of Christian perfection to John Fletcher's "baptism of the Holy Ghost." A similar shift in emphasis took place in American perfectionism, culminating finally in the advent of pentecostalism.[22] Wesley spoke of the Spirit as giving assurance; Palmer emphasized the Spirit's empowering.

> There is ever one standing in their midst, who baptizeth with the Holy Ghost and with fire. The gift is truly for the Marys and the Susannas as for the Peters and Johns. When the Holy Ghost descended, it fell alike upon them all. . . . There was a great work to be done, and therefore, they *all* . . . spoke as the Spirit gave utterance. . . . And who would dare to say that Christianity has lost any of its power. Spirit-beings men and women are still mighty in their sayings and doings.[23]

6. A final factor in the Methodist tradition which opened up leadership roles for women was its emphasis on social outreach. Wesley's concept of salvation—justification and sanctification—was never simply an individualistic vision, but incorporated a strong concept of social service. For Wesley, the kingdom of God was "not barely a future happy state in heaven, but a state to be enjoyed on earth, . . . the gospel dispensation, in which subjects were to be gathered to God by his Son, and a society to be formed, which was to subsist first on earth, and afterward with God in glory."[24] Holiness was to be both inward and outward. Though the Moravians counseled stillness, Wesley never gave up the good works he had practiced so assiduously at Oxford.

Simultaneously with their building of meeting houses, the early Methodists built schools, orphanages, and hostels. At Laytonstone, Mary Bosanquet started a charity school for destitute orphans, which became also a "preaching-house," "a sanctuary for the devout, and a home for preachers."[25] One of her assistants, Sarah Ryan, had been housekeeper at Wesley's earliest school in Kingswood.

American Methodists also were heavily involved in such

social issues as temperance, relief, abolition, and eventually, women's rights. Phoebe Palmer founded the Five Points Mission—a forerunner of the settlement house—in one of New York's worst slums. Wesleyan Methodist abolitionist Luther Lee defended the right of women to attend temperance conventions and preached the ordination sermon for Antoinette Brown, the first woman to be ordained—as a Congregationalist.[26] Quaker abolitionist Laura Haviland became a Methodist preacher.[27] The first women's rights convention was held in the Seneca Falls Wesleyan Methodist Church, and Methodist laywoman Frances Willard used the Women's Christian Temperance Union to further women's suffrage.

Yet as Palmer noted, "It is humiliating to refer to the manner in which female gifts of the highest order, and most manifestly intrusted by Christ, have been slighted and ultimately rejected" by the church.[28] Or as Catherine Mumford Booth cried,

> Oh, that the ministers of religion would search the original records of God's word in order to discover whether the general notions of society are not wrong on this subject, and whether God really intended woman to bury her gifts and talents, as she now does, with reference to the interests of His Church! O that the Church generally would inquire whether narrow prejudice and lordly usurpation has not something to do with the circumscribed sphere of woman's religious labors, and whether much of the non-success of the Gospel is not attributable to the restrictions imposed upon the operations of the Holy Ghost in this.[29]

Yet within Methodism and the wider Wesleyan milieu since the Wesleys, there has been a climate consistently conducive to the liberation of women from the patriarchalism of traditional Christianity and leading to the continued growth of all people into the fullness of Christ, in whom there is neither male nor female.

# Sanctification and Liberation in the Black Religious Tradition

## *James H. Cone*

Since the appearance of black theology in the late 1960s, much has been said and written about the theme of liberation in black religion.[1] Figures such as Henry Highland Garnet, David Walker, Daniel Payne, and Henry McNeil Turner have been widely quoted in black theological circles, because they related the Christian gospel to the politics of black liberation. For the same reason, such spirituals as "Go Down Moses," "O Freedom," and "Steal Away" are often quoted in contemporary black theological discourse. Black theologians feel the need to show the liberating character of black Christianity in our struggle for social and political justice. But in our effort to show that the gospel is political, we are sometimes in danger of reducing black religion to politics and black worship to a political strategy session, thereby distorting the essence of black religion. This point is forcefully stated—in fact overstated— by Cecil Cone in *Identity Crisis in Black Theology*.[2]

My concern here is to examine the spiritual foundation of black worship as reflected in its components of preaching, singing, shouting, conversion, prayer, and testimony. I will attempt to clarify the connection between the experience of holiness in worship and the struggle for political justice in the larger society.

A version of the material in this chapter appeared in *Theology Today* (July 1978) and is used here by permission.

JAMES H. CONE

# The Holy Spirit and Black Worship

Black worship is essentially a spiritual experience of the truth of black life. The experience is spiritual because the people encounter the presence of the divine Spirit in their midst; the worship is truthful because the Spirit's presence authenticates the people's experience of freedom by empowering them with courage and strength to bear witness, in their present existence, to what they know is coming in God's own eschatological future.

> Have I got a witness?
> Certainly Lord!
> Have I got a witness?
> Certainly Lord!
> Certainly, certainly, certainly Lord.

This call and response is an essential element of the black worship style. Black worship is a community happening wherein the people experience the truth of their lives as lived together in the struggle of freedom and held together by God's Spirit. There is no understanding of black worship apart from the presence of the Spirit who descends upon the gathered community, lighting a spiritual fire in their hearts. The divine Spirit is not a metaphysical entity, but the power of Jesus breaking into the lives of the people, giving them a new song to sing as confirmation of God's presence with them in historical struggle. It is the presence of the divine Spirit that accounts for the intensity with which black people engage in worship. There is no understanding of black worship apart from the rhythm of song and sermon, the passion of prayer and testimony, the ecstasy of shout and conversion, as the people project their humanity in the togetherness of the Spirit.

The black church congregation is an eschatological community that lives as if the end of time is already at hand. The difference between the earliest Christian community as

175

an eschatological congregation and the black church community is this: The postresurrection community expected a complete cosmic transformation through Jesus' immediate return, because they thought the end of time was at hand. The eschatological significance of the black community is found in the belief of the people that the Spirit of Jesus is coming to visit them in the worship service, each time two or three are gathered in his name, to bestow upon them a new vision of their future humanity. This eschatological revolution is not so much a cosmic change as a change in the people's identity; no longer are they named by the world, but by the Spirit of Jesus. Roberta Flack expresses the significance of this eschatological change in identity in her singing of "I told Jesus it would be all right if he changed my name. He told me that the world will turn away from you, child, if I changed your name." This change not only affects one's relationship with the world but also one's immediate family. "He told me that your father and mother won't know you, child, if I changed your name." Because the reality of the Spirit's liberating and sanctifying presence is so overwhelming on the believer's identity, the believer can still say with assurance, "I told Jesus it would be all right if he changed my name."[3]

The Holy Spirit's presence with the people is a liberating experience. Black people, who have been humiliated and oppressed by the structures of white society for six days of the week, gather together each Sunday morning in order to experience another definition of their humanity. The transition from Saturday to Sunday is not just a chronological change from the seventh to the first day of the week. It is rather a rupture in time, a kairos—an event that produces a radical transformation in the people's identity. The janitor becomes the chairperson of the deacon board; the maid becomes the president of Stewardess Board Number I. Everybody becomes Mr. or Mrs. and Brother or Sister. The last becomes first, making a radical change in the perception of self and one's calling in the society. Every person becomes "somebody," and one can see the people's recognition of their newfound identity by the way they stand and talk and carry themselves. They walk with the rhythm of assurance that they know where they are going, and they talk as if they know the truth about which they speak. It is this experience of being radically transformed by the power of the Spirit that defines the primary style of black worship. This transformation is found not only in the titles of deacon, stewardess, trustee, and usher, but also in the excitement of the entire congregation at worship. To be at the end of time, where one has been given a new name, requires a passionate response commensurate with the felt power of the Spirit in one's heart.

In the act of worship itself, the experience of liberation becomes a constituent of the community's being. In this context, liberation is not exclusively a political event but also an eschatological happening. It is the power of God's Spirit invading the lives of the people, "buildin' them up where they are torn down and proppin' them up on every leanin' side." When a song is sung in the right way, and the sermon is delivered in response to the Spirit, the people experience the eschatological presence of God in their midst. Liberation is no longer a future event, but a present happening in the worship itself. That is why it is hard to sit still in a black worship service; the people claim that "if you don't put anything into the service, you sure won't get anything out of it." Black worship demands involvement. Sometimes a sister does not plan to participate too passionately, but before she knows what is happening, "a little fire starts to burning and a little prayer-wheel starts to turning in her heart." In response to the Spirit and its liberating presence, she begins to move to the Spirit's power. How and when she moves depend upon the way the Spirit touches her soul and engages her in the dynamics of the community at worship. She may acknowledge the Spirit's presence with a song.

Everytime I feel the spirit
Moving in my heart I will pray.
Everytime I feel the spirit
Moving in my heart I will pray.

Upon the mountain my Lord spoke.
Out of His mouth came fire and smoke.
In the valley on my knees,
Asked my Lord, Have mercy, please.

Everytime I feel the spirit
Moving in my heart I will pray. . . .

However, song is only one possible response to the Spirit's presence. God's Spirit also may cause a person to preach, pray, or testify. "I believe I will testify to what the Lord has done for me" is an often-heard response in the black church. But more often the presence of the Spirit elicits what W. E. B. DuBois called the "frenzy" and what the people call the "shout," which refers not to sound but to bodily movement.[4] "When the Lord gets ready," the people claim, "you've got to move"—that is, "stand up and let the world know you are not ashamed to be known as a child of God."

There is no authentic black worship service apart from the presence of the Spirit—God's power to be with and for the people. It is not unusual for the people to express their solidarity with John on the Island of Patmos and to say with him, "I was in the Spirit on the Lord's day" (Rev. 1:10). Like John, black people believe that to be in the Spirit is to experience the power of another Presence in their midst. The Spirit is God's guarantee that the little ones are never—no not ever—left alone in their struggle for freedom. It is God's way of being with the people and enabling them to shout for joy, even when they have no empirical evidence in their lives to warrant happiness. The Spirit sometimes makes you run and clap your hands; at other times, you want just to sit still and perhaps pat your feet, wave your hands, and hum the melody of a song, "Ain't no harm to praise the Lord."

It is difficult for an outsider to understand what is going on in a black worship service. To know what is happening in this eschatological event, one cannot approach it as a detached observer in the role of a sociologist of religion or a psychologist, looking for an explanation not found in the life-experience of the people. One must come as a participant in black reality, willing to be transformed by one's encounter with the Spirit. If people are willing to let the Spirit hold sway, being open to what God has in store, then they will probably understand what is meant when they hear,

> Glory, glory, hallelujah
> Since I laid my burdens down.
> Glory, glory, hallelujah,
> Since I laid my burdens down.
>
> I'm going home to live with Jesus,
> Since I laid my burdens down.
> I'm going home to live with Jesus,
> Since I laid my burdens down.

It is the people's response to the presence of the Spirit that creates the unique style of black worship. Its style is an integral part of its content, and both elements point to the theme of liberation. Unlike whites, who often drive a wedge between content and style in worship (as in their secular/sacred distinction), blacks believe that a sermon's content is inseparable from the way it is proclaimed. Blacks are deeply concerned about *how* a thing is said in prayer and testimony and its effect upon those who hear it. The way I say "I love the Lord, he heard my cry" cannot be separated from my intended meaning as derived from my existential and historical setting. For example, if I am one who has just escaped from slavery and my affirmation is motivated by that event, I will express my faith-claim with the passion and ecstasy of one who was once lost and is now found. There will be no detachment in my proclamation of freedom. Only those who do not know bondage existentially can speak of liberation objectively. Only those who have not been in the "valley of death" can sing the songs of Zion as if they were uninvolved. Black worship is derived from a meeting with the Lord in the struggle to be free. If one has not met the Spirit of God in the struggle for freedom, there can be no joy and no reason to sing with ecstatic passion, "I am so glad that trouble don't last always."

## The Components of Black Worship

There are six principal components of black worship: preaching, singing, shouting, conversion, prayer, and testimony.

### Preaching

Expressing his admiration for the black preacher, W. E. B. DeBois called him, among other things, "a leader, a politician, an orator, a 'boss,' an intriguer, an idealist."[5] Dubois did not include "prophet" in his list, although certainly it is the black preacher's most important office. The black preacher is a prophet who speaks God's truth to the people. The sermon therefore is a prophetic oration, which "tells it like it is," according to the divine Spirit who speaks through the preacher.

In the black church, the sermon is not intended to be an intellectual discourse on things divine or human. That would make the preached Word a human word and thus dependent upon the intellectual capacity of the preacher. In order to separate the sermon from ordinary human discourse and thereby connect it with prophecy, the black church emphasizes the role of the Spirit. No one is an authentic preacher in the black church tradition until he or she is called by the Spirit. Persons, according to this tradition, should not decide to enter the ministry of their own volition. Preaching is not a human choice; it is a divine choice. Just as God called Amos from Tekoa, Jeremiah while he was only a youth, Isaiah in the temple, and Paul on the Damascus Road, so also he speaks directly to those whom he sets aside for the ministry. It is expected that the preacher will give an account of his calling—how and when the Lord touched his soul and set him aside for the proclamation of divine truth. A preacher might testify that it was late one Wednesday evening or early one Thursday morning. There is no rigidity about the time or the circumstances of the call. But it is important that the call be authenticated, so that the people know they are encountering God's Word through the sermon's oration, and not simply the personal interest of a given preacher.

In the black tradition, preaching as prophecy essentially is telling God's story, and "telling the story" is the essence of black preaching. It is proclaiming, with appropriate rhythm and passion the connection between the Bible and the history of black people. What have the Scriptures to do with our life in white society and the struggle to be "somebody" in it? The answer to that question depends upon the preacher's capacity to tell God's story so that the people will experience its liberating presence in their midst. That is why the people ask of every preacher, "Can the Reverend tell the story?" To "tell the story" is to act out, with the rhythm of the voice and the movement of the body, the truth about which one speaks. We can speak of the black preacher in the way B. D. Napier speaks of the Old Testament prophet: "The symbolic acts of the prophets are simply graphic, pictorial extensions of the Word, possessing both for the prophet and for his observers-hearers a quality of realism probably unfathomable psychologically to the Western mind."[6]

If the people do not say "Amen" or give some other

passionate response, it usually means that the Spirit has chosen not to speak through the preacher at the time. The absence of the Spirit could mean that the preacher was too dependent on his or her own capacity to speak or that the congregation was too involved in its own personal quarrels. Whatever the case, the absence of a "Hallelujah" and "Praise the Lord" when the preacher speaks God's Word is uncharacteristic of a black worship service, for these responses let the preacher know that he or she is on the right track, and that what is being said rings true to the Spirit's presence in their midst. An Amen involves the people in the proclamation and commits them to the divine truth that they hear proclaimed. It means that the people recognize that what the preacher is saying is not just Reverend So-and so's idea, but the claim that God is laying upon the people.

## Song

Next to preaching, song is the most important ingredient in black worship. Most black people believe that song opens their hearts for the coming of God's Spirit. That is why most church services are opened with a song and why most preachers would not attempt to preach without a "special" song which not only prepares the people for God's Word, but also intensifies the power of the Spirit's presence. Through song a certain mood is created in the congregation, and the people can experience the quality of the Spirit's presence. One cannot, through manipulation, force the Spirit to descend. The Spirit always remains free of human choice. By singing, the people know whether they have the proper disposition for the coming of the Spirit.

In many black congregations, there are special songs that are led by particular people, and no one would dare sing another's song. That would be a sure way to "kill the Spirit." I grew up in the Macedonia AME Church in Bearden,

Arkansas, and I can remember the special songs of several people in that congregation. My mother's song was,

> This little light of mine,
> I'm going to let it shine;
> This little light of mine,
> I'm going to let it shine,
> Let it shine, let it shine.

Sister Ora Wallace, unquestionably the best singer at Macedonia, would always sing,

> I'm workin' on the buildin'
> It's a true foundation,
> I'm holdin' up the blood-stained banner for my Lord.
> Just as soon as I get through,
> Through working on the buildin'
> I'm goin' up to heaven to get my reward.

Of all the songs of Macedonia, I will never forget Sister Drew Chavis' favorite, because she sang with intensity and passion that never failed to bring tears to the eyes of most of the people assembled.

> Precious Lord, take my hand,
> Lead me on, let me stand,
> I am tired, I am weak, I am worn.
> Through the storm, through the night
> Lead me on to the light,
> Take my hand, precious Lord,
> Lead me home.

By the time she reached the second stanza and began to sing "When my life is almost gone, Hear my cry, hear my call, Hold my hand lest I fall," the eyes of the entire congregation were wet, because they knew they had to cross the River Jordan. Thus they waited patiently for the familiar lines in the third verse, "At the river I stand, Guide my feet, hold my hand. Take my hand, precious Lord, Lead me home."

It is possible to "have church," as the people say, without outstanding preaching, but not without good singing. Good singing is indispensable for black worship, for it can fill the vacuum left by a poor sermon. There are those who would say that "a good sermon ain't nothing but a song." In recent years, taking their cue from their white counterparts, many black churches have replaced congregational singing with choir singing, thereby limiting the people's involvement in worship. While choirs have their place in certain restricted contexts, the true black service involves the entire congregation in song.

## Shouting and Conversion

Good singing naturally leads to shouting, which is often evidence that one has been converted. As elements of black worship, shouting and conversion belong together because they are different moments in a single experience. To shout is to "get happy." It happens in the moment of conversion and in each renewal of that experience in the worshiping community. Shouting is one's response to the movement of the Spirit as one encounters its presence in the worship sevice. For white intellectuals, including theologians, the shouting of black folks is perhaps the most bizarre event in their worship services. White intellectuals often identify the shouting in the black church with similar events in some white churches, attempting to discover a common sociological and psychological reason for the phenomenon. Such an approach is not only grossly misleading from my theological perspective, but also from the premises and procedures that white scholars claim guide their examination. How is it possible to speak of a *common* sociological and psychological reason for religious ecstasy among blacks and whites, when they have radically different social and political environments, thereby creating different psychological and religious orientations? It is absurd on sociological, psychological, or theological grounds to contend that the Ku Klux Klansman and the black person who escaped him are shouting for similar reasons in their respective church services. Because the worship services of whites and blacks arise out of differing historical and theological contexts, the people do not shout for the same reasons.

The authentic dimension of black people's shouting is found in the joy they experience when God's Spirit visits their worship and stamps a new identity upon their persons, in contrast to their oppressed status in white society. This and this alone is what the shouting is about. This experience is so radical that the only way to speak of it is in terms of dying and rising again. It is a conversion experience. In one sense conversion is a once-and-for-all event and is associated with baptism. In another sense, one is continually converted anew to the power of the Spirit, and this usually is connected with shouting. "God struck me dead," recalled a former slave, likening his conversion with the experience of dying.[7] But on the other side of death is the resurrection, a new life, and the determination to live for God. Since one cannot stay on the "mountaintop" but must return to the "valley of life," there is always the need to return to the place where one once stood, in order to experience anew the power of God's Spirit. On Sunday morning, at the altar call, the preacher invites all in the congregation to renew their determination to stay on the "Lord's journey" and "to work in his vineyard."

## Testimony and Prayer

One's determination is often renewed with prayer and also with testimony, when one stands before the congregation and bears witness to one's determination to keep on the "gospel shoes."A sister might say,

> I don't know about you, but I intend to make it to the end of my journey. I started on this journey twenty-five years ago,

and I can't turn back now. I know the way is difficult and the road is rocky. I've been in the valley, and I have a few more mountains to climb. But I want you to know this morning that I ain't going to let a little trouble get in the way of me seeing my Jesus.

Prayer, like song, creates the mood for the reception of God's Spirit and is the occasion when the people specifically request Jesus to come and be with them. The people believe that they can call Jesus upon the "telephone of prayer" and tell him their troubles; his line is never busy, and he is always ready to receive their call. It is not uncommon to hear someone say, "Jesus is on the main line; call him up and tell him what you want." Prayer is communication with the divine. That is why prayer before entering the pulpit is so important to most black preachers.

Harold Carter, a Baptist preacher in Baltimore, accurately describes the essence of black prayer: It is "more than a word spoken; it [is] an event to be experienced. The spirit of what happen[s] [is] as important as the words [being] spoken."[8] Black prayer should not be read, but heard, because the rhythm of the language is as crucial to its meaning as is the content of the petition. To understand black prayer, one needs to *hear* the deacon say,

> Almighty and all wise God our heavenly Father! Tis once more and again that a few of your beloved children are gathered together to call upon your holy name. We bow at your footstool, Master, to thank you for our spared lives. We thank you that we were able to get up this morning clothed in our right mind. For Master, since we met here, many have been snatched out of the land of the living and hurled into eternity. But through your goodness and mercy we have been spared to assemble ourselves here once more to call upon a captain who has never lost a battle.[9]

At this point in the prayer, the deacon is ready to go through his list of requests, which normally relate to the bestowal of strength on the people so that they can survive in a sin-sick world. After the requests, he moves toward the conclusion.

> And now, oh, Lord; when this your humble servant is done down here in this low land of sorrow; done sitting down and getting up; done being called everything but a child of God; oh, when I am done, done, done, and this old world can afford me a home no longer, right soon in the morning, Lord, right soon in the morning, meet me at the River of Jordan, bid the waters to be still, tuck my little soul away in your chariot, and bear it away over yonder in the third heaven where everyday will be a Sunday and my sorrows of this old world will have an end, is my prayer for Christ my Redeemer's sake, and Amen and thank God.[10]

One fact is clear from our examination of black worship: It is primarily a happening in the lives of the people. Both the content of what is said and the manner in which it is expressed emphasize that black worship is an eschatological event—a time when the people experience a liberation in their present of the way they believe life will be fully realized in God's coming future.

## Sanctification, Liberation, and the Struggle for Justice

On the basis of our interpretation of black worship as an eschatological event, it is not difficult to understand why Richard Allen, the founder of the African Methodist Episcopal (AME) Church, was so "confident that there was no religious sect or denomination [that] would suit the capacity of the colored people as well as the Methodist."[11] The process of salvation in terms of repentance, forgiveness, and new birth, so important for John Wesley, is also dominant in the black religious tradition generally, and in black Methodism in particular. Black worship is the actualization of the story of salvation as experienced in the lives of oppressed black people.

However, the claim that the black church was influenced

by Methodism and other forms of evangelical Protestantism does not mean that there are no essential differences between them. In fact, the dissimilarities are perhaps more important than the similarities, and it was for this reason that Richard Allen and other blacks walked out of St. George Methodist Church of Philadelphia in 1787 and later, in 1816, founded the AME Church. Similar events happened in other black/white Methodist contexts, giving rise to the AME Zion Church and much later to the Colored Methodist Episcopal Church.[12] The central difference between black and white Methodism was and is the refusal of black people to reconcile racism and social injustice with the experience of conversion and new birth. We do not believe it is possible to be sanctified and a racist at the same time. If conversion and new birth have any significance at all, they must involve the historical actualization of the experience of salvation in works of piety and mercy on behalf of the oppressed of the land. John Wesley seems to have recognized this historical vocation, since he not only took a radical stand against slavery but also insisted on the social character of the experience of salvation.[13] "Christianity," he wrote, "is essentially a social religion; and . . . to turn it into a solitary religion is indeed to destroy it."[14] But John Wesley notwithstanding, North American Methodism, unfortunately, did not institutionalize this stand on slavery.[15] The failure of white Methodism in this regard led to the creation of a white spirituality that is culturally determined by American values and thus indifferent to oppressed black people's struggle for social justice.

In contrast, black American spirituality was born in the context of that struggle. The contradiction between the experience of sanctification and human slavery always has been a dominant theme in black religion. It is found not only in the rise of independent black churches but also in our songs, stories, and sermons.[16] When the meaning of sanctification is formed in the social context of an oppressed community struggling for liberation, it is difficult to separate the experience of holiness from the spiritual empowerment to change the existing societal arrangements. If "I'm a chile of God wid soul set free" because "Christ hab bought my liberty," then I will find it impossible to tolerate slavery and oppression. Black slaves expressed this point in song.

> Oh Freedom! Oh Freedom!
> Oh Freedom, I love thee!
> And before I'll be a slave,
> I'll be buried in my grave,
> And go home to my Lord and be free.

The historical realization of the experience of salvation has always been an integral part of the black religious tradition. The idea that black religion was and is otherworldly and nothing more is simply not true. To be sure, black religion is not a social theory that can substitute for a scientific analysis of societal oppression. But it is a spiritual vision of the reconstruction of a new humanity in which people are no longer defined by oppression, but by freedom. This vision can serve as an important force in organizing people for the transformation of society. Because black people know that they are more than what has been defined for them, this knowledge of that "more" requires that they struggle to realize in society the freedom they experience in their worship life.

Sometimes this experience of God's gift of a new identity actualizes itself in political revolution, as found in the well-known insurrections of Gabriel Prosser (1800), Denmark Vesey (1822), and Nat Turner (1831).[17] Black religion is, by definition, the opposite of white religion; it was born in black people's political struggle to liberate themselves from oppression in the white church and in the society the white church justifies. Even when black slaves could not actualize their experience of salvation in revolutionary struggle, they often verbalized the distinction between black and white religion. Harriet Martineau recorded the comment to a mistress by one of her slaves, "You no holy. We be holy. You in no state of salvation." A similar point is emphasized in a joke about a "slave's reaction to the news that he would be rewarded by being buried in the same vault with his master: 'Well, Massa, one way I am satisfied, and one way I am not. I like to have a good coffin when I die [but] I afraid, Massa, when the debbil come to take you body, he make mistake and get mine.' "[18]

Sanctification in black religion cannot be correctly understood apart from black people's struggle for historical liberation. Liberation is not simply a consequence of the experience of sanctification—sanctification *is* liberation—that is, to be politically engaged in the historical struggle for freedom. When sanctification is defined in that manner, it is possible to connect it with socialism and Marxism—the reconstruction of society on the basis of freedom and justice for all.

Although black religion grounds salvation in history and refuses to accept any view of sanctification that substitutes inward piety for social justice, there is also an eschatological vision included in salvation. It is important to emphasize that this vision in black religion is derived from Scripture and is not in any sense a rejection of history. To reject history in salvation leads to passivity and religion then becomes the opiate of the people. Black religion, while accepting history, does not limit salvation to history. As long as people are bound to history, they are bound to law and thus to death. If death is the ultimate power, and life has no future beyond this world, then the heads of the state who control the military are ruling in the place of God. They have the future in their hands and the oppressed can be made to obey the law of injustice. But if the oppressed, while living in history, can see beyond it; if they can visualize an eschatological future beyond this world, then the "sigh of the oppressed creature," to use Marx's phrase, can become a revolutionary cry of rebellion against the established order. It is this revolutionary cry that is granted in the resurrection of Jesus. Salvation then is not simply freedom *in* history; it is freedom to affirm the future that is *beyond* history.

Indeed, because we know that death has been conquered, we are truly free to be human in history, knowing that we have a "home over yonder." That home, vividly and artistically described in the slave songs, is the gift of salvation granted in the resurrection of Jesus. If this "otherness" in salvation is not accepted seriously, there is no way to sustain the struggle against injustice. The oppressed will become tired, and they will be afraid of the risks of freedom. They will say, as the Israelites said to Moses when they found themselves between Pharoah's army and the Red Sea, "Is it because there are no graves in Egypt that you have taken us away to die in the wilderness? What have you done to us, in bringing us out of Egypt?" (Exod. 14:11 RSV). The fear of freedom and of the risks that attend the struggle is an ever-present reality. But the "otherness" of salvation, its transcendence beyond history, introduces a factor that makes a difference. The difference is not that we are taken out of history while living on earth—that would be an opiate. Rather it is a difference that plants our being firmly in history because we know that death is not the goal. The "transcendence factor" in salvation helps us to realize that our fight for justice is God's fight, too; and his presence in Jesus' resurrection has already defined what the ultimate outcome will be. It was this knowledge that enabled black slaves, although they lived in history, not to be defeated but to triumph over their limitations in history. To be sure, they sang about the fear of "sinking down" and the dread of being a "motherless child." They encountered trouble and the agony of being alone, where they "couldn't hear nobody pray." They encountered death and expressed it in song.

> Soon one mornin', death comes a creepin' in
>     my room.
> O my Lawd, O my Lawd, what shall I do?

Death was a terrible reality for black slaves; it often visited the slave quarters, leaving orphans behind.

> Death done been here, took my mother an' gone,
> O my Lawd, what shall I do?

> Death done been here, left me a motherless child,
> O my Lawd, what shall I do?

In these songs are expressed the harsh realities of history and the deep sense of dread at the very thought of death. But because the slaves knew that death had been conquered in Jesus' resurrection, they believed they also could transcend death and they interpreted salvation as a heavenly, eschatological reality. And that is what they sang.

> You needn't mind my dying,
> Jesus' goin' to make up my dying bed.

> In my room I know,
> Somebody is going to cry,
> All I ask you to do for me,
> Just close my dying eyes.

# The Methodist Witness and the African Situation

*Kwesi A. Dickson*

It is true to say that Africa is in the spotlight of world attention today. The reasons are many and varied, and it is important that we look at some of them, if even briefly, as a necessary preliminary to a discussion of Methodism in the African context.

## I

Africa is in the postindependence era; most of the countries of black Africa have achieved independence from colonial rule and have been running their own affairs for many years. On the one hand, the attainment of political independence was a necessity, if only because it removed an important cause of degradation and strife; on the other hand—and paradoxically—the political situation today is considerably more complex and a potential source of unrest. There is a general feeling that things have not gone as well as they might; the rule exercised by African governments over their own peoples has not always proved to be the panacea for social, economic, and political ills that it was expected to be. Of course, world inflation has had its impact on the uncertain economies of many African nations, but it remains a fact that this general inflationary trend often has been exacerbated by corrupt and incompetent rule, with the result that increasingly, the necessities of life are eluding many. Military regimes have sprung up in quite a few

African countries, and these have not always resulted in any more honest and capable governments than the civilian regimes they ousted.

Racialism has been and continues to be a potential source of much conflict, particularly in southern Africa; indeed, the situation could easily result in hostilities that could embroil the great powers, as we know only too well.

Another development has been discernible for some time and is the subject of much comment by certain African heads of state—the importation of outside rivalries into these tense spots in Africa. This phenomenon to a certain extent has been facilitated by African countries themselves, particularly those that have shown a penchant for adopting the cliches of Marxism and other such ideologies, in the mistaken assumption that those countries in which these ideologies predominate have solved all their social, economic, and political problems. Our own view is that these terms, and many others, must be recognized as the cliches they are, and African countries must devise their own solutions to their problems.

This brief statement does not pretend to be a competent analysis of the African situation, but it does indicate that the African continent, like most other areas of the world, has important problems that await solution. Of course, generalizing about Africa can be a hazardous undertaking; there are sufficient variations from one part of the continent to another to necessitate caution when speaking of Africa as a whole. We are even more conscious of this necessity as we turn to look at the Christian church in Africa. Here we shall consider West Africa in general, and Ghana in particular.

## II

As far as the Christian church is concerned, the last few decades have seen considerable expansion, a fact that has given rise to euphoric prognostications of further phenomenal growth. As an institution, the church has great visibility in Africa. Not only are most of the leading citizens products of church schools, but also the churches have—in some African countries, at any rate—either by themselves or in connection with the All Africa Conference of Churches, become increasingly vocal about various matters that hitherto have been considered to be the preserve of government and its various agencies. In speaking of the Christian church we have in mind not only the historic churches but also the numerous independent churches, which have experienced phenomenal growth; indeed, these latter churches seem to be attracting more attention, probably because of their attitude toward traditional beliefs, which enables their leadership to accept the fears of the worshipers with respect to witchcraft and the influence of malevolent spirits.

The pattern of evangelism employed in the early days of Methodist missions in Ghana (the early decades of the last century) contained certain contradictions that to this day have not been fully resolved. First, it was the avowed aim of the Methodist Missionary Society to foster an indigenous ministry in the mission areas, and an institution for this purpose was set up in Ghana within seven years after the arrival of the first missionary from England in 1835. However, though the candidates selected for training were Ghanaians, the ministry that emerged was not, strictly speaking, indigenous, since the aim of the training was to make the Ghanaian Methodist minister (or assistant missionary as he was called originally) a copy, as much as possible, of the English missionary.[1]

Second, there was the tendency to link the Christian message of new life to the necessity that the converts separate themselves from their traditional life; this has been amply documented by Brodie Cruickshank, an observer of the developments in those early days.[2] This tendency resulted either in the removal of the converts from the sphere of life in which they were to live and mature in their faith, or in a dual kind of existence—one for church consumption, another in accordance with traditional life.

Third, the gospel of grace, which was preached with such dedication and ethusiasm in the early days of Ghanaian missions, went hand in hand with the missionaries' insistence upon the observance of a great body of rules and regulations. Anyone who has read *The Ecclesiastical Principles and Policy of the Wesleyan Methodists*, the third edition of which was published in 1873, will be aware that the British missionary and his Ghanaian colleagues were expected to be familiar with a veritable battery of rules and regulations. They were under obligation to enforce these rules in a part of the world where customs and ways appeared to be particularly at variance with the mode of life being inculcated along with the preaching of Christ. The most striking proof of the influence of such regulations was the attitude of a group of Methodists who, in the 1860s, broke away from the church to form their own Methodist Society because, as they argued, the missionaries had become lax in the enforcement of rules relating to the sale of alcoholic beverages by members of the church. In reacting to this development, one of the Methodist missionaries on the scene, Alfred Taylor, noted, "It is only right to say that this rule has never been strictly observed in this District, and, I think, not in any other. I am likewise pretty sure that it is not observed at home."[3] This emphasis on rules, needless to say, led to misinterpretations of Methodist teaching on sanctification, which is the work of God, not of man.

The fourth contradiction, in those early days of Methodist missions in Ghana, was the tension between the spiritual and the secular felt by the missionaries—a dichotomy unknown in African culture. The missionaries criticized existing institutions and customs, such as human sacrifice and domestic slavery, and saw the need to meet concrete social problems, such as widespread unemployment; hence the conviction expressed by Thomas Birch Freeman, a nineteenth-century missionary, to the effect that "the Church should be both Christian and industrious; that its members, young and old, should develop a sense of the value of steady and vigorous industry, and for this purpose they should be introduced to large-scale agriculture on well-organized plantations."[4] However, as the historian F. L. Bartels quite rightly observes, "the missionaries themselves were frequently torn between their instructions in the *Twelve Rules of a Helper* and their desire to improve the economy and make the Church self-supporting; they were torn between the instruction ' you have nothing to do but save souls' and the secular demands of a model farm."[5] This uncertainty about the church's role in the world is to be encountered in the Methodist Church in Ghana and elsewhere in Africa today.

Contradictions such as these have not been unknown in other denominational histories, to be sure. Impeccable policy statements often have been set aside in the realities of the field situation. Thus the 1659 instruction by the Sacred Congregation for the Propagation of the Faith, noting that nothing can be "more absurd than to transport France, Spain or Italy or any other part of Europe to China" may have been inspired, at least in part, by the work of such missionaries as Roberto de Nobili, the seventeenth-century Italian Jesuit; but a restatement had to wait for Vatican II, in our own time. And our own experience in West Africa suggests that the Roman Catholic Church will have to wait a long time for the full implications of such an instruction to be worked out.

The result of the pattern of evangelism employed in the nineteenth century has been that the Methodist Church in Ghana, and elsewhere in Africa, tends to have a middle-class image. The minister's outfit, the silver communion vessels, and so on, seem to set the church apart from life as the ordinary man experiences it. And in the last decades, the church seldom has been heard to speak on behalf of the underprivileged and the powerless, or against misrule and mismanagement. Indeed, in at least one African country the Methodist Church has gone out of its way to give a kind of official recognition to a head of state whose rule is blatantly oppressive and not in the best interest of the people.

At the risk of being repetitive, we shall now place side by side the two elements in the work of the early preachers. On the one hand, they gave much attention to Christian perfection. Personal journals and letters witness to their having been very conscious of this teaching that is part of the Methodist heritage, and indeed to this day, at synods and conferences the ministers are regularly asked whether they continue to preach "our doctrines." The answer has always been in the affirmative. On the other hand, the edge of this teaching has been blunted by the fact that, at worst, the church has tried to separate its members from life as they know it in the particularity of their circumstances, and at best, has pretended not to be aware of its members' involvement. It has been argued that John Wesley's "theology and ethics projected themselves quite naturally into a concern for the present life of man" and that he believed that "Christianity should be relevant in terms of the economic life."[6] The truth of the matter is that Methodist preaching and teaching have not seemed to constitute a potential force for change in the context of Africa. Some reasons already have been given but we shall now look at religion's role in society in a broader perspective.

In his *Religion and Revolution,* Guenter Lewy examines in some detail the dual role of religion in society. Religion, he writes, "may provide legitimation for the existing social order, give emotional support to the fundamental values of a society . . . and lessen social tension by stressing supramundane values"; however, religion may also provide "strong support for an attack on the *status quo* by those who are dissatisfied—politically, economically, socially, or spiritually."[7] There is a sense in which Methodism, in the early days of its establishment in Africa, legitimized the existing social order, if we understand that what was being legitimated was the Europeanizing of Africa that was being inculcated along with the preaching of the gospel. Every attempt was made to ensure that the social order conformed to what Europeans would consider legitimate in the circumstances, with the European in the role of the harbinger of civilization. In this connection the missionary often worked hand in hand with the colonial government, as did Thomas Birch Freeman, one of the most celebrated of the missionaries to Ghana. Freeman, it must be added, did come to realize how unwise it was to link Christianity to westernism.[8]

The attractiveness of westernism ensured that Africans would make every effort to meet the preconditions for entering into the European social class. It could be argued that the missions saw their goal to be the reform of institutions, if by "institutions" we refer to the traditional African social, economic, and religious institutions, which were looked upon as evil. Thus a new social order, conforming to European standards, was hoped for; and every attempt was made to discredit the traditional social order. To complicate the picture further, the aim of missionary preaching, at least in the context of the early days, was to convert individuals to Christ as well as to the world of the European, and consequently, to a certain extent, to a reconciliation with the ruling colonial power.

This is not meant to suggest that Methodism did not inculcate a sense of freedom. It has been pointed out often enough that the Methodist system of organization is such that it encourages people to think and act for themselves. The Sunday schools, which in the early days provided an opening for the illiterate to obtain a first glimpse of a new world (in those days Sunday schools tended to have the character of literacy classes); the class meetings, which encouraged free discussion and a sense of social responsibility by engendering the feeling that each member had a responsibility for the others, in sickness and in health, in sorrow and in joy; and in general, the organization of the Methodist societies, which placed the minister in the position of the first among equals and hence fostered the spirit of give and take, with its consequent mutual strengthening—these are characteristics of Methodism as it has been experienced in Africa. No wonder that only some thirty years or so after the arrival of the first Methodist missionary in Ghana, a splinter group had come into being and thought well enough of the parent church to call itself the Methodist Society; no wonder that there are in Ghana today more independent churches founded by former Methodists than by members from any other historic church!

## III

Raking up the past is sometimes an unpleasant undertaking; in some circles it is felt that no useful purpose is served by wishing for a pattern of evangelism that was more or less unthinkable, given the nature of the ethnographic material available in the early decades of the last century. It was necessary, nevertheless, to essay this brief historial analysis, for two reasons.

First, World Methodism is aware—and thank God for this!—that the age of missions is not over. In recent discussions concern has been expressed over the lack of enthusiasm for missions, and Methodist societies everywhere have been urged to intensify their efforts to be more effective instruments of God in the dissemination of his Word. However, the mission field is not limited to Africa, Asia, and the Caribbean; it is all these and England, America, and Europe, too—in short, the world is the mission field. The gospel of Christ must be heard again in those very countries that formed the missionary societies which took the gospel to Africa and Asia. It is important, then, that the past be kept in mind even as we press on toward the future.

Second, it is a fact that the consequences of the pattern of evangelism of the last century are still with the peoples of Africa today. Most of the Methodist churches in Africa are independent and are headed by indigenous leadership, and in at least one African country, the Methodist Church has evolved a very distinctive pattern of organization and ethos. Some churches still receive missionaries, often referred to euphemistically as fraternal workers, but these are asked for by the African churches themselves, and as in Ghana, such workers come under the authority of the local conferences. As a matter of fact, it is not unknown for the church in one African country to ask for help in the form of personnel from another African country, rather than from England. Despite such signs of a coming of age the Methodist churches in Africa, generally speaking, have preserved the character they had under foreign mission boards and conferences. On the whole, the African leadership has not been in a hurry to make the church relevant to the circumstances of today. The orders of service, music, and sermons tend to relate to a world that is not familiar to most African Christians.

It is a measure of the Methodist Church's effectiveness that several of its theologians, in company with theologians from the other historic churches, are questioning the present image of the Christian church and asking that her theology be reconsidered. Until recently, the progress toward steering the church away from overattachment to the past has tended to be cosmetic. Of course, it would not be quite true to say that until African theologians began to speak, no theologizing whatsoever had been done. Africans had theologized in their singing and praying and preaching, but the theologizing was unsystematized and uncoordinated. Now African theologians are asking that a closer look be taken at the church's theology, with a view to attempting a propositional articulation of the Christian faith from the standpoint of the particularity of the African situation. Various comments made in recent years would seem to suggest that there are three theological options open to Africans. Black theology and liberation theology will be very briefly discussed here, if only for the reason that well-known proponents of these theologies have contributed chapters to this book. The third option, of course, is usually referred to as African theology.

## Black Theology

The expression "black theology" has been used by both black American theologians and theologians from South Africa. James Cone, perhaps one of the most articulate of black American theologians, has stated that "the task of Black Theology . . . is to analyze the black man's condition in the light of God's revelation in Jesus Christ with the purpose of creating a new understanding of black dignity among black people, and providing the necessary soul in that people, to destroy white racism."[9] He goes on to say that it is not possible to "want God without blackness, Christ without obedience, love without death." Cone appears to mean that the true test of a Christian is complete identification with the dispossessed and the rejection of the kind of structures that bring about such oppression. As James Cone starts from the situation of the American black, Manas Buthelezi of South Africa starts from the African, in the context of the present existential situation. Buthelezi speaks of the African as being alienated in South African society; he also gives attention to the economic domination that has contributed to the second-rate citizenship of Africans in that country. Though he does a certain amount of socioeconomic analysis, he seems to place more emphasis on cultural analysis, seeing the South African system as doing all it possibly can to prevent the black citizens from an understanding of themselves.[10]

Both Cone and Buthelezi begin where theologizing should begin—at Christ, in the context of society as it exists and functions in particular localities. Theology must have a particularity; it must arise from concrete life situations. One need only recall the various theories of atonement to realize how the ransom theory fitted the conditions of unrest and brigandage characteristic of the patristic age; the satisfaction theory, the conditions of medieval age, with its feudalism and chivalry; and the forensic or penal substitution theory, the conditions of the post-Reformation period, when ideas of law and jurisprudence were very much in vogue. However, both Cone and Buthelezi have been criticized: While some think Buthelezi's socioeconomic analysis could be deeper, there are others who believe that the tone of reconciliation seems to be missing from the Cone construction of theology. It is a fact that the black situations in America and in South Africa are not the same as the situation in West Africa, though this is not to say that all is well in West Africa. As indicated earlier, the social, economic, and political situation in independent black Africa is far from ideal. All the same, there are many in West and East Africa who would, while appreciating the theologizing being done by the blacks of America and South Africa and recognizing that they do have something to say to the world, nevertheless insist that African traditional culture has such a hold on people, both literate and illiterate, and such richness and meaningfulness, that it is extremely relevant to the social, economic, and political realities of our time—so much so that even Buthelezi's cultural bias is inadequate.

## Liberation Theology

Liberation theology is, of course, a well-known subject, widely discussed in and outside Latin America, where it could be said to have had its origin. It is worth noting, however, that liberation theology is not entirely the preserve of Latin America theologians. One only need refer to Dorothee Soelle's *Political Theology* to see that the European political theology overlaps the Latin American liberation theology; that both theological expressions proceed on the premise that the "social situation is . . . . potentially transformable," to use Soelle's words.[11] In a recent conference in Tanzania, between African theologians and Latin American theologians, there was a certain amount of unanimity on the question of the need to relate theology to the actuality of one's circumstances. Nevertheless the Latin Americans felt, quite rightly, that African theologians were so preoccupied with culture that they tended to lose sight of the socioeconomic situation, while the African theologians refused, again quite rightly, to accept the view that the socioeconomic situation fully defined the circumstances within which meaningful theologizing could be done.[12] While it would be wrong to assume that all liberation theologians have the same emphases, it is nevertheless true that one could be critical of the distinction between praxis and worship that seems to be drawn by some; after all, for the Christian, worship is at the very heart of praxis. Furthermore, while acknowledging that oppression is evil, it is a fact that *all* men have sinned and fallen short of the glory of God. Quite apart from these considerations, theologians of West, Central, and East Africa tend to speak of African theology, which they see as arising from understanding the Christian message in the light of African life and thought.

## African Theology

African theology remains somewhat ill-defined. Some have expressed themselves to the effect that it is no more than a restatement of orthodoxy in culturally recognizable terms; quite possibly this is what African theologians in general have been understood as saying. One might question whether this is doing theology at all, since it merely would be giving a cosmetic touch to a system that has been defined in terms of a different social, economic, and political context. That several African theologians have tended to define their theology in this way may account for the fact that there is still a preoccupation with trying to settle matters of methodology. Any reader of Aylward Shorter's *African Christian Theology* soon discovers that the author is discussing background matters rather than attempting a propositional articulation of the African view of the Christian faith. Again, Shorter argues that "an African Christian Theology . . . must grow out of a dialogue between Christianity and the theologies of the African Traditional Religions."[13] In so writing Shorter is reflecting an approach that would seem to be favored by several African theologians. However, there are others who would consider this approach restrictive since it would ignore other important parameters. I favor the view that sees the dialogue as being between the Christian message, on the one hand, and the African religiocultural traditions, on the other. This calls for two important undertakings: a serious study of the Christian message that would involve an examination of the biblical record for a rediscovery of God's ways and his dealings with man (after all, in considering the biblical text, one ultimately is seeking direction for one's own time and the clarification of one's own situation) and a review of the religiocultural traditions in the light of impinging agents of change.

African traditional religion is not a thing of the past; it effects the lives of many, even of those who would deny that it influences their lives. Also, though traditional culture *has* been affected by various forces such as western literary education, money economy, industrialization, Christianity, Islam, and so on, there is a greater inclination among the literate classes now, than perhaps thirty years ago, to identify with African traditional culture. Hence it would be wrong to say that to permit traditional culture to play a role in theologizing would be to tie theology to a thing of the past. In this connection it is significant that Shorter devotes a chapter to the developments in religious thought in Western Tanzania; the point is that one should take into account the changes that have come about over the years as a result of contact with the outside world. While it would be wrong to tie theologizing to an analysis of a religiocultural tradition that does not exist, forms of traditional culture that persist into the present are of utmost importance and must be taken into consideration.

There are other factors that will need to play a part in the development and articulation of African theology. African theologians cannot afford to lose sight of the Christian theological heritage of the worldwide church. God has done something for humankind that has brought the church into being, and the experiences of the world church over these many centuries should be of interest to the protagonists of African theology. It is from this standpoint that I believe Methodism has a contribution to make to African thinking. Of course, it is the very brave man who would say exactly what John Wesley's view of a particular situation would be, had he addressed himself to it; it is difficult enough to relate his words to situations of his own time and in his own country. Wesley would have been bewildered had he come out to Africa as a missionary in the early decades of the last century. We imagine, however, that he would have continued to proclaim his important convictions: All men need to be saved, and in Christ, God has made his forgiveness available. These are convictions that cannot be dispensed with—they are at the core of the gospel of Christ. All Christian theology must start there.

John Wesley also might have had some difficulty with the view expressed at a consultation of African theologians at Ibadan, Nigeria, in 1966: If God is the Father of us all, then his revelation in Christ cannot be totally discontinuous with the African experience of God. That was not by any means a new insight, for Wilfred Cantwell Smith had stated it in even broader terms in his *Faith of Other Men* a few years earlier.[14] As a matter of fact, in 1944 a Ghanaian, J. B. Danquah, wrote in *The Akan Doctrine of God*, "The Spirit of God is abroad, even in the Akan of the Gold Coast."[15]

We must also consider the much discussed characteristic of African traditional life and thought: Religion and life are inseparable; or if you like: Praxis and worship go together. There is no distinction between them, chronological or otherwise—no possibility of separating and relegating them to different spheres. There is no question of God being given leave from duty so that human beings may act. The traditional African cultural life, informed by traditional religion, enshrines such values as care for the underprivileged, brotherhood, and communality; the chief's rule is to be benign, not dictatorial (if dictatorial, there are constitutional means for ending it); all are to have access to the good things of life (in East Africa it is not theft if one who is starving makes use of what does not belong to one); hospitality is to be made available even to the total stranger; the aged are to be cared for (homes for the aged are as yet unknown). In other words, the African cultural situation covers the same concerns that have necessitated a thorough socioeconomic analysis by Latin American theologians.

When we look at all these characteristics it becomes clear that traditional African society has as its aim the integration of all its members, ensuring that inequalities in talents and circumstances do not lead to some being uncared for and deprived. It is true, and it is often remarked, that communalism in Africa has been shaken by westernism, with its emphasis on the individual. But the triumph of individualism over communalism may be more apparent than real. Even in European and American societies, if the psychologists are to be believed, communalism has not disappeared completely. Harvey Cox might argue that impersonal relationships contribute to the city person's freedom, but it cannot be denied that larger societies would be unable to operate without communal relationships. In the African situation communalism is not on its way out. Cities are growing, but the expected individualism has been tempered by the creation of a great variety of societies which provide that sense of belonging that is such an important characteristic of smaller societies and that the city is otherwise reluctant to supply.

Methodism's organizational structures may have contributed to a sense of belonging, but its theology has tended to emphasize the individual. This may be one of the factors that has led to the phenomenon whereby its members live the gospel only in certain situations. The reverse is true in the African setting—communalism ensures that religion is lived in every circumstance of life; this is an important problematic, to which African theology is seeking to address itself.

# A Liberating *Pastoral* for the Rich

*Dow Kirkpatrick*

## I

The word *pastoral*, as it is pronounced in Spanish, conveys a richness I do not sense in English usage. Perhaps that is because I have heard the word so often in conversations with Latin Americans who are deeply committed to the struggle on behalf of the dispossessed. It does not slip easily off their tongues, but comes out of profound, sacrificial, risk-taking involvement in liberation.

"Pastoral" here is used to define the whole action of the church when it conceives that *faithfulness to the gospel requires solidarity with the oppressed.*

Members of our congregations resent being called rich, and various devices are used to ease this discomfort:

—deny we are rich;
—blame the poor for their own condition;
—give to charity from our surplus, but without attacking the root causes of poverty;
—appeal to the universality of grace ("Isn't salvation for everyone—for the rich, too?").

The answer is yes, but Jesus said it is harder for us—so difficult, in fact, as to border on the impossible (Mark 10:27). The late C. S. Lewis put it graphically in a short poem.

---

In Spanish, the word *pastoral* (pronounced *pastorál)* is used as a noun and traditionally refers to the care of souls—the shepherding of the flock. Here it refers to the church's commitment to its people in their need. Ed.

> All things (e.g. a camel's journey through
> A needle's eye) are possible, it's true.
> But picture how the camel feels, squeezed out
> In one long bloody thread from tail to snout.[1]

The first movement toward conversion is repentance, and the first act of repentance is acknowledgment of one's true condition. Our condition is that we are rich. Most of the world is poor. The world system produces victims and beneficiaries; we are beneficiaries. This raises the question, *Is there a liberating "pastoral" for the rich?*

My response arises out of more than thirty-five years of parish ministry in the United States and five years of residence in Latin America, which is the only continent on earth where two facts exist side by side: (*a*) The majority of the people are oppressed and poor; and (*b*) The majority are Christian. There I have chosen to live—not with the notion that I can become one of them, but because God is speaking a fresh word today among the poor. *My* people need to hear that word, and there is no other place—no other way—but to hear it from those in whose midst it is being spoken.

## II

A new moment may be given us as we answer this question: How would it affect the shape of our *pastoral*—the care of the souls for which we are responsible—*if we believed the gospel now preached to us by the poor?* That gospel is offered in five strong affirmations.

We are Pharaoh.
The God of the Bible is known only by doing justice.
In Jesus, God became poor.
"Evangelism" is confronting the atheism of our worship.
Hope for the liberation of the rich is available—as a gift from the poor.
(Notice: Our churches do not seriously believe that any one of these statements is true.)

DOW KIRKPATRICK

## We Are Pharaoh

The contradiction between the oppressed and the oppressor—is it fundamental or is it a matter of degree? The rich believe it is a matter of degree. ("What those people need is more of what we've got—hard work, thrift, food, education, health.") Three times, Pharaoh is recorded as calling the Jews lazy because they couldn't keep up production schedules after he had placed an embargo on straw! This attitude is based on the now discredited philosophy of developmentalism, which assumes that the poor can lift themselves, as we think we have done. Its corollary is, "As the rich get richer, the poor will get richer."

"No!" the poor remonstrate. "The contradiction is fundamental. We must be poor so you can be rich. Underdevelopment that ensures cheap raw materials and labor is the essential foundation for the affluence of developed economies." This accusation confuses the people in our churches. There is some resentment, but more perplexity, because of the superficial and limited nature of the faith we have taught them. They are people of goodwill, who have no desire to profit from the poverty of others. They wish for everyone what they themselves enjoy. Within the boundaries of their individual lives, they are generous. This is precisely where we have misled them. We are guilty of preaching a theology of vivisection—of cutting a living whole into sections. We have taught them that it is possible to isolate themselves from their own total reality. They believe there are generous and good choices available to them in this abstracted aloneness.

Would it have made any difference if Jimmy Carter had been Pharaoh? There is no evidence the Pharaoh was not a "good man" with streaks of compassion. But he was the Pharaoh—responsible for an economy that would collapse without slave labor.

The contradiction between the Jews and Pharaoh is fundamental. Regardless of Pharaoh's prayer life, love of family, or benign feelings toward his servants, he is on top—they are on the bottom. If they move, he moves. If they are liberated, he is drowned.

Can Pharaoh be liberated? The record gives the answer—not in terms of an alternative to drowning, but in Moses' radicalization. Moses was a part of Pharaoh, until the day of his anger. The moment he saw an Egyptian beating a slave, was the moment Moses broke with his class—it was his conversion. He ceased being part of Pharaoh and became brother to Jewish slaves. Solidarity resulted in exile. As a refugee, he built a new life—job, wife, family, and wealth. Then he was confronted by the God of the burning bush.

Why do we blot from our preaching God's self-definition, written here in the most significant revelation prior to that of Jesus Christ? "I am the God [who has] heard their outcry against their slave-masters . . . and have come down to rescue them. . . . Come now; I will send you . . . and you shall bring my people . . . out" (Exod. 3:6-11 NEB).

> Now [Moses] will suffer the persecution of the totality that is Egypt, because he must somehow shoulder the injustice and enslavement of his people in order to free them.
>
> The slave is the epiphany of God. If a person opens up to the slave . . . he opens up to God; if he shuts out the slave . . . he shuts out God. The person who does not commit himself to the liberation of the slaves in Egypt is an atheist.[2]

The herdsman met God and answered the call to solidarity with his oppressed brothers. He thus became a shepherd/ pastor. The first element of a liberating *pastoral* for the rich is to call the Pharaoh church to the Moses solidarity.

DOW KIRKPATRICK

## The God of the Bible
## Is Known Only by Doing Justice

The poor say there is no mystery as to why the rich have revised the biblical message. The Scriptures have no purpose but to reveal God. If we are not taught by the oppressed how to read the Bible, we are in danger of not knowing the one true God. "The time has come," writes Mexican biblical scholar José Porfirio Miranda, "for Christianity to break a long chain of hypocrisy and collusion with the established powers and decide if its message is or is not going to be the same as the Bible's."[3] Miranda asserts that "a focal point of the Bible's irreconcilability with Western civilization" is to be found in the biblical way to know God, and he gives his version of the explicit passage in Jeremiah 22:15-16:

> Your father ate and drank like you,
> but he practiced justice and right;
> this is good.
> He defended the cause of the poor and the needy;
> this is good.
> *Is not this what it means to know me?* It is
> Yahweh who speaks.

Justice is not a quality, a consequence of being, insists José Míguez Bonino. Nor is it a sign of previous knowledge. He cites Jeremiah also: "Let him who glories glory in this, that he understands and knows me, that I am the Lord who practice steadfast love, justice, and righteousness in the earth" (9:24 RSV). Here, according to Míguez,

> . . . the basis for the identification between "knowing God" and "practising justice" becomes clear: it is Yahweh's own character. . . . The character of the knowledge is determined by the object: the God of the covenant [who] cannot be known except by becoming totally committed to and involved in his own action.[4]

*213*

Referring to Habakkuk 2, Míguez comments on "the 'both-and' formula which we love to use when we don't know how to integrate things which in the Bible are one. The language of the prophets is much bolder: to do justice *is* to know Yahwah." John's message is no different from that of the prophets, says Míguez. "Neither . . . contemplates the possibility of a theoretical, abstract, contemplative 'knowledge of God.' . . . There is no relation to God outside an active engagement," as classically summarized in the statement, "Everyone who loves is a child of God and knows God, but the unloving know nothing of God" (I John 4:8, NEB).[5]

Why do these seemingly obvious biblical insights elude us? In order to preserve the unjust system that produces rich and poor, a dualism must be read into our message. According to Miranda, however, the only way to affirm the transcendence of God is to break this dualism.

> The God who does not allow himself to be objectified, because only in the immediate command of conscience is he God, clearly specifies that he is knowable exclusively in the cry of the poor and the weak who seek justice. To know God directly is impossible, not because of the limitations of human understanding but rather, on the contrary, because Yahweh's total transcendence, his irreducible and unconfused otherness, would thereby disappear. . . . Transcendence [means] a God who is accessible only in the act of justice.[6]

Our rich parishes will ask, "Is not a Marxist reading of Scripture as suspect of bias as a capitalistic exegesis? If our wealth perverts our reading, why are we to believe the eyes of the poor are more clear?" In *The Liberation of Theology,* Juan Luis Segundo offers a methodology to avoid this error. The "hermeneutic circle" is the continuing revision of our interpretation of the Bible, dictated by the continuing transformation of our viewpoint on reality that is made necessary by the Scriptures themselves.

*Firstly* there is our way of experiencing reality, which leads us to ideological suspicion. *Secondly* there is the application of our ideological suspicion to the whole ideological superstructure in general and to theology in particular. *Thirdly* there comes a new way of experiencing theological reality that leads us to exegetical suspicion, that is, to the suspicion that the prevailing interpretation of the Bible has not taken important pieces of data into account. *Fourthly* we have our new hermeneutic, that is, our new way of interpreting the fountainhead of our faith (i.e., Scripture) with the new elements at our disposal.[7]

I suggest this process more appropriately should be called the hermeneutic *spiral,* because the dialectic between social reality and the Bible means that, each time around, more insight is opened up, both into the Scriptures and into social reality. Beatriz Melano Couch depicts this process.

The hermeneutics of the theology of liberation is done in a dialectic relationship between reality as it is described by modern social sciences and then reflection on the Scriptures, going back and forth from the "reading" of reality to the "reading" of the Scriptures and vice versa. . . . It is a reflection which is being born of the way we experience reality in Latin America; this reflection points out the contradictions of our own society, the contradictions within our own selves, between the church and the gospel, between the Bible and academic theology. I would insist that these reflections have to spring from suffering; by this I mean from the immersion in conflict and in struggle to survive as free human beings.[8]

In this hermeneutic spiral the poor and oppressed possess a view of reality closer to that of the Bible than do the rich oppressors.

The second element of a liberating *pastoral* for the rich consists, therefore, of reading Scripture from the perspective of poverty and slavery. "Blessed are you poor, for yours is the kingdom of God" (Luke 6:20 RSV).

## In Jesus, God Became Poor

The third word from the poor is most offensive of all. Scripture is unambiguous in its attitude toward the rich and the poor. The Magnificat declares: "The hungry he has satisfied with good things / the rich sent empty away" (Luke 1:53 NEB). (Not the *wicked* rich—simply "the rich.") Christ announced his ministry as in continuity with Isaiah 61: "He has sent me to announce good news to the poor" (Luke 4:18 NEB). (No news for the rich?) The incarnational passage in Philippians offers a life-style for Christ's followers: He "made himself nothing, assuming the nature of a slave" (2:7 NEB). The radical nature of kenosis, the emptying act of birth in a manger, is made explicit by Paul in II Corinthians: "He was rich, yet for your sake he became poor" (8:9 NEB). Enrique Dussel asks,

> What did God do? He sent his Son into the system of sin; although of divine origin, Jesus took on the form of a slave. He became in a certain way the son of a despised race, a despised class, and a despised nation. Jesus, then, became oppressed; but he gave a consciousness, an awareness of liberation. He revealed this to the people and was condemned for having revealed it.[9]

Christology from a Latin American perspective is being enacted most significantly by Leonardo Boff, a Brazilian Franciscan, and Jon Sobrino. Sobrino, as a member of the Jesuits, who are targets of government violence in El Salvador, knows the threat of the political nature of the death of Christ. In a conversation, he said, "God is love, but love is an abstraction. When he expresses his love he does it with partiality. He has to take a concrete standpoint. That standpoint is poverty." In *Christology at the Crossroads*, Sobrino explains why God in Jesus inserted himself into humanity by identifying with a specific class, the poor.

First, the poor are the people who understand the meaning of the kingdom best, even though their knowledge and understanding comes by way of contrariety.

Second, Jesus reinforces his experience of the necessity for justice through his contact with the poor.

Third, Jesus' service to the totality is concretized directly in his service to the poor.

Fourth, in his own personal life he experiences poverty. . . .

Fifth, Jesus undergoes the experience of class-identity, and specifically the consequences of his fellowship with the group known as the poor. The power wielded by the other major group in society is directed against him.

It would be anachronistic to look to Jesus for an analysis of classes such as we find in the work of present-day sociology. Yet his general attitude makes it clear that in trying to understand justice Jesus adopts a stance that is rooted in the poor and is meant to benefit them. . . . In that sense the first principle for concretizing moral values is nothing else but the first principle of Christology itself: i.e., incarnation. One must deliberately adopt some partial stance in order to comprehend the totality. To look for some stand that will give us the totality directly is to do the very opposite of incarnation [profound disincarnation].[10]

The third requirement of a liberating *pastoral* for the rich, then, is to become poor in the sense that God in Christ entered into solidarity with the protest from, and for, the poor.

## *"Evangelism" Is*
### *Confronting the Atheism of Our Worship*

A liberating pastoral will be a *transformational* evangelism rather than the *neonostalgic* evangelism currently so popular in the churches of the rich. The contradictions between authentic and inauthentic evangelism may be described in five areas.

1. *Conversion.* Neonostalgic evangelism makes no demand for conversion. It is a call to persons to join churches or groups that are most compatible with their accustomed life-style and value-system. The design is to keep church life—like pornography—at a level acceptable to prevailing community standards. Authentic evangelism will demand conversion—a radical break with one's class—and commitment to the new creation.

2. *Numerical Growth.* Neonostalgic evangelism defines itself as numerical growth. Orlando Costas, director of the Institute of In-Depth Evangelism in San Jose, Costa Rica, gives a critical analysis of evangelism conceived of as church growth in terms of numbers alone. He broadens the definition of church growth to four areas: numerical, organic, contextual and incarnational. Neonostalgic evangelism (my term), he says,

—focuses only on numerical growth to the sacrifice of the others;
—is based on a shallow hermeneutic;
—makes the locus of theology the church instead of Christ;
—truncates the witness to a portion only of the human, which is possible because of an ambiguous concept of man and sin;
—suffers from an anthropological-functionalistic syndrome, which sees change and stability only in terms of strategy, rather than ethics.[11]

In a forthcoming essay, Costas includes a case study of Chilean Protestantism, which is largely pentecostal and has found a congeniality with the junta in their shared anticommunism.

First of all, *numerical* and *organic* growth in themselves do not necessarily mean that a church is indeed growing. It may be . . . simply getting fat. The Chilean example illustrates the problem of "ecclesial obesity," an excessive fatness which may preclude (or at least cloud) the presence of the kingdom.[12]

3. *Christendom*. The Latin American Bishops' Conference in Medellin (1968), in their report on "Pastoral Care of the Masses," observed,

> To date the pastoral attitude has been one of preservation of the faith through the administration of the sacraments. . . . This type of pastoral care was suited to an age in which the social structures coincided with the religious ones, the structures that communicate values (family, school, etc.) were permeated by Christian principles, and the faith was transmitted, one might say, by the very inertia of tradition.[13]

Neonostalgic evangelism is the effort to maintain a "Christendom" relationship with society. This is being attempted at a time when Christendom has broken up, never to be reconstituted.

Transformational evangelism focuses instead on church growth as contextual and incarnational. In a commencement address at Fuller Theological Seminary, Costas said that, too often, evangelism "has been so amoral, so uncontextual [that] it represents the politics of the kingdom of darkness. Nothing pleases the devil more than congregations that are alienated from their historical context, from the cause of justice and from the humiliating situation of the downtrodden."[14] Authentic evangelism denounces any god who alienates the church from its context, thus paralyzing its incarnational mission.

4. *Human Rights*. José Comblin of Chile asserted, "If the United States would end its commitment to the doctrine of National Security, this entire system of military repression [in Latin America] would collapse."[15] In an article in *Servir*, Pablo Richard sees the task of giving a theological answer to the doctrine of national security as the "central nucleus of evangelism." The mission of the church is the defense of human rights and the criticism of the model of development imposed in the name of national security.

It treats of a central problem: the destruction of people as people. According to this theology, the destruction of people implies the destruction of the church, because without people there is no church. . . . The church, representative of the people, confronts the state and this confronting is evangelizing.[16]

5. *Atheism.* All the characteristics of a transformational evangelism are integrated into this: The task of evangelism is to confront the atheism of our worship—a lesson from Cuba.

"The Confession of Faith of the Presbyterian-Reformed Church in Cuba—1977" declares,

> The Church teaches that the "atheism" of the ideology sustained by the Socialist Revolution, makes more clearly evident the atheism of the "believers" who are not capable of "discerning the signs of the times" in the midst of the new society being constructed, in which the radical transformations of the unjust structures make possible the creation of a more integrally reconstructed human being.

In scripture, atheism is not viewed as the denial of God's existence, but as worship of the wrong god. The prohibition of idols is the confrontation of atheism in worship. In our churches there is a widespread assumption that capitalism is theistic and Marxism is atheistic, but Sergio Arce, rector of the Evangelical Seminary in Matanzas, Cuba, claims that atheism is a product of Western culture, rather than a specific Marxian phenomenon.[17] "The first task of evangelism," he said in a conversation, "is to confront Christians who are not atheists of the head, but are atheists of the heart. Marx was an atheist of the head, but not of the heart."

The fourth element of a liberating *pastoral* for the rich, therefore, and the central evangelistic task, is the confrontation of the atheism of our worship.

DOW KIRKPATRICK

## Hope for the Liberation of the Rich Is Available— As a Gift from the Poor

Dussel points to the source of our hope. "The process of liberation itself is the only thing which will make it possible for the oppressor to undergo a real conversion. Hence only the underdeveloped nations of the world can enable the affluent nations to discover a new, more human model of human life."[18] Paulo Freire made the same point in a letter to Hugo Assmann, "I get the impression that the Third World could become a source of inspiration for theological renewal. . . . The developed countries are prevented from exercising any prophetic role by their nature as societies whose future lies in the maintenance of their present affluence."[19]

Behind the truth of all this is the promise and call of Jesus: "Blessed are the poor in spirit, for theirs is the kingdom." Are we left out because we are rich? Only if we refuse to become poor. The ambiguity of these two words is avoided by biblical clarity.

*Material poverty* is the lack of economic goods necessary for human life worthy of the name. The Bible consistently regards material poverty as degrading, subhuman, against the will and purpose of God and to be vigorously struggled against. More importantly, it is rooted in sin, the injustice of oppression. No one is called by Jesus to this.

*Spiritual poverty* is not to "spiritualize" material poverty—a device of colonizers. It is to be poor in spirit—to be those poor who are blessed "*because* the Kingdom of God has begun," as Gustavo Gutiérrez says. "From the time of Zephaniah (seventh century B.C.), those who waited the liberating work of the Messiah were called 'poor.' . . . They are blessed because the coming of the Kingdom will put an end to their poverty by creating a world of brotherhood."[20] To be poor in spirit is to have no other sustenance for hope but God. It is to have a joyful life of expectancy because God is destroying the causes of material poverty.

The materially poor have the advantage of being further removed than the rich from the deceitful temptation of wealth's promise. Being human, the poor may be subverted into believing that material riches will liberate them. The call to spiritual poverty delivers both—the materially rich and the materially poor—from the temptation to expect that material wealth will produce hope.

Jesus invites the materially rich to salvation through becoming poor in spirit. It is a conversion more radical than divesting ourselves of our money. We are to surrender dependence on everything except this God who has entered history to bring total justice. Such conversion may mean giving up most or all of one's material wealth, or it may not. If the surrender is made, it must in no sense be charity. The giving must signal the uprooting of injustice. And whatever is retained must give the same signal.

The materially poor are liberated by becoming poor in spirit; by recognizing, rejoicing, and participating in the work of God to eliminate the roots of injustice that made them materially poor. The materially rich are liberated by becoming poor in spirit by recognizing, rejoicing, and participating in the work of God to eliminate the roots of injustice that made them materially rich. This is the style of life Gutiérrez calls "poverty as solidarity and protest." Its authenticity can always be tested by the pattern of the incarnation of God as the human poor, in Jesus.

The fifth requirement of the liberating *pastoral* for the rich, therefore, is to become poor in the sense that qualifies us for the benefits of the beatitudes.

## III

The cover design for the series *Latin American Philosophy and Liberation* reproduces an Aztec drawing from a wall of the Museum of Anthropology in Mexico City.[21] Human figures, male and female, carry totems symbolizing their roles in the community. The most interesting feature is the trail of bare footprints winding through the entire logo. They mark the Aztec pilgrimage to freedom. The people of God always move with uncertain, sometimes erratic, but eschatological steps—toward hope born from a future that invades the present.

Hugo Assmann—a Brazilian, who in faithfulness has been forced from his home country and also from Uruguay, Bolivia, and Chile, and who now lives in Costa Rica (*Theology for a Nomad Church* is a most appropriate title for his book)—tells us what it ultimately means to put our feet in this way.

> Once set on this path the Latin American theologian is still going to find himself alone, almost devoid of links with the Christian reference-points of the past. . . . He is a conscious "apostate" from the idealisms of the past and those that are arising again today. Like any apostate rebelling iconoclastically against the idols of the past, he finds it difficult . . . to make his brothers understand that he is not just an iconoclast but an opener of new horizons on the use of the name of God.[22]

# Notes

## Chapter 1. Theodore Runyon

1. Moltmann, *Religion, Revolution and the Future* (New York: Charles Scribner's Sons, 1969), pp. 138, 93-107.
2. Cf. *The Works of John Wesley*, vol. 5 (Grand Rapids: Zondervan Publishing House, 1958), p. 224 (hereafter cited as *Works*).
3. John Wesley, *Explanatory Notes upon the New Testament* (London: Epworth Press, 1952), p. 22, Matt. 3:2 (hereafter cited as *Notes*).
4. *Works*, 5, p. 337.
5. *Ibid.*, 11, pp. 74, 72.
6. *Ibid.*, p. 78.
7. *The Letters of John Wesley*, ed. John Telford, vol. 8 (London: Epworth Press, 1931), p. 265 (hereafter cited as *Letters*).
8. *Works*, 7, pp. 125-26.
9. Halévy, *England in 1815: A History of the English People in the Nineteenth Century*, vol. 1 (London: T. F. Unwin, 1924; New York: Peter Smith, 1949).
10. Elie Halévy, *The Birth of Methodism in England* (Chicago: University of Chicago Press, 1971), pp. 1, 70.
11. Cf. Robert F. Wearmouth, *Methodism and the Working-Class Movements of England 1800–1850* (London: Epworth Press, 1937).
12. Semmel, *The Methodist Revolution* (New York: Basic Books, 1973; London: Heinemann, 1974).
13. This is substantially the claim of the German edition of Garth Lean's *John Wesley, Anglican,* trans. and intro. by Klaus Bockmühler as *John Wesley: Model einer Revolution ohne Gewalt* (Giessen: Brunnen Verlag, 1969).
14. Cf. E. J. Hobsbawm, "Methodism and the Threat of Revolution in Britain," *History Today,* vol. 7 (February 1957), pp. 119ff.
15. E. P. Thompson, *The Making of the English Working Class* (London: Victor Gollancz, 1964), p. 36.
16. *Works*, 9, pp. 191-465.
17. Cf. "The End of Christ's Coming," *Works,* 6, pp. 267ff.

18. Míguez Bonino, *Doing Theology in a Revolutionary Situation* (Philadelphia: Fortress Press, 1975), p. 16.

19. Segundo, *The Liberation of Theology* (Maryknoll, N.Y.: Orbis Books, 1976), pp. 142, 145, 147, 150.

20. *Works,* 10, p. 456; 8, p. 68.

21. *Letters,* 2, p. 189.

22. George C. Cell, *The Rediscovery of John Wesley* (New York: Henry Holt, 1935), p. 361; John Peters, *Christian Perfection and American Methodism* (Nashville: Abingdon Press, 1956), p. 21.

23. Gordon Rupp, *Principalities and Powers* (Nashville: Abingdon Press, 1952), p. 97; Colin Williams, *John Wesley's Theology Today* (Nashville: Abingdon Press, 1960), p. 175.

24. At least one scholar, Jürgen Weissbach, is convinced that this in fact is what Wesley did. Cf. *Der neue Mensch im theologischen Denken John Wesleys, Beiträge zur Geschichte des Methodismus,* No. 2 (Stuttgart: Christliches Verlaghaus, 1970), p. 218.

25. Cf. *Works,* 12, p. 399.

26. Cf. Joseph Petulla, *Christian Political Theology* (Maryknoll, N.Y.: Orbis Books, 1972), p. 12.

27. Karl Marx, *The Economic and Philosophic Manuscripts of 1844,* intro. by Dirk J. Struik (New York: International Publishers, 1964), p. 24.

28. The usual translation of *sinnlich* in Marxist literature is "sensuous," a term with misleading overtones for most English readers. *Sinnlich* refers to the empirical world known by the senses. Wesley's own term, "sensible world," would be a more felicitous translation, were it not archaic English.

29. Note the parallel to the Hegelian notion of fulfillment through self-expression by positing the "other," a process that begins with God himself in creation.

30. Marx, *Economic and Philosophic Manuscripts,* pp. 113-14.

31. *Ibid.,* pp. 110, 111, 109.

32. *Ibid.,* p. 114.

33. Weber, *Grundlagen der Dogmatik,* vol. 2 (Neukirchen-Moers: Neukirchener Verlag, 1962), p. 363.

34. This goal of the renewal of the race and of the very cosmos is reiterated in a teleologically oriented series of sermons (*Works,* vol. 6)—"God's Love to Fallen Man," "The General Deliverance," "The Mystery of Iniquity," "The End of Christ's Coming," "The General Spread of the Gospel," and "The New Creation"—as well as his long "Treatise on Original Sin" (vol. 9).

35. *Works,* 6, pp. 512-13.

36. Jeremy Taylor, *The Rule and Exercises of Holy Living* (London: Ward, Lock & Co., n.d.), p. 3.

37. Piette, *John Wesley and the Evolution of Protestantism* (New York: Sheed & Ward, 1937), pp. 306-7

38. *Works,* 5, p. 202. Cf. 11, p. 367.

39. *The Journal of John Wesley,* ed. Nehemiah Curnock, vol. 2 (London: Robert Culley, 1909), p. 467 (hereafter cited as *Journal*).

40. *Luther's Works,* vol. 6 (Philadelphia: Muhlenberg Press, 1932), pp. 451-52.
41. *Journal,* 1, pp. 475-76. Curnock's suggestion that it may have been Luther's "Preface to Galatians" rather than "Preface to Romans" that was read seems unlikely. While it is true that the Galatians preface was circulating at the same time and was read by Charles Wesley, there is no section in that preface that would as readily fit John's account: " . . . while he was describing the change which God works in the heart through faith in Christ." Moreover, there is so much in the "Preface to Galatians" that would have offended Wesley—and did offend him three years later—it is unlikely that he could have heard any gospel word coming through it (cf. *Luther's Works,* vol. 26 [St. Louis: Concordia, 1963], pp. 4-12).
42. *Letters,* 1, p. 188.
43. *Journal,* 1, p. 423.
44. *Works.* 7, p. 236.
45. *The Poetical Works of John and Charles Wesley,* vol. 1 (London: Wesleyan Methodist Conference Office, 1868), p. xxii (hereafter cited as *Poetical Works*).
46. This often-made point of the activity of love is given fresh interpretation by Mildred Bangs Wynkoop, *A Theology of Love* (Kansas City: Beacon Hill Press, 1972).
47. *Works,* 5, p. 299.
48. *Letters,* 5, p. 264.
49. *Works,* 6, p. 48.
50. Cf. *Works,* 5, p. 3, regarding traditional concern.
51. Weissbach, *Der neue Mensch,* p. 217.
52. *Works,* 9, pp. 466-509.
53. Albert Outler, ed. *John Wesley* (New York: Oxford University Press, 1964), pp. 367ff.
54. See *Journal,* 2, p. 499, for Wesley's description of this quietism.
55. Cf. John Simon, *John Wesley and the Methodist Societies,* 2nd ed. (London: Epworth Press, 1937), pp. 9-15.
56. As quoted by Wesley, *Works,* 9, pp. 502ff.
57. *Letters,* 1, p. 207.
58. *Journal,* 1, p. 420.
59. *Works,* 5, pp. 305-6.
60. *Ibid.,* pp. 296, 302.
61. *Poetical Works,* 1, p. xxii.
62. *Works,* 5, p. 296.
63. *Ibid.,* p. 295. (Italics mine.)
64. Ludwig Feuerbach, *The Essence of Christianity,* foreword by H. Richard Niebuhr and intro. by Karl Barth (New York: Harper & Brothers, 1957), pp. 66, 33, 26.
65. Karl Marx and Friedrich Engels, *On Religion,* intro. by Reinhold Niebuhr (New York: Schocken Books, 1964), pp. 69ff.
66. Cf. Outler, *Wesley,* pp. 28, 345-449. Note the frequency of such phrases as "we quibble over words," e.g. Outler, *Wesley,* p. 369; *Works,* 8, pp.

340-41; *Letters,* 5, p. 264. Cf. Peter Brown's essay on "Human Understanding," which Wesley reprinted as an appendix to his own *Compendium of Natural Philosophy,* vol. 2 (New York: Bangs and Mason, 1823): "Divine metaphor is the substituting our ideas of sensation, which are direct and immediate with words belonging to them, for the things of heaven, of which we have no direct idea, or immediate conception. . . . The words, figuratively transferred from one thing to another, do not agree with the things to which they are transferred, in any part of their literal sense" (pp. 436-37). To be sure, this stricture does not apply to "revealed truth." But theology as such is always an admixture of revelation and human analogy and metaphor and therefore an inexact science at best.

67. Cf. *Works,* 9, pp. 513-14. Wesley was also aware of the human tendency to project, and the inadequacy of those projections, e.g. Peter Brown's comments in Wesley's *Natural Philosophy:* "The multiplying and enlarging our own perfections in number or degree only, to the utmost stretch of our capacity, and attributing them so enlarged to God, is no more than raising up an unwieldy idol of our own imagination, without any foundation in nature" (p. 434). Cf. Míguez Bonino, *Doing Theology,* p. 81.

68. *Works,* 5, p. 46.

69. *Ibid.,* p. 47.

70. *Ibid.,* 11, pp. 366-446.

## Chapter 2. José Míguez Bonino

1. *Journal,* 2, p. 488 ff.

2. *"Sicut non potest discerpi Christus in partes, ita inseparabilia sunt haec duo, quae simul et coniunctim in ipso percipimus; iustitiam et sanctificationem,"* Calvin, *Institutes,* 3: 11, 6. (The English translation quoted leaves out the last words, "justice and sanctification," which I have added in the text.)

3. Barth, *Church Dogmatics,* 4:2, p. 504.

4. *Ibid.,* p. 508.

5. Semmel, *Methodist Revolution,* p. 8.

6. Barth, *Dogmatics,* 4:2, p. 502.

7. John Deschner, *Wesley's Christology: An Interpretation* (Dallas: Southern Methodist University, 1960), p. 78. I disagree with Deschner's implicit presupposition that an evangelical theology must make justification the absolute norm. This forces Deschner to decide on a question Wesley would not allow and thus tends to distort the perspective of the evaluation.

8. This is how G. C. Berkouwer summarizes Wesley's concern in the discussion with Zinzendorf in *Faith and Sanctification* (Grand Rapids: Eerdmans Publishing Co., 1952), p. 51. Berkouwer himself is in sympathy with Wesley at this point. At another point, he gives a good characterization of his own position with the same emphasis:

"Sanctification, if it is to be at all, must not take place merely on some underground level of psychic life, quite in defiance of all outside disturbance, but must be the redemptive touch of our faith on all of life"(p. 13).

9. *Works,* 11, p. 53 ff.
10. Friedrich Engels, *The Condition of the Working Class in England in 1844* (Moscow: Foreign Languages Publishing House, 1962). The original German was published in 1845.
11. Quoted by Semmel, *Methodist Revolution,* p. 162.
12. Barth, *Dogmatics,* 4:2, p. 520.
13. *Letters,* 4, p. 158; 6, p. 175.
14. *Works,* 6, p. 2.

## Chapter 3. Rupert E. Davies

1. *Works,* 5, p. 60-61.
2. Gutiérrez, *A Theology of Liberation* (Maryknoll, N.Y.: Orbis Books, 1973), p. 15.
3. Cecil Cone, *The Identity Crisis in Black Theology* (Nashville: AMEC, 1975), pp. 92-122.
4. James Cone, *Black Theology and Black Power* (New York: Seabury Press), pp. 138-52.
5. *Works,* 7, p. 347.
6. James Cone, *A Black Theology of Liberation* (Philadelphia: J.B. Lippincott Co., 1970).

## Chapter 4. John Kent

1. Semmel, *Methodist Revolution.* Cf. R. R. Palmer, *The Age of Democratic Revolution,* vol. 2 (Princeton, N.J.: Princeton University Press, 1964), p. 466.
2. See, for instance, Thompson, *English Working Class,* 2nd ed., (1968). Also Perkins, *The Origins of Modern English Society 1780–1880* (London: Routledge & Kegan Paul, 1969).
3. When he visited England in the 1840s and 1860s, Finney did not seem to be particularly interested in social reform, as it is said that he was in America (see ch. 6 and 7 in this volume).
4. Cf. Hobsbawm, *Labouring Men* (London: Wiederfeld & Nicholson, 1964); also his "Methodism and Threat of Revolution," *History Today,* pp. 115-24.
5. Sarah Hennell and her brother Charles, together with Charles Bray (an ex-Methodist), were the center of the group of Coventry rationalists who helped to educate the young George Eliot. The passage quoted is from Hennell's *Thoughts in the Aid of Faith* (London: G. Manwaring, 1860).
6. William Reginald Ward, *Early Victorian Methodism: The Correspondence of Jabez Bunting* (London: Oxford University Press, 1976), pp. 303, 309.

7. Spencer, *Social Statics* (London: John Chapman, 1851), p. 64; (New York: D. Appleton, 1865), p. 78.
8. William Butler Yeats, *A Vision* (London: Macmillan & Co., 1962), p. 25.
9. John Hick, ed., *The Myth of God Incarnate* (London: S.C.M. Press, 1977; Philadelphia: Westminster Press, 1977), p. 202.
10. John Frank Kermode, *The Sense of an Ending* (London, New York: Oxford, 1967), p. 39.
11. Weil, *First and Last Notebooks,* trans. Richard Rees (London, New York: Oxford, 1970), pp. 295, 296. Simone Weil was born in Paris in 1909 and died in England as a war exile in 1943. She was one of the most remarkable religious writers of her generation—her best-known book, *Waiting for God,* was published in 1950.
12. Adorno, *Negative Dialectics,* trans. E. B. Ashton (New York: Seabury Press, 1973), p. 320.
13. Weil, *Notebooks,* p. 130.

## Chapter 5. Thomas W. Madron

1. J. O. Lindsay, ed., *The New Cambridge Modern History,* vol. 7 (Cambridge: The University Press, 1957), p. 241.
2. Kathleen Walker MacArthur, *The Economic Ethics of John Wesley* (New York: Abingdon Press, 1936), pp. 35-36.
3. Lindsay, *Modern History,* p. 245.
4. *Ibid.,* pp. 245-46.
5. MacArthur, *Economic Ethics,* p. 44.
6. Oscar Sherwin, *John Wesley: Friend of the People* (New York: Twayne Publishers, 1961), p. 41.
7. *Works,* 7, pp. 205, 353. Cf. William R. Cannon, *The Theology of John Wesley* (New York: Abingdon Press, 1946), pp. 250, 252.
8. *Letters,* 2, p. 376.
9. John Locke, "Of Property," *Two Treatises on Government* (New York: Hafner Publishing Co., 1947), pp. 133-34.
10. *Works,* 7, pp. 308-9.
11. *Ibid.,* 6, p. 136. For further information on Wesley's concept of property and its implications, see MacArthur, *Economic Ethics,* pp. 123-24 and Sherwin, *Friend of the People,* p. 41.
12. *Works,* 6, p. 376.
13. For Wesley's exposition of this "economic formula," see *Works*, 6, pp. 127-34. This sermon was published in 1760.
14. *Works,* 6, p. 376.
15. *Notes,* p. 409, Acts 4:32. Cf. note on Acts 4:35.
16. The Bennet Minutes of the first Conference, as quoted by Richard M. Cameron, *Methodism and Society in Historical Perspective* (New York: Abingdon Press, 1961), pp. 69, 70.
17. As quoted by Wearmouth, *Working-Class Movements,* p. 203.
18. As late as 1760, a pamphlet sought to dissuade Methodists from "their

Notion of the Community of Christian Men's goods" (p. 33). Alexander Jephson, *A Friendly and Compassionate Address to All Serious and Well-disposed Methodists,* as quoted by Wellman J. Warner, *The Wesleyan Movement in the Industrial Revolution* (London: Longman's Green Ltd., 1930), p. 156. The conviction that Methodism stood for such a notion persisted so strongly that Thomas Coke, after the death of Wesley, was forced to issue an official denial.

19. Max Weber, *The Protestant Ethic and the Spirit of Capitalism,* trans. Talcott Parsons (New York: Charles Scribner's Sons, 1958), pp. 142-43.

20. *Works,* 1, p. 285.

21. MacArthur, *Economic Ethics,* p. 123. See, for example, the following rejections of such a position: *Letters,* 3, p. 122; *Works,* 3, pp. 71, 367; 4, p. 180; 7, p. 1. Warner, *Wesleyan Movement,* contends that the logical deduction from Wesleyan thought would follow the lines Weber suggested, but that Wesley refused to make the deduction (p. 161). On the contrary, it would seem that Wesley's thought does not lead, logically or otherwise, to Weber's interpretation.

22. R. H. Tawney, *Religion and the Rise of Capitalism* (New York: Mentor Books, New American Library, 1961), p. 161.

23. *Letters,* 5, pp. 352, 354. Apparently he referred to the enclosure movement.

24. H. Richard Niebuhr, *The Social Sources of Denominationalism* (New York: Abingdon Press, 1961), p. 70.

25. *Works,* 2, p. 415.

26. Maldwyn Edwards, *John Wesley and the Eighteenth Century,* 3d ed. (London: Epworth Press, 1955), p. 148.

27. *Works,* 2, pp. 269-70; 3, p. 482.

28. *Works,* 11, pp. 53-59.

29. *Letters,* 5, pp. 349-51.

30. *Ibid.,* pp. 351-54. Cf. MacArthur, *Economic Ethics,* pp. 106-8.

31. *Letters,* 6, pp. 175-76.

32. Sherwin, *Friend of the People, p. 113.*

33. *Works,* 6, p. 132-33.

34. Sherwin, *Friend of the People,* p. 38.

35. See, for example, *Works,* 1, p. 506; 3, p. 61; *Letters,* 3, p. 26. Cf. Simon, *Methodist Societies,* 3rd ed. (1952), p. 178; MacArthur, *Economic Ethics,* p. 124; Sherwin, *Friend of the People,* p. 45.

36. Sherwin, *Friend of the People,* p. 110.

37. *Works,* 7, p. 31.

38. Sherwin, *Friend of the People,* p. 132.

39. *Ibid.; Works,* 2, pp. 17, 81; 3, p. 270; Edwards, *Wesley and Eighteenth Century,* p. 154; MacArthur, *Economic Ethics,* pp. 115-16.

40. *Works,* 4, p. 296.

41. *Journal,* (London: Epworth Press, 1916, reprinted 1960), 8, p. 49.

42. *Works,* 4, pp. 85-86.

43. John Snell, "The Political Thought of Adam Ferguson," *The Municipal University of Witchita Bulletin* (May 1950), pp. 10-11.

44. Edwards, *Wesley and Eighteenth Century,* p. 184. For MacArthur's

evaluation of Wesley's economic position, see *Economic Ethics,* pp. 111-12. In commenting on Wesley's economic views, J. A. Faulkner, *Wesley as Sociologist, Theologian, Churchman* (New York: Methodist Book Concern, 1918) says, "It only touches the surface of a condition that needed severer remedies—remedies that none in England then proposed and few now propose" (p. 12).

45. H. E. Luccock and Paul Hutchinson, *The Story of Methodism* (New York: The Methodist Book Concern, 1925) note that Wesley "saw the evils, and he made Methodism the kind of religious movement which expressed its sanctification by its devotion to the removal of those evils" (p. 210).

### Chapter 6. Timothy L. Smith

1. Documentation for this, as for other points in this essay where the work is cited, appear in Timothy L. Smith, *Revivalism and Social Reform in Mid-Nineteenth-Century America* (Nashville: Abingdon Press, 1957), pp. 105, 116-17.

2. *Ibid,* pp. 181, 184-85. Cf. Donald Dayton, *Discovering an Evangelical Heritage* (New York: Harper & Row, 1976), pp. 73-85; Donald G. Mathews, "Orange Scott: The Methodist Evangelist as Revolutionary," *The Antislavery Vanguard: New Essays on the Abolitionists,* ed. Martin Duberman (Princeton, N.J.: Princeton University Press, 1965), pp. 71-101.

3. Bertram Wyatt-Brown, *Lewis Tappan and the Evangelical War Against Slavery* (Cleveland: Case Western Reserve Press, 1969), pp. 129-30.

4. Smith, *Revivalism,* pp. 104-5, 108-13; Dayton, *Evangelical Heritage,* pp. 15-24, 35-43.

5. Wyatt-Brown, *Tappan,* p. 131.

6. Charles G. Finney, *Lectures to Professing Christians* (New York: John S. Taylor, 1837), nos. 17, 19, 20. This work has appeared in many subsequent editions.

7. George M. Marsden, *The Evangelical Mind and the New School Presbyterian Experience: A Case Study of Thought and Theology in Nineteenth-Century America* (New Haven: Yale University Press, 1970), pp. 59-87; Nathaniel W. Taylor, "The Revolution in the Presbyterian Church," *The Quarterly Christian Spectator,* vol. 9 (December 1837), pp. 597-646, a little-noticed article in which Taylor equated New School doctrine with the New England Theology and raised the slavery issue (p. 629); Smith, *Revivalism,* pp. 26-27, 185-87.

8. Taylor, "Revolution," *Christian Spectator* (December 1837), pp. 599, 604-17. Sidney E. Mead, *Nathaniel William Taylor, 1786–1858: A Connecticut Liberal* (Chicago: University of Chicago Press, 1942), underplays the perfectionist ethics in Taylor's theology.

9. Robert Merideth, *The Politics of the Universe: Edward Beecher, Abolition, and Orthodoxy* (Nashville: Vanderbilt University Press, 1968), pp. 73-84.

10. Edward Beecher, "The Nature, Importance, and Means of Eminent Holiness Throughout the Church," *The American National Preacher: Or Original Sermons—Monthly*, vol. 10 (June and July 1835), pp. 193-94, 197, 203. Merideth, *Politics of the Universe*, pp. 91-101, shows the relationship of these sermons to Beecher's friendship and alliance with abolitionist Elijah P. Lovejoy, from 1834 to Lovejoy's death at the hands of a mob in October, 1837.

11. These articles in *The Christian Spectator*, vol. 7, appeared unsigned, as did all the others of which I presume Taylor to be the author: "Man's Dependence on the Grace of God, for Holiness of Heart and Life" (March 1835), pp. 76-89; "The Nature and Application of Divine Influence in the Salvation of Man" (June 1835), pp. 301-21; "An Inquiry into the True Way of Preaching on Ability," pp. 223-57; "The Scriptural View of Divine Influence" (December 1835), pp. 591-97, in which the discussion of the work of the Holy Spirit (pp. 595-97) seems to me to lay down the basis in logic for Charles G. Finney's later use of the terminology "baptism of the Holy Ghost."

12. William Ellery Channing, *The Perfect Life, in Twelve Discourses* (Boston: Roberts, 1873). I have recently discovered that the "Dr. C." to whom Charles G. Finney refers in his *Memoirs* (New York: A. S. Barnes and Co., 1876), pp. 356-57, is identified in the manuscript version (Oberlin College Archives) as William Ellery Channing.

13. Wyatt-Brown, *Tappan*, p. 131.

14. Aileen S. Kraditor, *Means and Ends in American Abolitionism: Garrison and His Critics in Strategy and Tactics, 1834–1850* (New York: Pantheon Books, 1967), pp. 59, 79-82.

15. *Ibid.*, pp. 90-91. Cf. pp. 24-25, showing Garrison's agreement with the New Divinity and hence, with Finney and Mahan, on the nature of depravity and of free will, a context for Garrison's thought of which Kraditor is largely unaware.

16. Philip Bruce, "An Extract of a Letter . . . to Bishop Coke, dated Portsmouth, Virginia, March 25, 1788," *The Arminian Magazine* [American], vol. 2 (November 1790), pp. 563-64, came to my attention through my student, Thomas C. Johnsen. Cf. the idea of sanctification as liberation from sin through love, "the inward law of the gospel, *the law of the Spirit of life*," in a sermon by "Dr. Cutworth," vol. 1 (September 1789), pp. 444-45.

17. George Claude Baker, *An Introduction to the History of Early New England Methodism, 1789–1839* (Durham, N.C.: Duke University Press, 1941), pp. 37-38, 45-82; Smith, *Revivalism*, pp. 154-59, 169-72, 184-85; letter from James B. Finley, Dayton, Ohio, December 3, 1819, to the editor, *The Methodist Magazine*, vol. 3 (January 1820), pp. 34-40, quoting statements by Indian chiefs praising the liberating power of the "good Spirit" from addiction to whisky; "State Legislation on The Temperance Question," *The A. M. E. Christian Recorder* (August 17, 1854), p. 70.

18. Norris Magnuson, *Salvation in the Slums: Evangelical Social Work,*

*1865–1920* (Metuchen, N.J.: Scarecrow Press, 1977), pp. 165-78 and generally, pp. 101-2, 117, 124-26, 140-42; Smith, *Revivalism,* pp. 148-77; William Arthur, *The Tongue of Fire; or, The True Power of Christianity* (New York; Fleming H. Revell Co., 1880), pp. 52-57, 110-32, 145-46.

19. Accounts of British Methodist overseas missions in *The* [American] *Methodist Magazine,* vol. 1 (1819), pp. 30-36, 193-200, 313-19, and *passim,* do not refer at all to the doctrine of sanctification, though the journal shows Methodists in the United States were continually interested in the subject. For the Moravians, see their American journal, *The United Brethren Missionary Intelligencer and Religious Miscellany . . . ,* vol. 2 (First Quarter 1825), pp. 9-10. Cf. *Periodical Accounts Relating to the Missions of the Church of the United Brethren,* vol. 1 (1790), pp. 7-15.

20. Robert T. Handy, *A Christian America: Protestant Hopes and Historical Realities* (New York: Oxford University Press, 1971), pp. 27-35; Thomas H. Skinner, review of *Thoughts on Evangelizing the World, The Christian Spectator,* vol. 9 (June 1837), pp. 291-295; "Encouragement to Effort, for the Speedy Conversion of the World," *CS,* 7 (March 1835), pp. 1-8.

21. Garth M. Rosell, "The Millennial Roots of Early Nineteenth-Century Reform: An Examination of Charles G. Finney's Theology of Social Action" (paper presented to the Hopkins-Harwichport Seminar in American Religious History, 1975).

22. Typical of many others is Asa Rand's description of Lyman Beecher's New Divinity as resembling "in its prominent features and bearing *Wesleyanism,*" a "strange mingling of evangelical doctrine with Arminian speculation, . . . tending to produce spurious conversions," *The Baptist Weekly Journal of the Mississippi Valley* (August 9, 1833).

23. "Wesleyan Methodism on the 'Witness of the Spirit,' " *Christian Spectator,* vol. 9 (June 1837), pp. 176-82 and *passim,* and W.M.B., "Letter to the Christian Spectator on the Witness of the Spirit," *Methodist Magazine and Quarterly Review,* vol. 8 (October 1837), pp. 457-76, review the controversy.

24. Wyatt-Brown, *Tappan,* pp. 65-70, 129-31, 138-41.

25. *Ibid.,* pp. 109-14, 121-28; Kraditor, *Means and Ends,* pp. 22-25, 78-81; Finney, *Memoirs,* pp. 333-43.

26. William G. McLoughlin, *Modern Revivalism: Charles Grandison Finney to Billy Graham* (New York: Ronald Press Co., 1959), pp. 108-113, misunderstands Finney's choice of role as that of pietistic withdrawal from social action, an interpretation which the events at Oberlin, described hereafter, do not sustain. Cf. Dayton, *Evangelical Heritage,* pp. 15-24.

27. Edward H. Madden, *Civil Disobedience and Moral Law in Nineteenth-Century American Philosophy* (Seattle: University of Washington Press, 1968), pp. 44-45 and *passim.* Cf. D. H. Meyer, *The Instructed Conscience: The Shaping of the American National Ethic* (Philadelphia: University

of Pennsylvania Press, 1972), pp. 89-97, on Mahan as moral philosopher; Finney, *Memoirs,* pp. 340-51; Asa Mahan, *Out of Darkness Into Light* . . . (Boston: The Willard Tract Repository, 1876), pp. 125-31, 133-36.

28. Asa Mahan, *Scripture Doctrine of Christian Perfection,* 4th ed. (Boston: D. S. King, 1840), pp. 185-87.

29. *Ibid.,* pp. 186-87. Cf. Mahan, *Out of Darkness,* pp. 139-47.

30. Mahan, *Scripture Doctrine, pp. 163-93,* prints this lecture, which includes the cited personal testimony; the quotation is from p. 172. This volume, printed on a Methodist press in Boston, uses Wesleyan terms such as "perfect love" and "entire sanctification" freely.

31. Finney, *Memoirs,* p. 340; Finney, *Lectures to Christians,* p. 213.

32. Charles G. Finney, "Letters to Readers," *The Oberlin Evangelist* (hereafter cited as *OE*), vol. 1 (January 30, 1839).

33. Finney, *Skeletons of a Course of Theological Lectures,* vol. 1 (Oberlin: James Steele, 1840), p. 24.

34. Finney, manuscript of *Memoirs,* Oberlin College Archives. Garth Rosell called my attention to this passage.

35. *OE,* 1 (March 14, 1839), p. 51; (March 27, 1839), p. 57.

36. Dayton, *Evangelical Heritage,* p. 47.

37. *OE,* 1 (September 11, 1839), p. 157.

38. *Ibid.*

39. *OE,* 2 (April 22, 1840), pp. 67-68.

40. *OE,* 1 (January 1, 1839), pp. 9-10.

41. *OE,* 1 (January 16, 1839), pp. 18-19.

42. *OE,* 1 (January 30, 1839), pp. 26-27.

43. *OE,* 1 (February 13, 1839), p. 34.

44. *Ibid.*

45. *OE,* 1 (February 27, 1839), p. 41.

46. *OE,* 1 (March 13, 1839), p. 50.

47. *Ibid.,* pp. 50-51; *OE,* 1 (March 27, 1839), pp. 59-60.

48. *OE,* 1 (April 10, 1839), pp. 49, 65-67.

49. *OE,* 1 (April 24, 1839), pp. 74-75; (June 19, 1839), pp. 106. Cf. Mahan, *Scripture Doctrine,* pp. 52-58, 101-3, on Romans 7 and 8; Cutworth's sermon, *Arminian Magazine,* pp. 429, 444, 446, on the "law of the Spirit of life" in Romans 8.

50. *OE,* 1 (May 22, 1839), pp. 89, 90; (June 5, 1839), p. 97; (June 19, 1839), p. 106 for the quotation; for the other two lectures, the issues for July 3 and July 17.

51. *OE,* 1 (August 14 1839), pp. 137-38. Cf. Finney's letter "To Ministers of the Gospel of all Denominations," *OE,* 2 (June 3, 1840), p. 92, also using the terminology "baptism of the Holy Ghost" freely. The two references thus bracket the writing of the summary lectures, published in Charles G. Finney, *Views of Sanctification* (Oberlin, Ohio: James Steele, 1840), in which the term does not appear, but in which Finney explains his preference for "entire sanctification" over "entire consecration," on both biblical and practical grounds (pp. 194-95).

52. *OE,* 1 (August 28, 1839), p. 147.

53. *OE,* 1 (August 14, 1839), p. 138.
54. *OE,* 2 (May 6, 1840), p. 76. Cf. the letters in the same series in the two succeeding issues: (May 20, 1840), p. 84; (June 3, 1840), p. 92. Finney composed these letters shortly after completing the last seven lectures in the series on Christian perfection, printed in *OE* from January through mid-April, 1840, and in July of the same year, in his *Views of Sanctification.* These concluding lectures recapitulated the logic of the earliest ones in the series and do not employ the terminology of Pentecost, which led scholars (including myself), who previusly relied chiefly on that volume and neglected to read the *Evangelist* carefully, to suppose that Finney did not at this state teach the doctrine of the baptism of the Holy Spirit.
55. *OE,* 1 (August 14, 1839), p. 140.
56. I am instructed on this point by Joseph H. Smith, "The Psychoanalytic Understanding of Human Freedom: Freedom From and Freedom For," *The Journal of the American Psychoanalytic Association,* vol. 26 (1978), pp. 87-107.

### Chapter 7. Donald W. Dayton

1. *Newsweek* (October 25, 1976).
2. George Gallup, Jr., "US in Early Stages of Religious Revival?" *Journal of Current Social Issues,* vol. 14 (Spring 1977), pp. 50-55.
3. Dean Kelley, *Why Conservative Churches are Growing* (New York: Harper & Row, 1972).
4. Ralph Winter, review of several recent books on evangelicalism, *Christianity Today* (April 9, 1976), p. 38.
5. Heinrich Bornkamm thus explicates *The Heart of Reformation Faith* (New York: Harper & Row, 1965).
6. Ian Bradley, *The Call to Seriousness* (New York: The Macmillan Co., 1976), p. 22.
7. For this concept, cf. Winthrop Hudson, "The Methodist Age in America," *Methodist History,* vol. 12 (April 1974), pp. 3-15; C. C. Goen, "The 'Methodist Age' in American Church History," *Religion in Life,* vol. 34 (1964–65), pp. 562-72.
8. David F. Wells and John D. Woodbridge, *The Evangelicals* (Nashville: Abingdon Press, 1975), reissued in paperback (Grand Rapids: Baker, Book House, 1977) with a new chapter on the holiness/pentecostal traditions—added in part in response to criticisms of the book by Timothy Smith and myself.
9. Martin Marty, *The New Shape of American Religion* (New York: Harper & Row, 1959), p. 28.
10. Cf. James E. Hamilton, "Academic Orthodoxy and the Arminianizing of American Theology," *Wesleyan Theological Journal,* vol. 9 (Spring 1974), pp. 52-59.
11. Smith, *Revivalism.*
12. Claude Welch, *Protestant Thought in the Nineteenth Century,* vol. 1 (New Haven: Yale University Press, 1972), p. 201.

13. Robert Whalen, "Millenarianism and Millennialism in America, 1790–1880" (Ph.D. dissertation, State University of New York at Stony Brook, 1972).

14. See his various writings on the subject, but especially Ernest R. Sandeen, *The Roots of Fundamentalism* (Chicago: University of Chicago Press, 1970).

15. Cf. especially the pioneering work of Smith, *Revivalism* and *Called Unto Holiness* (Kansas City: Nazarene Publishing House, 1962); Melvin Dieter, "Revivalism and Holiness" (Ph.D. dissertation, Temple University, 1973); and the work of Charles Jones, *Perfectionist Persuasion* (Metuchen, N.J.: Scarecrow Press, 1974) and *A Guide to the Study of the Holiness Movement* (Metuchen, N.J.: Scarecrow Press, 1974).

16. Robert Mapes Anderson, *Vision of the Disinherited: The Making of American Pentecostalism* (New York: Oxford University Press, 1979), p. 5.

17. See for example, Ronald Nash, *The New Evangelicalism* (Grand Rapids: Zondervan, 1963).

18. Richard Quebedeaux, *Young Evangelicals* (New York: Harper & Row, 1973).

19. Howard Lindsell, *Battle for the Bible* (Grand Rapids: Zondervan Publishing House, 1976).

20. Dayton, *Evangelical Heritage.*

21. Carl Henry, *Uneasy Conscience* (Grand Rapids: Eerdmans Publishing Co., 1947).

22. Cf. John Oliver, "A Failure of Evangelical Conscience," *The Post American,* vol. 4 (May 1975), pp. 26-30.

23. Roger Anstey, *The Atlantic Slave Trade and British Abolition, 1760–1810* (Atlantic Highlands, N.J.: Humanities Press, 1975).

24. Anne C. Loveland, "Evangelicalism and 'Immediate Emancipation' in American Antislavery Thought," *Journal of Southern History, vol. 32 (May 1966).*

25. John L. Hammond, "Revival Religion and Anti-Slavery Politics," *American Sociological Review,* vol. 39 (April 1974).

26. Cf. Luther Lee, "Women's Right to Preach the Gospel," *Five Sermons and a Tract by Luther Lee,* ed. and intro. Donald W. Dayton (Chicago: Holrad House, 1975).

27. B. T. Roberts, *Ordaining Women* (Rochester, N.Y.: Earnest Christian Publishing House, 1891).

28. Seth Cook Rees, *The Ideal Pentecostal Church* (Cincinnati: Martin Wells Knapp at the Revivalist Office, 1897), p. 41.

29. Mrs. J. Fowler Willing, "Women and the Pentecost," *Guide to Holiness,* vol. 68 (January 1898), p. 21.

## Chapter 8. Nancy A. Hardesty

1. Robert F. Wearmouth, *Methodism and the Common People of the Eighteenth Century* (London: Epworth Press, 1945), p. 223.

2. Abel Stevens, *The Women of Methodism* (New York: Carlton & Porter, 1866), pp. 10-11.
3. See Stevens, *Women of Methodism;* Henry Moore, *The Life of Mrs. Mary Fletcher* (New York: Carlton & Lanahan, 1856), and *An Account of the Experience of Hester Ann Rogers* (New York: Hunt & Eaton, 1889); Annie E. Keeling, *Eminent Methodist Women* (London: Charles H. Kelly, 1889); John Kirk, *The Mother of the Wesleys* (London: Henry James Tresidder, 1864); Helen Knight, *Lady Huntington and Her Friends* (New York: American Tract Society, 1853).
4. W. H. Withrow, *Barbara Heck* (London: Robert Culley, 1893).
5. Outler, *John Wesley* (1974), p. 99.
6. Robert G. Tuttle, Jr., *John Wesley* (Grand Rapids: Zondervan Publishing House, 1978), pp. 47, 58.
7. *Ibid.,* p. 195.
8. Stevens, *Women of Methodism,* pp. 63-64.
9. *Ibid.,* p. 82.
10. Phoebe Palmer, *Promise of the Father* (Boston: Henry V. Degen, 1859), pp. 115, 117.
11. Stevens, *Women of Methodism,* p. 64.
12. Adam Clarke, *Commentary* (Nashville: Abingdon, 1883), Galatians 3:28 (vol. 6, p. 402).
13. See for example, Luther Lee, *Woman's Right to Preach the Gospel* (Syracuse: the Author, 1853); Phoebe Palmer, *Promise of the Father;* Catherine Mumford Booth, *Female Ministry* (London: n.p., 1859; reprinted, New York: Salvation Army Headquarters, 1975); David Sherman, "Woman's Place in the Gospel," preface to John O. Foster, *Life and Labors of Mrs. Maggie Newton Van Cott* (Cincinnati: Hitchcock & Walden, 1872), preface; Frances Willard, *Woman in the Pulpit* (Boston: D. Lothrop Co., 1888); Roberts, *Ordaining Women.*
14. *Works,* 6, pp. 350-60.
15. Adam Clarke, *Memoirs of the Wesley Family* (New York: Lane & Tippett, 1848; reprinted Taylors, S.C.: Van Hooser Publications, 1976), p. 412.
16. *Ibid.,* p. 387.
17. *Ibid.,* p. 393.
18. Charles G. Finney, *Lectures on Revivals of Religion,* ed. William G. McLoughlin (Cambridge: Belknap Press, Harvard University Press, 1960), pp. 207, 372*n.*
19. Phoebe Palmer, *The Way of Holiness* (New York: the Author, 1854), pp. 19, 63-4, 38.
20. Richard Wheatley, *The Life and Letters of Mrs. Phoebe Palmer* (New York: W. C. Palmer, Jr., 1876), p. 67.
21. Walter C. Palmer and Phoebe Palmer, *Four Years in the Old World* (New York: W. C. Palmer, Jr., 1870), p. 635.
22. Donald W. Dayton, "The Doctrine of the Baptism of the Holy Spirit: Its Emergence and Significance," *Wesleyan Theological Journal,* vol. 13 (Spring 1978), pp. 114-26; "Theological Roots of Pentecostalism" (Ph.D. dissertation, University of Chicago, 1980).

23. Phoebe Palmer, "Model Revival," *Guide to Holiness,* vol. 46 (September 1864), p. 61.
24. *Notes,* Matt. 3:2 (p. 22).
25. Stevens, *Women of Methodism,* p. 61.
26. Lee, *Five Sermons.*
27. Laura S. Haviland, *A Woman's Life-Work* (Chicago: Publishing Association of Friends, 1889).
28. Palmer, *Promise of the Father,* p. 361.
29. F. de L. Booth-Tucker, *The Life of Catherine Booth,* vol. 1 (London: Salvation Army Headquarters, 1892), p. 86.

## Chapter 9. James H. Cone

1. The earliest publication on black theology was by James H. Cone, *Black Theology and Black Power;* see also James Cone, *A Black Theology of Liberation, The Spirituals and the Blues* (New York: Seabury Press, 1972), and *God of the Oppressed* (New York: Seabury Press, 1975). Other writers on the subject include J. Deotis Roberts, *Liberation and Reconciliation: A Black Theology* (Philadelphia: Westminster Press 1971) and *A Black Political Theology* (Philadelphia: Westminster Press, 1974); Major Jones, *Black Awareness: A Theology of Hope* (Nashville: Abingdon Press, 1971); William Jones, *Is God a White Racist?* (Garden City, N.Y.: Doubleday & Co., 1973); Cecil Cone, *The Identity Crisis in Black Theology.* For a historical account of the development of black religion and black theology, see Gayraud S. Wilmore, *Black Religion and Black Radicalism* (Garden City, N.Y.: Doubleday & Co.,1972) and G. Wilmore and J. Cone, eds., *Black Theology: A Documentary History, 1966–1979* (Maryknoll, N.Y.: Orbis Books, 1979).
2. Cecil Cone, *Identity Crisis.*
3. From "I Told Jesus," Roberta Flack's record album, "First Take," Atlantic Recording Corp., New York, 1969.
4. W.E.B. DuBois, *The Souls of Black Folk* (New York: Fawcett Publications, 1968), pp. 141-42.
5. *Ibid.,* p. 141.
6. "Prophet, Prophetism," *The Interpreter's Dictionary of the Bible,* George A. Buttrick *et al.,* vol. 3 (Nashville: Abingdon Press, 1962), p. 912.
7. See Clifton Johnson, ed., *God Struck Me Dead* (Philadelphia: Pilgrim Press, 1969).
8. Harold Carter, *The Prayer Tradition of Black People* (Valley Forge, Pa.: Judson Press, 1976), p. 21.
9. A prayer offered in South Nashville, Tennessee, in the summer of 1928 and reproduced in Langston Hughes and Arna Bontemps, *Book of Negro Folklore* (New York: Dodd, Mead, & Co., 1958), p. 256.
10. Ibid., pp. 256-57.
11. Richard Allen, *The Life Experience and Gospel Labors of the Right Reverend Richard Allen* (Nashville: Abingdon Press, 1960), p. 29. For

biographies of Allen, see Charles Wesley, *Richard Allen: Apostle of Freedom* (Washington: Associated Publishers, 1935) and Carol V. R. George, *Segregated Sabbaths: Richard Allen and the Emergence of the Independent Black Churches 1760–1840* (New York: Oxford University Press, 1973).

Wesley's description of the order of salvation emphasizing repentance, justification, new birth, and assurance are prominently present in Allen's account of his conversion experience:

"I was awakened and brought to see myself, poor, wretched and undone, and without the mercy of God must be lost. Shortly after, I obtained mercy through the blood of Christ, and was constrained to exhort my old companions to seek the Lord. I went rejoicing for several days and was happy in the Lord, in conversing with many old, experienced Christians. I was brought under doubts, and was tempted to believe I was deceived, and was constrained to seek the Lord afresh. I went with my head bowed down for many days. My sins were a heavy burden. I was tempted to believe that there was no mercy for me. I cried to the Lord both night and day. One night I thought hell would be my portion. I cried unto Him who delighteth to hear the prayers of a poor sinner, and all of a sudden my dungeon shook, my chains flew off, and, glory to God, I cried. My soul was filled. I cried, enough for me—the Saviour died. My confidence was strengthened that the Lord, for Christ's sake, had heard my prayers and pardoned all my sins. I was constrained to go from house to house, exhorting my old companions, and telling to all around what a dear Saviour I had found." (*Life Experience,* pp. 15-16)

12. The best history of black religion is Wilmore, *Black Religion and Black Radicalism.* For an account of the rise of black Methodism, see Harry V. Richardson, *Dark Salvation* (New York: Doubleday & Co., 1976). Unfortunately Richardson's book fails to point out the significance of the relation between black faith and history. Careful attention to the theological importance of this relationship would have disclosed the difference between black and white spirituality in Methodism. Richardson seems to be unaware not only of the recent rise of black theology, but also of the *theological* importance of the rise of independent black Methodist churches and also of the emergence of the Black Methodists for Church Renewal in contemporary United Methodism. He includes only one sentence on black theology and one short paragraph on BMCR, in the context of "Protest Movements."

Although it is old, Carter G. Woodson, *History of the Negro Church* (Washington: Associated Publishers, 1945), is still very important. See also James Cone, "Negro Churches (in the United States)," *Encyclopaedia Britannica,* vol. 12, Macropaedia, 15th ed. (1974), pp. 936-37.

13. See *Works,* 11, pp. 59-60.

14. Cited in Wearmouth, *The Social and Political Influence of Methodism in the Twentieth Century* (London: Epworth Press, 1957), p. 185. Despite Wesley's emphasis on works of piety and mercy, his view of

salvation seems to see social justice as a secondary ingredient of salvation and at most, a mere *consequence* of it.

15. In the beginning, American Methodism took a radical stand on slavery. In 1780 at the Baltimore Conference, Methodists condemned slavery as "contrary to the laws of God, man, and nature, and hurtful to society." And four years later at the Christmas Conference of 1784, they "voted to expel all slaveholding of Methodist societies . . . who would not, within twelve months after due notification, perfect a legal document to manumit all their slaves when they reached certain specific ages. The conference also voted to expel immediately all Methodists who bought (except for the purpose of liberation) or sold slaves." However, by the beginning of the nineteenth century cotton had become king, and the Methodist, like other white churches, allowed the change in social reality to influence its stand on slavery. Not only did it suspend the 1784 rules within six months, but in 1816 a General Conference committee reported that "emancipation is impracticable" (Cited in H. Shelton Smith, *In His Image, But . . . : Racism in Southern Religion, 1780–1910* [Durham, N.C.: Duke University Press, 1972], pp. 37, 38, 45). For a historical account, see Donald G. Mathews, *Slavery and Methodism* (Princeton: Princeton University Press, 1965).

16. For a theological interpretation of slave songs, often called Negro spirituals, see *The Spirituals and the Blues*. In *God of the Oppressed,* songs, sermons, stories, and prayers were primary sources for a black theology of liberation.

17. Wilmore interprets these insurrections in *Black Religion and Black Radicalism*, ch. 3. For a detailed account of more than 200 slave revolts, see Herbert Aptheker, *American Negro Slave Revolts* (New York: International Publisher, 1943).

18. Lawrence W. Levine, *Black Culture and Black Consciousness* (New York: Oxford University Press, 1977), pp. 34, 35.

### Chapter 10. Kwesi A. Dickson

1. Kwesi Dickson, "The Minister—Then and Now," *Religion in a Pluralistic Society,* ed. J. S. Pobee (Leiden: E.J. Brill, 1976).

2. Bruce G. (Brodie) Cruickshank, *Eighteen Years on the Gold Coast,* vol. 2 (London: Frank Cass, 1853).

3. Methodist Mission Society Archives, London (letter, January 1868).

4. F. L. Bartels, *The Roots of Ghana Methodism* (London: Cambridge University Press, 1965), p. 66.

5. *Ibid.,* p. 68.

6. Thomas W. Madron, "Some Economic Aspects of John Wesley's Thought Revisited," *Methodist History,* vol. 4 (October 1965), p. 45.

7. Guenter Lewy, *Religion and Revolution* (New York: Oxford University Press, 1974), pp. 583-84.

8. Methodist Mission Society Archives, London (Freeman's 1847 Report).

9. James Cone, *Black Theology and Black Power,* pp. 117, 150.

10. Cf. Manas Buthelezi, "An African Theology or a Black Theology," *The Challenge of Black Theology in South Africa,* ed. Basil Moore (Atlanta: John Knox Press, 1973), pp. 29-35.
11. Dorothee Soelle, *Political Theology* (Philadelphia: Fortress Press, 1974), p. 60.
12. Sergio Torres and Virginia Fabella, eds., *The Emergent Gospel* (Maryknoll, N.Y.: Orbis Books, 1978).
13. Aylward Shorter, *African Christian Theology* (London: Geoffrey Chapman, 1975; Maryknoll, N.Y.: Orbis Books, 1977), back cover.
14. Wilfred Cantwell Smith, *The Faith of Other Men* (New York: Harper & Row, 1972).
15. J. B. Danquah, *The Akan Doctrine of God,* 2nd ed., intro. Kwesi A. Dickson (London: Frank Cass, 1968), p. 187.

## Chapter 11. Dow Kirkpatrick

1. C. S. Lewis, "Epigrams and Epitaphs No. 8," *Poems,* ed. Walter Hooper (London: Geoffrey Bles, 1964), p. 134. © 1964 by the Executors of the Estate of C. S. Lewis. Reprinted by permission of Harcourt Brace Jovanovich, Inc. British Commonwealth rights granted by Collins Publishers.
2. Enrique Dussel, *History and the Theology of Liberation* (Maryknoll, N.Y.: Orbis Books, 1976), pp. 4-7.
3. José Porfirio Miranda, *Marx and the Bible* (Maryknoll, N.Y.: Orbis Books, 1974), pp. 16, 44.
4. José Miguez Bonino, *Christians and Marxists* (London: Hodder & Stoughton, 1976; Grand Rapids: Eerdmans Publishing Co., 1976), pp. 33, 38.
5. *Ibid.,* pp. 35-38. Cf. Miranda's study of John, *Being and the Messiah* (Maryknoll, N.Y.: Orbis Books, 1977).
6. Miranda, *Marx and Bible,* p. 48.
7. Segundo, *Liberation of Theology,* p. 9.
8. Beatriz Melano Couch, in *Theology in the Americas,* ed. Sergio Torres and John Eagleson (Maryknoll, N.Y.: Orbis Books, 1976), pp. 305-6.
9. Dussel, *Ibid.,* p. 288.
10. Jon Sobrino, *Christology at the Crossroads* (Maryknoll, N.Y.: Orbis Books, 1976), p. 124.
11. Orlando Costas, *The Church and Its Mission: A Shattering Critique from the Third World* (Wheaton, Ill.: Tyndale House, 1974), pp. 90, 131-49.
12. Costas, "Church Growth as a Multidimensional Phenomenon: Some Lessons from Chile," *Occasional Bulletin of Missionary Research* (forthcoming).
13. "The Church in the Present-day Transformation of Latin America in the Light of the Council. II: Conclusions" (Washington: U.S. Catholic Conference, Division for Latin America, 1973), p. 102.
14. Costos, "Mission Out of Affluence," *Missiology: An International Review,* vol. 1 (October 1973), p. 419.

15. Personal conversation (December 1976).
16. Pablo Richard, "The Theology of Liberation in the Political Situation of Latin America," *Servir,* vol. 13 (January 1977), pp. 47-48.
17. Alice Hageman and Philip Wheaton, eds., *Religion in Cuba Today* (New York: Association Press, 1971), pp. 168-69, 236-37.
18. Dussel, *History and Theology of Liberation,* p. 146.
19. Hugo Assmann, *Theology for a Nomad Church* (Maryknoll, N.Y.: Orbis Books, 1976), p. 73.
20. Gutiérrez, *Theology of Liberation,* pp. 296-302.
21. *Latin American Philosophy and Liberation* (Mexico City: Editorial Edicol).
22. Assmann, *Nomad Church,* p. 124.

# Bibliography

## Primary Sources

*The Works of the Rev. John Wesley,* 3rd. ed., ed. Thomas Jackson.
14 vols. London: Wesleyan-Methodist Book Room, 1829–31.
Reprinted, Grand Rapids: Zondervan Publishing House, 1958;
Grand Rapids: Baker Book House, 1979.

*The Journal of John Wesley,* ed. Nehemiah Curnock. 8 vols.
London: Robert Culley, 1909–1916. Reprinted, London: Epworth Press, 1938.

*The Letters of John Wesley,* ed. John Telford. 8 vols. London:
Epworth Press, 1931.

*Wesley's Standard Sermons,* ed. Edward H. Sugden. 2 vols.
Reprinted, London: Epworth Press, 1921; 5th ed., 1961.

*Explanatory Notes upon the New Testament.* London: William
Bowyer, 1755. Reprinted, London: Epworth Press, 1952.

*The Poetical Works of John and Charles Wesley,* ed. G. Osborn. 13
vols. London: Wesleyan Methodist Conference Office, 1868–
1872.

## Secondary Sources

Andrews, Stuart. *Methodism and Society.* London: Longmans
Group, 1970.

Anstey, Roger. *The Atlantic Slave Trade and British Abolition.*
Atlantic Highlands, N.J.: Humanities Press, 1975.

Armstrong, Anthony. *The Church of England, the Methodists and
Society, 1700–1850.* London: University of London Press, 1973.

Baker, F. "Methodism and the '45 Rebellion." *London Quarterly
and Holborn Review,* 172 (1947) 325-33.

Barclay, Wade Crawford. *Early American Methodism,* Vol. 2, *To
Reform the Nation.* New York: Board of Missions, 1950.

## BIBLIOGRAPHY

Bebb, E. Douglas. *Wesley: A Man with a Concern*. London: Epworth Press, 1950.

Bence, Clarence L. *John Wesley's Teleological Hermeneutic*. Ann Arbor, Michigan: University Microfilms, 1980.

Berkouwer, C. G. *Faith and Sanctification*. Grand Rapids: Eerdmans Publishing Co., 1952.

Booth, Catherine. *Aggressive Christianity*. New York: Salvation Army Headquarters, 1890.

Booth, William. *The Doctrine and Discipline of the Salvation Army*. New York: Salvation Army Headquarters, 1890.

———. *In Darkest England and the Way Out*. New York, London: Funk & Wagnalls, 1890.

Bready, John W. *England Before and After Wesley*. New York: Harper & Brothers, 1938.

Bucke, Emory S., ed. *The History of American Methodism*. 3 vols. New York: Abingdon Press, 1964.

Cameron, Richard. *Methodism and Society in Historical Perspective*. New York: Abingdon Press, 1961.

Cannon, William. *The Theology of John Wesley*. New York: Abingdon-Cokesbury Press, 1946.

Carter, Henry. *The Methodist Heritage*. New York: Abingdon-Cokesbury Press, 1951.

Cell, George C. *The Rediscovery of John Wesley*. New York: Henry Holt & Co., 1935.

Cox, Leo George. *John Wesley's Concept of Perfection*. Kansas City: Beacon Hill Press, 1964.

Davies, Rupert and Rupp, Gordon, eds. *A History of the Methodist Church in Great Britain*. London: Epworth Press, 1965.

Dayton, Donald W. *Discovering an Evangelical Heritage*. New York: Harper & Row, 1976.

Deschner, John. *Wesley's Christology*. Dallas: Southern Methodist University Press, 1960.

Dieter, Melvin. "Wesleyan-Holiness Aspects of Pentecostal Origins," *Aspects of Pentecostal-Charismatic Origins*. Ed. Vincent Synan. Plainfield, N.J.: Logos International, 1975.

Dunlap, E. Dale. "Tuesday Meetings, Camp meetings and Cabinet meetings: A Perspective on the Holiness Movement in the Methodist Church in the U.S. in the 19th century." *Methodist History*, 13 (April 1975).

Edwards, Maldwyn. *Methodism and England*. London: Epworth Press, 1943.

———. *This Methodism*. London: Epworth Press, 1939.

## BIBLIOGRAPHY

————. *John Wesley and the Eighteenth Century*. London: Epworth Press, 1955.

————. *After Wesley: A Study of the Social and Political Influence of Methodism in the Middle Period, 1771–1849*. London: Epworth Press, 1948.

————. "Methodism and the Chartist Movement." *London Quarterly and Holborn Review*, 191 (1966) 301-10.

Flew, R. Newton. *The Idea of Perfection in Christian Theology*. Oxford: Oxford University Press, 1934.

French, Goldwin. *Parsons and Politics*. Toronto: Reyerson Press, 1962.

Gilbert, A. D. *Religion and Society in Industrial England*. London: Longman, 1976.

Green, John Brazier. *John Wesley and William Law*. London: Epworth Press, 1945.

Halévy, Elie. *The Birth of Methodism in England*. Chicago: University of Chicago Press, 1971.

————. *A History of the English People in the 19th Century*, Vol. I, *England in 1815*. London: T. F. Unwin, 1924; 2nd ed., New York: Peter Smith, 1949, pp. 389-459, 588-91.

Hammond, John. "Revival Religion and Anti-Slavery Politics." *American Sociological Review*, 39 (April 1974).

Hammond, J. L. and Hammond, Barbara. *The Town Labourer, 1760–1832*. London: Longmans, Green, 1917.

Harding, F.A.J. *The Social Impact of the Evangelical Revival*. London: Epworth Press, 1947.

Haywood, C. Robert. "Was John Wesley a Political Economist?" *Church History*, 33 (1964) 314-21.

Hildebrandt, Franz. *From Luther to Wesley*. London: Lutterworth Press, 1951.

Himmelfarb, Gertrude. *Victorian Minds*. New York: Alfred A. Knopf, 1968, pp. 275-99.

Hobsbawm, Eric J. *Labouring Men: Studies in the History of Labour*. London: Wiederfeld & Nicholson, 1964.

————. "Methodism and the Threat of Revolution in Britain." *History Today*, 7 (February 1957) 115-24.

————. *Primitive Rebels*. Glencoe, Ill.: Free Press, 1959.

Hughes, Robert D. "Wesleyan Roots of Christian Socialism." *The Ecumenist*, 13 (May-June 1975).

Hynson, Leon. "Social Concerns of Wesley: Theological Foundations." *Christian Scholars Review*, 4 (1974).

————. "John Wesley and Political Reality." *Methodist History*, 12 (October 1973).

BIBLIOGRAPHY

———. "The Church and Social Transformation: An Ethics of the Spirit." *Wesleyan Theological Journal,* 2 (Spring 1976).

Inglis, Kenneth S. *Churches and the Working Class in Victorian England.* London: Routledge & Kegan Paul, 1963.

Jones, Charles. *Perfectionist Persuasion.* Metuchen, N.J.: Scarecrow Press, 1974.

Jones, E. L. and Mingay, G. E. *Land, Labor and Population in the Industrial Revolution.* London: Edward Arnold, 1967.

Jones, Peter D'A. *The Christian Socialist Revival 1877–1914.* Princeton, N.J.: Princeton University Press, 1968.

Källstad, Thorvald. *John Wesley and the Bible.* Uppsala: Uppsala University Press, 1974.

Kent, John. "M. Elie Halévy on Methodism." *Proceedings of the Wesley Historical Society,* 34 (March 1953–December 1954) 84-91.

———. *The Age of Disunity.* London: Epworth Press, 1966.

Kingdon, R. M. "Laissez-faire or Government Control: A Problem for John Wesley." *Church History,* 26 (1957) 342-54.

Law, William. *A Serious Call to a Devout and Holy Life.* New York: Stanford and Swords, 1850.

———. *A Treatise on Christian Perfection.* London: G. Moreton, 1893.

Lean, Garth. *John Wesley, Anglican.* London: Blanford Press, 1964. (German trans., *John Wesley—Modell einer Revolution ohne Gewalt.* Giessen: Brunnen Verlag, 1969).

Lecky, William E. H. *A History of England in the 18th Century.* New York: D. Appleton & Co., 1878.

Lee, Umphrey. *The Historical Background of Early Methodist Enthusiasm.* New York: Columbia University Press, 1931.

———. *John Wesley and Modern Religion.* Nashville/New York: Abingdon-Cokesbury Press, 1936.

Lerch, David. *Heil und Heiligung bei John Wesley.* Zürich: Christliche Vereinsbuchhandlung, 1941.

Lindstrom, Harald. *Wesley and Sanctification.* London: Epworth Press, 1950.

Lyles, A.M. *Methodism Mocked: The Satiric Reaction to Methodism in the Eighteenth Century.* London: Epworth Press, 1960.

Madron, Thomas W. "John Wesley on Race: A Christian View of Equality." *Methodist History,* 2 (July 1964) 24-34.

———. "Some Economic Aspects of Wesley's Thought Revisited." *Methodist History,* 4 (October 1965) 33-45.

MacArthur, Kathleen Walker. *The Economic Ethics of John Wesley*. New York: Abingdon-Cokesbury Press, 1936.

Marquardt, Manfred. *Praxis und Prinzipien der Sozialethik John Wesleys*. Goettingen: Vandenhoeck & Ruprecht, 1977.

Mathews, Donald G. *Slavery and Methodism*. Princeton: Princeton University Press, 1965.

Matlock, L. C. *The Antislavery Struggle and Triumph in the Methodist Episcopal Church*. New York: Negro Universities Press, 1881. Reprinted, 1969.

Mayor, Stephen. *The Churches and the Labour Movement*. London: Independent Press, 1967.

McConnell, Francis J. *John Wesley*. New York: Abingdon-Cokesbury Press, 1939.

Monk, Robert C. *John Wesley: His Puritan Heritage*. Nashville: Abingdon Press, 1966.

Moore, Robert. *Pit-Men, Preachers and Politics*. Cambridge: Cambridge University Press, 1974.

Moore, Robert L. *John Wesley and Authority: A Psychological Perspective*. Missoula, Mont.: Scholars Press, 1979.

Noro, Yoshio. "Wesley's Understanding of Christian Perfection." *Wesleyan Studies*, 3 (1967).

North, Eric McCoy. *Early Methodist Philanthropy*. New York: Methodist Book Concern, 1914.

Outler, Albert. *Evangelism in the Wesleyan Spirit*. Nashville: Tidings, 1971.

————, ed. *John Wesley*. New York: Oxford University Press, 1964.

————. "Methodism's Theological Heritage," *Methodism's Destiny*. Ed. Paul Minus. New York: Abingdon Press, 1969.

Perkin, Harold. *The Origins of Modern English Society*. London: Routledge and Kegan Paul, 1969.

Peters, John L. *Christian Perfection and American Methodism*. New York: Abingdon Press, 1956.

Piette, Maximim. *John Wesley in the Evolution of Protestantism*. New York: Sheed & Ward, 1937.

Rattenbury, J. Ernest. *Wesley's Legacy to the World*. London: Epworth Press, 1928.

Rattenbury, Owen. *Flame of Freedom: The Romantic Story of the Tolpuddle Martyrs*. London: Epworth Press, 1931. (German trans., *Flammen der Freiheit: Die Geschichte der Märtyrer von Tolpuddle*. Bern: Gotthelf Verlag, 1934.)

Richardson, Harry V. *Dark Salvation*. Garden City, N.Y.: Doubleday & Co., 1976.

Rupp, E. Gordon. *Principalities and Powers*. New York: Abingdon Press, 1952.

Sangster, W. E. *The Path to Perfection*. New York: Abingdon Press, 1943.

Schilling, S. Paul. *Methodism and Society in Theological Perspective*. New York: Abingdon Press, 1960.

Schneeberger, Vilem. *Theologische Wurzeln des sozialen Akzents bei John Wesley*. Zürich: Gotthelf Verlag, 1974.

Sherwin, Oscar. *John Wesley, Friend of the People*. New York: Twayne Publishers, 1961.

Semmel, Bernard. *The Methodist Revolution*. New York: Basic Books, 1973.

Smith, Timothy L. *Revivalism and Social Reform*. Nashville: Abingdon Press, 1957. Reprinted, Gloucester, Mass.: Peter Brown, 1976.

————."Slavery and Theology: The Emergence of Black Christian Consciousness in 19th Century America." *Church History,* 41 (December 1972) 1-16.

————."Social Reform: Some Reflections on Causation and Consequence," *The Rise of Adventism*. Ed. Edwin Gaustad. New York: Harper & Row, 1974.

Soloway, R. A. *Prelates and People*. London: Routledge and Kegan Paul, 1969.

Sommer, J. W. Ernest. *John Wesley und die soziale Frage*. Breman: Verlaghaus der Methodistenkirche, 1930.

Starkey, Lycurgus. *The Work of the Holy Spirit: A Study in Wesleyan Theology*. New York: Abingdon Press, 1962.

Taylor, E. R. *Methodism and Politics 1791–1851*. Cambridge: Cambridge University Press, 1935.

Taylor, Jeremy. *Holy Living and Dying*. New York: D. Appleton, 1841.

Thompson, D. D. *John Wesley as Social Reformer*. Freeport, N. Y.: Books and Libraries Press, 1898. Reprinted, 1971.

Thompson, Edward P. *The Making of the English Working Class*. London: Victor Gollancz, 1964.

Turner, George Allen. *The Vision Which Transforms*. Kansas City: Beacon Hill, 1964.

Tuttle, Robert G., Jr. *John Wesley, His Life and Theology*. Grand Rapids: Zondervan Publishing House, 1978.

Tyerman, L. *The Life and Times of the Rev. John Wesley, M. A.* 3 vols. London: James Sangster & Co., 1876.

Urwin, E. C. and Wollen, Douglas. *John Wesley, Christian Citizen:*

# BIBLIOGRAPHY

*Selections from His Social Teachings.* London: Epworth Press, 1937.

Walters, Orvill S. "The Concept of Attainment in John Welsey's Christian Perfection." *Methodist History*, 10 (April 1972) 12-29.

Ward, W. R. *Religion and Society in England 1790–1850.* New York: Schocken Books, 1973.

Warner, Wellman J. *The Wesleyan Movement in the Industrial Revolution.* London: Longmans, Green, 1930.

Wearmouth, Robert F. *Methodism and the Common People of the 18th Century.* London: Epworth Press, 1945.

———.*Methodism and the Working-Class Movements of England.* London: Epworth Press, 1937.

———.*The Social and Political Influence of Methodism in the 20th Century.* London: Epworth Press, 1957.

———.*Some Working-Class Movements of the 19th Century.* London: Epworth Press, 1948.

Weissbach, Jürgen. *Der neue Mensch im theologischen Denken John Wesleys, Beiträge zur Geschichte des Methodismus*, No. 2. Stuttgart: Christliches Verlaghaus, 1970.

Whiteley, J. H. *Wesley's England: A Survey of 18th Century Social and Cultural Conditions.* London: Epworth Press, 1945.

Williams, Colin W. *John Wesley's Theology Today.* New York: Abingdon Press, 1960.

Wynkoop, Mildred Bangs. *A Theology of Love.* Kansas City: Beacon Hill Press, 1972.

Yates, Arthur S. *The Doctrine of Assurance.* London: Epworth Press, 1952.

# Contributors

**James H. Cone**—Charles A. Briggs Professor of Systematic Theology, Union Theological Seminary, New York. Author of *Black Theology and Black Power, A Black Theology of Liberation, The Spirituals and the Blues, God of the Oppressed;* co-authur of *Black Theology: A Documentary History 1966–1979.*

**Rupert E. Davies**—Warden of the New Room (Wesley's Chapel), Bristol, England. Formerly principal of Wesley College, Bristol. Author of *The Problem of Authority in the Continental Reformers, Religious Authority in an Age of Doubt, Christian Theology of Education, What Methodists Believe, Methodists and Unity: The Church in Our Times*; co-editor of *Catholicity of Protestantism, History of the Methodist Church in Great Britain.*

**Donald W. Dayton**—Librarian and associate professor of historical theology, Northern Baptist Theological Seminary, Lombard, Illinois. Author of *Discovering an Evangelical Heritage.*

**Kwesi A. Dickson**—Professor and sometime head of the Department of Religion, University of Ghana, Legon (Accra). Author of *Aspects of Religion and Life in Africa;* co-editor of *Biblical Revelation and African Beliefs.*

**Nancy A. Hardesty**—Assistant professor of American church history, Candler School of Theology, Emory University, Atlanta. Co-author of *All We're Meant to Be: A Biblical Approach to Women's Liberation, Great Women of Faith.*

**John Kent**—Professor of theology, University of Bristol, England. Author of *The Age of Disunity, From Darwin to Blatchford: The Role of Darwinism in Christian Apologetic*; co-editor of *Church Membership and Intercommunion, Holding the Fort: Studies in Victorian Revivalism.*

**Dow Kirkpatrick**—Missionary of the United Methodist Board of Global Ministries on special assignment to interpret developments in Latin American Christianity to North American Christians. Formerly pastor of First United Methodist Church, Evanston, Illinois. Author of *Six Days and Sunday*; co-founder of the Oxford Institute; editor of Institute books cited in the preface of this volume.

**Thomas W. Madron**—Director of academic computing and research services, Western Kentucky University, Bowling Green, Kentucky. Author of *Small Group Methods and the Study of Politics, Political Parties in the United States.*

**José Míguez Bonino**—Dean of graduate studies, Protestant Institute of Advanced Theological Studies (associated with Union Theological Seminary), Buenos Aires, and a president of the World Council of Churches. Author of *Doing Theology in a Revolutionary Situation, Christians and Marxists, Room to Be People;* editor of *Out of the Hurt and Hope.*

**Theodore Runyon**—Professor of systematic theology and director of Methodist and ecumenical studies, Candler School of Theology, Emory University, Atlanta. Co-author of *Protestant Parish;* editor of *What the Spirit is Saying to the Churches,* Jürgen Moltmann's *Hope for the Church.*

**Timothy L. Smith**—Professor of history and director of program in American religious history, The Johns Hopkins University, Baltimore. Author of *Called unto Holiness: The Story of the Nazarenes, Revivalism and Social Reform: American Protestantism on the Eve of the Civil War.*